DUKE UNIVERSITY PRESS · SOCIOLOGICAL SERIES
☆ ☆ ☆
Charles A. Ellwood and Howard E. Jensen
Consulting Editors

SOCIOCULTURAL CAUSALITY, SPACE, TIME

SOCIOCULTURAL CAUSALITY, SPACE, TIME

☆ ☆ ☆

*A Study of Referential Principles of
Sociology and Social Science*

BY

PITIRIM A. SOROKIN

NEW YORK
RUSSELL & RUSSELL · INC
1964

HM
24
.56
1964

EDITORIAL NOTE

THE HISTORY of the various sciences shows an accelerated curve of development as each in turn has arrived at methodological maturity. For the formulation of adequate basic assumptions concerning the nature of the phenomena in any field of research enables each succeeding generation of scientists to invent and apply techniques more appropriate to their task, and to labor co-operatively in creating a constantly accumulating body of generally accepted fact and theory. Until such methodological foundations have been laid, a science remains divided into conflicting schools, and the cumulative effect of joint effort waits upon the achievement of basic agreements among scientific workers in the field. Even in a matured science, when its expanding frontiers force it to reconsider its methodological foundations, the tendency to divide into schools is again manifested, and progress in these new areas of research is correspondingly retarded.

Beginning with the social physicists of the seventeenth century, many attempts have been made to find a shortcut to methodological maturity in the social sciences by adopting or adapting the referential principles and methods of the natural sciences to sociocultural phenomena. All such attempts have assumed a fundamental similarity between physical, biological, and sociocultural phenomena which the author of this volume has demonstrated not to exist. Any empirical sociocultural system consists of (1) a system of meanings (2) embodied in material objects or vehicles and (3) employed by human agents. Since the vehicles and agents are physical, chemical, and biological objects, they can be studied by the natural sciences, but their significance as components in sociocultural systems is not thereby disclosed. The component of meaning is an essential aspect of sociocultural reality, and for this there is no genuine analogue in the physical, chemical, and biological fields. Consequently, natural science methodology cannot merely be transferred to the social science field; it must be translated and transformed.

Professor Sorokin here attempts to show the transformations through which the concepts of cause, space, and time must pass if they are to be applicable to sociocultural phenomena. But the chief significance of the book is that it points the way to methodological maturity in the social sciences. This will be achieved, not by imitatively borrowing and superficially adapting the referential principles of physics, chemistry, and biology, but in precisely the same way in which these sciences themselves achieved it, "through the discovery and application of the theory and technique adequate to the nature of the phenomena studied."

HOWARD E. JENSEN and
CHARLES A. ELLWOOD, *Duke University.*

PREFACE

THIS VOLUME deals mainly with three referential principles of social science and sociology: sociocultural causality, sociocultural space, and sociocultural time. The prevalent sociological conceptions of the causal relationships of sociocultural phenomena, of time, and of space are taken from the natural sciences. While adapted to a study of physico-chemical and partly of biological phenomena, these concepts are far from being adequate for the study of the sociocultural world. To many sociocultural phenomena they are inapplicable; in other cases, inadequate; in still other instances, actually misleading. In order to become adequate referential principles for sociology and social science, the prevalent naturalistic conceptions in these three fields need drastic modifications. Since these principles, as they are used in macrophysics, are found to be inadequate in the field of even subatomic physics, they are still less serviceable in that of the social sciences.

This volume shows why and in what way these principles are deficient when applied to sociocultural phenomena, and it offers a constructive modification of these principles so as to render them adequate for a study of sociocultural phenomena and their relationships.

In less detail, a similar task is performed by the volume in regard to other referential principles and methodological rules borrowed by the social sciences from the natural sciences. Each of these is subjected to a destructive criticism, followed by a positive reconstruction.

Taken as a whole, the volume aims at a liberation of sociology and the social sciences from voluntary servitude to the natural sciences. If this servitude were fertile and fruitful, no objection could be raised against it. Unfortunately, however, in spite of endless efforts of the past and of the present, it has invariably proved sterile in its scientific and cognitive results. Hence the advisability, even the necessity, of terminating this servitude and of declaring the independence of the social sciences and sociology. In order that such an independence may rest upon a firm foundation, sociology and the social sciences must have their own set of referential principles and their own peculiar methods suited to the nature of the phenomena they deal with. The treatise presents an exposition of just such principles. A fundamental revision of the prevalent naturalistic principles and methods along the lines developed in this work appears to be imminent; as a matter of fact, it is already under way. Since the positivistic "natural-science sociology" becomes increasingly sterile, such a revolution can only be welcomed.

The author acknowledges his indebtedness to the American Book Company for its generous permission to quote liberally from his *Social and Cultural Dynamics*. Sincere thanks are due also the Harvard Committee for Research in the Social Sciences for its financial assistance in the editing, typographical preparation, and typing of this manuscript; Professors Charles A. Ellwood and Howard E. Jensen for most helpful advice and constructive criticism; and the Duke University Press for generous co-operation in the publication of this work.

P.A.S.

Harvard University.

CONTENTS

SOCIOCULTURAL CAUSALITY, SPACE, TIME

CHAPTER I

DECLARATION OF INDEPENDENCE OF SOCIOLOGY AND THE SOCIAL SCIENCES FROM THE NATURAL SCIENCES

MANY SOCIOLOGICAL empiricists still regard sociology as an *alter ego* of the natural sciences, particularly of the physicochemical sciences, in its structure, method, and referential principles. They continue to try to apply the principles and methods of the physicochemical sciences to the field of the social sciences and to erect a system of "social physics," "cultural physics," "social mechanics," or "natural-science sociology."[1]

If the claims advanced by this school of sociological thinkers were realizable, they would mean the complete absorption of sociology and the social sciences into the physicochemical sciences. If sociocultural phenomena could be adequately explained in terms of the physicochemical sciences, this would mean that they were simply physicochemical phenomena and nothing more. In that case, no sociology or social

---

[1] These attempts were initiated a long time ago, when social science and science in general first emerged in human history. They invariably made their appearance and flourished during periods of rising sensate culture, declining during periods of dominant ideational culture. Cf. P. A. Sorokin, *Social and Cultural Dynamics* (New York, 1937), II, 446 ff. *et passim*. The various theories are presented and criticized in P. A. Sorokin, *Contemporary Sociological Theories* (New York, 1928), chap. i. Typical of recent attempts of this kind are: G. A. Lundberg, *Foundations of Sociology* (New York, 1939) [see my criticism of it in the *American Journal of Sociology* (March, 1940)]; S. C. Dodd, *Dimensions of Society* (New York, 1942), and P. W. Bridgman, *The Intelligent Individual and Society* (New York, 1938). Bridgman, though an eminent physicist, is much less "physicochemical" in his interpretation of social phenomena and much more "sociocultural" than Professors Lundberg, Dodd, and other sociologists and psychologists. J. F. Brown, *Psychology and the Social Order* (New York, 1936), and K. Lewin, *Principles of Topological Psychology* (New York, 1936), are only mildly and inconsistently "physicochemical" and "mechanistic." Other references are G. Devereux, "Conceptual Scheme of Society," *American Journal of Sociology* (March, 1940); E. D. Chapple, *Measuring Human Relations: An Introduction to the Study of the Interaction of Individuals* (Provincetown, 1940); and M. Lins, *Espaço-Tempo e relações sociaes* (Rio de Janeiro, 1940). Other recent works are cited in later pages. Then comes a series of works of pseudobehaviorists, already outdated. An analysis and a criticism of these are given in Sorokin, *Sociological Theories*, pp. 617 ff. Cf. also C. A. Ellwood, *Methods in Sociology* (Durham, 1933), chaps. i-v; and H. O. Taylor, *Fact: The Romance of Mind* (New York, 1932).

science would be needed; for "physicochemical sociology" would be merely another way of designating the physicochemical sciences. No basis exists for a duplication of the same science under two different names. Hence the utter futility of any sociology or social science under these conditions. Thus the claims in question, if realizable, would lead, not to the creation of "a natural-science sociology," but to the disappearance of sociology itself, as a mere dilettantish superfluity.

THE DISSIMILARITY BETWEEN SOCIOCULTURAL PHENOMENA AND PHYSICOCHEMICAL AND BIOLOGICAL PHENOMENA

Fortunately—or unfortunately—these claims have never been substantiated and cannot be, for a number of most important reasons. One of these is the fundamental disparity between sociocultural phenomena and physicochemical—or even purely biological—phenomena.[2] *It consists in a profound difference between the componential structure of sociocultural phenomena on the one hand, and that of physicochemical and purely biological phenomena on the other. Any empirical sociocultural phenomenon consists of three components: (1) immaterial, spaceless, and timeless meanings; (2) material (physicochemical and biological) vehicles that "materialize, externalize, or objectify" the meanings; and (3) human agents that bear, use, and operate the meanings with the help of the material vehicles.*

Plato's *Republic,* Shakespeare's *Hamlet,* or the "Venus of Milo," for example, each represents, first of all, a system of meanings, and, second, a material product that objectifies or externalizes these meanings. Third, if these sociocultural phenomena are still vital, they have human agents that articulate, bear, use, and operate these meanings through the instrumentality of the material vehicles. The same may be said of any sociocultural phenomenon grounded in empirical reality and existing as a living unity.[3]

[2] For a more detailed analysis of this disparity, cf. Sorokin, *Social and Cultural Dynamics,* Vol. IV, chaps. i and ii. These chapters are reproduced in this and the following paragraphs in abridged form.

[3] If a sociocultural phenomenon—such as the recently exhumed ancient cultures—lacks human agents, then it is but the mummified shell of a once vital and now defunct cultural phenomenon. If a meaning is not objectified through a set of material vehicles, it remains in the realm of pure meanings, instead of being grounded in empirical sociocultural reality, and is hence objectively nonexistent. If, finally, a phenomenon lacks a component of meaning, it is not a sociocultural but merely a physicochemical or biological phenomenon. For details, cf. *ibid.*

Physicochemical and purely biological phenomena do not have the component of immaterial meanings. The essence of hydrogen, water, iron, stone, electricity, heat, light, sound, protoplasm, or any other physical substance or force or biological organism inheres in its physical or biological properties. It does not possess any traits absolutely different from its physical or biological attributes. It does not serve as a mere instrumentality for the objectification and externalization of this or that system of meanings, such as Plato's system of philosophy, externalized by a book, or Bach's *Mass in B Minor,* externalized by its score or its phonograph recording. Hence the unabridgeable chasm between the componential structure of sociocultural phenomena and that of physicochemical or purely biological phenomena.

A wealth of practically self-evident considerations and factual observations makes this difference unquestionable:

(1) *As soon as we deprive any sociocultural phenomenon of its component of meaning, it ceases to be a sociocultural phenomenon and becomes a mere physical or biological phenomenon.* A book stripped of its meanings or ideas becomes simply a material object with certain physical and chemical properties. A "Venus of Milo" proves to be nothing but a piece of marble with a given chemical and physical composition. Beethoven's *Missa Solemnis* resolves itself into a complex of sounds, or air vibrations. The Sun-God is transformed into a mere self-luminous heavenly body. The national flag turns out to be simply a piece of cloth attached to a stick; money, nothing but paper, silver, or gold. An automobile becomes an aggregation of steel, aluminum, and rubber. War is seen as a maze of physical motions; religious services, as a species of motions and sounds. The same is true of any other sociocultural phenomenon; as soon as it is divested of its component of meanings, it ceases to be a sociocultural phenomenon.

(2) What is still more important—*in sociocultural phenomena, the component of meanings is radically different from the component of material vehicles and can in no wise be identified with physical and biological properties.*

(3) *The component of meanings makes of a given sociocultural phenomenon something radically dissimilar to the physicochemical and biological properties of its vehicles.*

Let us comment briefly on the second and third points: That the component of meanings is different from that of the material vehicles is incontrovertibly established by the fact that *one and the same meaning* (for instance, that of the Christian credo, of Aristotle's *Politics,* or of Dante's *Divine Comedy*) *can be materialized or objectified by means of a variety of vehicles:* reading aloud, singing, or phonograph records, all of which depend on the use of sound or air waves; paper and printed or handwritten characters (manuscripts and books of various shapes, sizes, colors, and styles of letters); and the like. The meaning of each of these cultural phenomena—their inner aspect— remains constant, whereas the material vehicles vary markedly; and vice versa.

The same material shell can serve as a vehicle for externalizing the widest range of meanings or inner aspects of cultural phenomena. The same paper is employed for externalizing religious, philosophic, scientific, juridical, and pornographic or obscene meanings and values. Victrola records of the same make, chemical composition, color, and size objectify now Mozart's *Requiem,* now the *Saint Louis Blues,* now Shakespeare's *Hamlet,* and thousands of other quite different meanings. Sounds of the same kind convey all the variety of meanings objectified by words, by music, and by sound signals. Identical canvas, paint, and brushes, and other chemical, physical, and material object conductors, are utilized to externalize infinitely different meanings. Exactly the same material thing, such as a fifty-dollar bill, may signify payment for debt, a wage, gratitude for service, a bribe, or even compensation for murder; and it may possess countless other meanings and values.[4]

In this respect, the blanket character of money, as a vehicle capable of externalizing or materializing the widest range of meanings and values, is especially conspicuous. On the other hand, such a meaning as "private property" incorporates itself in material things of the most diverse character, from stocks and bonds, money, land, and buildings even to slaves and the pound of flesh we read of in *The Merchant of Venice.* The same is true of the action of time: a given material shell remains, but its meaning changes; or the meaning remains the same while the vehicle changes. A building that was once a church is now converted, as in Soviet Russia, into a Communist clubhouse. Many

<hr />

[4] See esp. the analysis of money from this standpoint in G. Simmel, *Philosophie des Geldes* (Leipzig, 1900), and P. Rykatchev, *Vlast Deneg (The Power of Money)* (Moscow, 1911). For the details, cf. P. A. Sorokin, *Sistema Soziologii (System of Sociology)* (St. Petersburg, 1920), Vol. I, chaps. iv and vii.

actions (ceremonies and rituals) that in the past meant one thing now mean something quite different. Cultural anthropology and history are full of examples of external shells that have changed their meaning. On the other hand, the external forms of the same meaning—for instance, politeness—are changing in time and space, and are expressing themselves now in one set of extreme manners and actions and now in a different set.

The undeniable identity of the meaning or value articulated by the most diverse empirical vehicles, and the identity of the material— external—vehicle incorporating highly different meanings, furnish incontrovertible evidence of the existence of these two components in practically all cultural phenomena; of their profound disparity; and, what is still more important, of the looseness of the relationship between the inner meaning or aspect of cultural phenomena and their external or material vehicles.[5]

The last point—the loose relationship between the inner aspect, or the component of meanings, and the external vehicle, or vehicle component, of cultural phenomena—needs to be stressed particularly. The above analysis shows that these two aspects or components are not "monogamously" tied together; each of them may "marry" another partner—the meaning, another vehicle; and that vehicle, still another meaning. Such "polyandry" or "polygamy" is a general rule and often has a wide range. Sometimes the marriage assumes the most striking and unexpected form. An ordinary physical stick becomes the sacred churinga of the Australian bushman. A piece of cheap cloth on a stick, worth five cents, becomes a vehicle of the most complex and significant value—the sacred flag of the country, in whose behalf multitudes of lives may be sacrificed. In these material objects, as purely physicochemical things, there is nothing impressive, magnificent, appalling,

---

[5] That is to say, the meaning aspect of sociocultural phenomena is a meaning different from, independent of, and superimposed upon, the meaning of the vehicles as purely physical, chemical, or biological objects or events. As material objects, they also have meaning as, for instance, a stick, a ring, the sun. But when a stick becomes a churinga (the most sacred religious object of the Australian bushman), when a ring becomes an engagement ring, and when the sun becomes the Sun-God, or the symbol of wisdom, joy, and life, these cultural meanings are superimposed upon the basic meaning that identifies these material objects as such with all their chemical, physical, or biological properties. The sociocultural meaning expressed by the material vehicles is the significance imposed upon that of the vehicles as such. It is, so to speak, a meaning of the second or third degree imposed upon the natural meaning of the objects as material phenomena.

adorable, divine, or sacred. In their inherent (physicochemical or biological) qualities, they are rather mediocre. And yet they often become the incarnation of supreme values for a man or a group.

A study of the material vehicles of so-called "sacred objects" and "great men"—such as religious relics, state flags and other patriotic symbols, regimental colors, family relics, the insignia of justice, the persons who function in the role of material vehicles of great value (saints, popes, kings, presidents, dictators, men of genius, and so on)—reveals the looseness of the relationship between the inner and external aspects of cultural phenomena with particular clearness. Even in the case of kings and similar human incarnators of values, the incarnation is not due to some specifically noteworthy physical and biological properties; as organisms or individuals, they frequently do not differ in any special way from the rest of mankind. Their "sacredness," "sacrosanctness," "heroism," or "greatness" is due to the fact that they are the incarnation of values superimposed upon or imputed to them by a given culture or society.

All this means that, as a rule, the inner meaning or value of a cultural phenomenon may be incarnated in almost any form of material vehicle; and vice versa. There is no specified causal relationship between the inherent nature of the external vehicle and the meaning it incorporates. The purely physicochemical properties of the vehicle as such do not ordinarily explain or warrant the fact of its becoming an incarnation of a given meaning; and vice versa. The purely physical properties of a churinga or totemic animal cannot account for its becoming a sacred object—the more so as there are plenty of similar sticks not endowed with such a value. The same is true of the physical properties of the stick and cloth of the national flag, or of those of the chalice or Communion cup, some specimens of which are of clay, others of silver or gold or glass, and each of a different size, color, shape, and pattern. Their value or sacredness is superimposed upon them, and as such is fundamentally different from their inherent physicochemical and biological nature. From these premises may be derived a series of important conclusions:

(1) Different material objects and phenomena—for instance, a wooden ikon of Christ, a chalice, and the sign of the cross—which, from the standpoint of their inherent (physicochemical or biological) qualities in nowise belong to the same class of phenomena, and hence

cannot be considered as identical, can and must be put in the same class of *religious cultural phenomena* because of the identity of the meaning or value they articulate. In other words, phenomena which, in their material nature, are dissimilar or not identical often become similar or identical in their cultural nature. Visual painting, the qualitative colossality of art objects, the rapid increase of scientific discoveries, utilitarian ethics, the prevalence of mediocre or pathological types of human beings as the subjects of literature and art, nominalism and individualism—these phenomena are certainly different from one another in their inherent (perceptional) qualities, and from this standpoint they cannot be identified as varieties of the same class of phenomena. And yet, as I have demonstrated in my *Social and Cultural Dynamics,* they all belong to the same class of cultural phenomena—namely, the sensate type of culture—and are but the embodiments of its system of mentality. In other words, they are species of the same genus of cultural phenomena. The same may be said of the manifold embodiments of ideational and idealistic culture.

(2) Identical material objects and actions—for instance, a man carrying a gun—are assigned to quite different classes of cultural phenomena, now "criminal," now "noncriminal," by virtue of the difference in meaning or value imputed to such objects and actions, though physically they are identical. Thus a ten-dollar bill may be "legitimate property" of the possessor, or it may be the evidence of "theft." The same sounds—let us say "two and two make four"—are mere gibberish to a person who does not understand English; but they make a perfectly comprehensible and meaningful proposition to one who knows English. Physically, the phenomenon is the same; culturally, it is profoundly different to those who understand and those who do not understand English. Before his elevation to the dignity of pope or king, a person is one individual. Culturally and socially, he becomes an entirely different individual after his elevation to either of those positions, though physically, biologically, and perhaps even psychologically he remains unchanged.

To sum up: *What materially or physically is identical is often fundamentally different culturally, by virtue of the difference of meaning or value imputed to it. This means that application of the principles of identity and difference from a cultural standpoint, on the basis of the identity or difference of the meanings expressed by the material*

objects, actions, and other phenomena, often leads to results funda-
mentally different from those arrived at on the basis of the inherent
physicochemical and biological properties. What is identical from the
standpoint of physical and biological properties is frequently different
when viewed from the cultural standpoint, and what is different when
regarded from the point of view of the inherent properties is often
identical from the cultural standpoint.

(3) From these propositions it follows that *a series of very different*
material things and phenomena which, by virtue of their physicochem-
ical and biological qualities, appear to be independent and unrelated to
one another causally, and hence do not belong to the same class, not
being bound into a single unity or system by their intrinsic properties,
may nevertheless exhibit definite unity, and constitute an identical class
and a well-integrated system of interdependent factors, if they all em-
body the same meaning, value, or principle. The bond that unites all
these external vehicles into one and the same class, or into one real
system of interdependent parts, is not the identity of their inherent
(physicochemical and biological) qualities (which by definition are
different), nor spatial juxtaposition, nor causal interdependence due to
their physical and biological properties, but, rather, either the identity
of the meanings they express or the consistent system of meanings and
values they incarnate.

The number and diversity of material objects and phenomena associated, let us say, with a given religion or science or law are enormous
—practically infinite—if we view them from the standpoint of their
inherent qualities. Yet they all belong to the same class of cultural
phenomena—religious, scientific, or juridical—if they are embodiments
of these values. Consider the objects and other phenomena that incarnate a definite system of religion, say, the Roman Catholic faith.
These are multifarious in character and are scattered over the whole
planet. We can discover no causal relationship between them if we
consider *only their intrinsic* qualities, as, for instance, those of a church
building, water, a chalice, ceremonial vestments, a cross, a prayerbook,
the rosary, fasting, the actions of kneeling or intoning certain words,
and thousands of other things that enter into the system of vehicles
of the Roman Catholic religion.

A visiting behaviorist from Mars would never have the slightest
suspicion that this heterogeneous conglomeration of material things,

overt actions, and physicochemical or biological phenomena could belong to the same cultural class—could be bound by definite ties and form a part of one closely integrated system. Yet there is not the slightest doubt that they are all external manifestations of the same system of values and meanings—that of the Roman Catholic religion. As such, they are mere parts of this system, and hence are tied together, even causally. *Their common membership in one and the same system of meanings throws over all of them a causal net of interdependence which would otherwise be absent.*

Let us take another example: Harvard University. Externally, a collection of fantastically numerous and heterogeneous objects, persons, actions, and other phenomena make up this cultural system, with its various buildings; the enormous diversity of objects in its museums, laboratories, classrooms, offices, and dormitories; the multiplicity of persons connected with it; and the manifold activities that they carry on. What identity can there be between glass flowers, guinea pigs, corpses (in the Medical School), Egyptian paintings in the Fogg Art Museum, brooms in the cellars, pipes and cigarettes in the offices, and the like? What causal connections can exist between such an extraordinary diversity of persons, objects, and activities on the basis of their physicochemical or biological qualities? What unity can be expected in such amazing heterogeneity? None! Yet, we well know that these various factors are all parts of a single system of meanings and values in which they perform certain definite functions. What is more, most of them are parts of a single causal system, sustaining a tangible causal interdependence. This interdependence is due, not to their inherent physical or biological properties, but to the fact that they are vehicles, or instrumentalities, of the same system of meanings and values. Without this meaningful component, they would possess no causal interdependence. They would be a mere congeries of multifarious phenomena.

All this furnishes a further illustration of the seemingly paradoxical fact that the *"immaterial" factor of meaning or value not only makes identical what is otherwise different, and different what otherwise is identical, but frequently casts a net of causal relationships of empirical interdependence over phenomena which otherwise, on the basis of their inherent qualities only, would be causally independent.*

The last point brings us to a concise preliminary analysis of the difference between pure causal systems and sociocultural systems, between the pure chance relationships of physical phenomena and the congeries relationships of sociocultural phenomena.

PURELY CAUSAL AND MEANINGFUL-CAUSAL SYSTEMS

Two or more physical phenomena may sustain either causal, or chance, relationships toward one another. The causal relationship is characterized by the tangible static or dynamic, one-sided or mutual, dependence of these phenomena. If *A* is given, *B* is given; if *A* changes, *B* changes in a certain definite way. If such dependence or interdependence is lacking between *A* and *B*, they stand, not in a causal, but solely in a chance relationship toward one another. The totality of the phenomena bound by the tie of causal interdependence constitute a causal system, in contradistinction to a mere congeries of phenomena devoid of such interdependence. In purely physical and biological phenomena, this dependence rests simply upon the physical or biological properties of *A* and *B*. No component of immaterial meaning is involved.[6] A pure causal system may hence be defined as follows: *Any system characterized by the existence of a tangible one-sided or mutual dependence of its parts upon one another, of the whole upon its parts, and of the parts upon the whole is a causal system, provided that this dependence is due to the physicochemical or biological properties of the whole and of its parts.*

An assembled automobile is a causal system. An unassembled automobile, with the parts scattered on the floor of the factory, is a mere congeries of physical objects. Causal systems may be concrete or discrete, continuous in space or discontinuous, durable or short-lived, heterogeneous or homogeneous. A conglomeration of physical and biological phenomena which lacks the triple dependence postulated by the foregoing definition is not a causal system and represents simply a chance conglomeration, or congeries.[7]

In contradistinction to purely causal systems and chance congeries, the empirical sociocultural systems are characterized by the identical dependence and interdependence of their parts upon one another and upon the whole, and of the whole upon the parts; but this interdependence is not entirely due (and is sometimes due not at all) to the physical and biological properties of the parts, but principally, and

[6] For a detailed analysis of causal systems, cf. Sorokin, *Dynamics*, Vol. IV, chaps. i and ii.

[7] For details and bibliography, see *ibid.*

sometimes exclusively, to the fact that the parts are the vehicles of the same system of meanings. No matter what may be their physical or biological properties, and even though these attributes are entirely unrelated to one another causally, if any conglomeration of physical objects and other phenomena become the instrumentalities of the embodiment or objectification of the same system of meanings, these vehicles become parts of a sociocultural system, and therefore dependent or interdependent causally, provided they and their human agents are in contact with one another.

Such is the fundamental difference between purely causal systems in the physical and biological realms and empirical sociocultural systems that are meaningful-causal. As has been said, an aggregation of sociocultural phenomena that do not display this dependence is simply a sociocultural congeries, or a fortuitous concatenation of sociocultural phenomena.

These definitions of sociocultural systems and congeries call for a few further words of clarification respecting what is meant by *system of meanings* and a mere *congeries of meanings.* A group of meanings may represent either a *congeries* of meanings unrelated to one another, such as "snow-triangle-symphony-electricity-war," or a *system* of meanings logically interdependent and presenting a new unified meaning, such as: "Two and two make four." Congeries of meanings assume the form either of isolated meanings or of groups of unrelated propositions. The statements "Two and two make four" plus "Napoleon lost the Battle of Waterloo" plus "J. S. Bach lived before Beethoven" constitute a congeries of systems of meanings. The three propositions are logically unrelated to one another. Likewise, a system of meanings may be composed of isolated propositions (each with its subject and predicate) or of a series of connected propositions constituting a syllogism, such as: "All men are mortal"; "Socrates is a man"; "Therefore Socrates is mortal." A syllogism is a system of meanings made up of at least three separate systems. A theory may consist, in turn, of several connected syllogisms, thus affording a still vaster system of meanings, composed of subsystems, each of which is made up of a number of subsubsystems; and so on.

Newton's *Principia,* Euclid's *Geometry,* and Kant's *Critique of Pure Reason* are (for the most part) systems of meanings, each of which is composed of many subsystems, which in their turn are made up of subsubsystems, until we come to single propositions, each of which represents a system of isolated meanings.

The same is true of Homer's *Iliad,* Beethoven's *Missa Solemnis,* the Christian credo, the civil code of Napoleon, or a capitalist or feudal social system, viewed as pure systems of meanings. (For the present, it is unessential that all parts and elements of these systems of meanings should constitute a unified system and should be necessary elements of each of these systems. Granted that some parts or elements are incidental congeries, the rest nevertheless compose a system.)

The next important problem is: What is the criterion that makes of a *group of meanings either a congeries or a system?* It is evidently not a question of time or space, because meanings are timeless and spaceless. It is also not a causal relationship, because the very conception of cause and effect as an empirical relation presupposes time and space and is therefore inapplicable.

The most general criterion of a system of meanings, in contradistinction to a congeries of meanings, is logical compatibility and the specific dependence or interdependence of each meaning element upon other meaning elements, of the meaning elements upon the whole system, and of the system upon the elements. The specific dependence is *logical dependence or interdependence* for all propositions and systems of propositions that constitute a form of judgment. It is *esthetic dependence or interdependence* for all the *art meanings or values* expressive of consistence or harmony—a kind of esthetic logic different from the logic of verbal propositions. Since an enormous proportion of meanings and their systems can be reduced to propositions (all the theories of science; articulated creeds and beliefs; the norms of law and ethics, mores and customs; the principles of political, economic, and social organization; all the articulated theories and judgments concerning art values; a vast proportion of rituals and ceremonies, with their meanings articulated verbally or through other media of expression), the principle of *logical* dependence and interdependence covers practically the overwhelming majority of meanings. The rest are covered by the principle of *esthetic or expressive* dependence or interdependence, a somewhat different branch of generic logical dependence.

All the groups of meanings that tangibly exhibit these forms of compatible dependence or interdependence are systems of meanings. The rest are congeries.

Any proposition—such as A is B or A is not B—is a system of meanings, because in it the subject, A, depends upon B, B depends upon A, and the whole proposition depends upon A, B, and the copula; and each part—subject, copula, and predicate nominative—depends upon the whole. If any part is changed in its meaning, the meanings of all the other parts and of the whole change; and so also changes that of any part if the whole is changed. This is still more true of a syllogism (its major and minor premises and its conclusion), and even more so of a chain of syllogisms or of an entire theory. By the tie of compatible logical dependence, they all are bound together into a unity, or system, and aim to present a new unified meaning or system of meanings.

In logical congeries, each meaning or system of meanings is either unrelated to or incompatible with another logically; therefore, they are not dependent or interdependent upon one another. From the simple congeries of meanings "table-Stalin-triangle-musical score-azalea-vital-ism-automobile," one can take any of the meanings, and the rest will not be changed in any way. One can add to this miscellany of meanings hundreds of others, and yet, though the aggregation will increase, the given congeries will undergo no logical change, since there is neither a logical whole nor parts, nor an element of mutual dependence.

Most scientific and philosophical theories, law codes, ethical and religious systems, and systems of fine arts (such as the works of Bach or Beethoven, Dante or Shakespeare) represent such systems of meanings and are sometimes made up of many subsystems and sub-subsystems.[8]

To sum up: *The most general criterion of a system of meanings, in contradistinction to a congeries of meanings, is the logical or esthetic dependence of the parts upon one another, the parts upon the whole, and the whole upon the parts. Additional characteristics of the two main types of the more closely integrated systems of meanings are: (1) the identity of the meaning permeating all the parts; (2) the harmonious and logico-esthetically necessary co-ordination of the meanings and subsystems of meanings in one new indivisible unity.* Where these criteria are absent, we have a congeries. Where there is an inner conflict or logico-esthetic contradition, we have congeries of meanings;

[8] For a further analysis, cf. *ibid.*

because the split, the incompatibility, the contradiction, is the opposite of oneness, or unity. Finally, it should be added that, in the given conglomerations of meanings, the transition from a pure congeries to the most highly unified systems of meanings is gradual; there are groups of meanings which are in part a system, in part a congeries. In most of the even highly integrated and complex systems of meanings, there are almost always some elements that are congeries; and in many a congeries, there are some elements united into a system.

The Relationship between Pure Systems of Meanings and Pure Causal Systems—Empirical Sociocultural Systems as Meaningful-causal Systems

A pure system of meanings may exist in the mind without any definite externalization or objectivization in material vehicles. *But as soon as it is to be transmitted to other persons (intentionally or unintentionally)—as soon as it begins to be socialized—it must be clothed in some sort of external vehicle; because without some vehicle that serves as a conductor, the meaning cannot be transmitted and socialized, and therefore cannot become an empirical sociocultural system.*

Hence the following inferences:

(1) Any assortment of external vehicles, regardless of their intrinsic properties, is an empirical sociocultural system, grounded in sociocultural reality, if the assortment externalizes a system of meanings in the above sense.

(2) If it externalizes a congeries of meanings in the above sense, such an assortment is an empirical sociocultural congeries.

This gives a fairly definite answer to the question as to which sociocultural phenomena are sociocultural systems and which are sociocultural congeries. The decisive criterion is whether the meanings represent a system. If they do, no matter what empirical, "space-time" vehicles are employed, they constitute an empirical, sociocultural system.

A religious, juridical, scientific, or political system of meanings incorporates itself in an incredibly large and varied assortment of vehicles. Nevertheless, all the important vehicles, however different physically, are found to be interdependent parts of one and the same social system. Medieval architecture and sculpture constituted "the Bible in stone." The meanings of the Christian religion were articulated also by medieval painting, literature, music, and drama—even by a considerable proportion of medieval political, economic, and social institutions. However different physically the materials used in medieval architecture, sculpture, painting, literature, music and political, familial, and social institutions, in their essential parts they all incorporated the same system of meanings and were even causally interdependent.

There remain two other problems that should be clarified: First, is there any difference between the fictitious and the real meaningful system as actually functioning in empirical sociocultural reality? Second, what is the relationship, if any, between meaningful and causal sociocultural systems? The problems are obviously related. As to the first question, it is couched in the wrong terms. There is no such thing as a fictitious meaningful system; such a system would be a mere congeries of meanings—not a system in the sense defined above. But there is a difference between a *pure system of meanings* not externalized, not socialized, and therefore nonexistent as an empirical sociocultural phenomenon, and a *system of meanings grounded in such a reality,* externalized by and incorporated in space-time objects and other phenomena, and functioning as a system in such a framework.

There is a pure system of Euclid's *Geometry* or Newton's *Principia* or Beethoven's *Eroica*. But in a society and culture of children, as well as among many grownups who are not familiar with these systems, and in all societies and cultures that existed before the discovery and socialization of these systems, the latter were not grounded empirically in any society or culture. Therefore they were nonexistent as empirical, sociocultural systems (of science or art). In order to become empirical sociocultural systems, they had to be supplemented by a component of material vehicles that objectified and socialized them, and by a component of human agents that could apply and give effect to these systems of meanings. Only when they acquired this three-componential structure did they become empirical sociocultural systems. Hence, *as soon as a system of meanings is objectified, socialized, or grounded in empirical sociocultural reality, as soon as it becomes a three-componential system, it becomes a causal system as well.*

When a system of meanings such as Harvard University was objectified in vehicles and socialized in human agents, its principal vehicles and human agents became tied to one another as embodiments of the meaningful system of Harvard University. They began to function as its instrumentalities, and as such—since the system was a unit—became parts of the whole, regardless óf the inherent (physical, chemical, and biological) properties of the several vehicles and human agents. By virtue of these material properties alone, the heterogeneous physical objects and agents that make up Harvard University would not be tied together and could not be causally interdependent upon one another. But because of the fact that they are instrumentalities of the same system of meanings, all the chief vehicles and agents are dependent and interdependent upon one another in their relationships, functionings, and changes. A change of administration affects tangibly all of the principal vehicles and agents; an increase or decrease of funds (vehicles) affects the rest of the vehicles (libraries, laboratories, museums) and agents; a change of the important agents (professors and students) affects the vehicles and other agents; and so on. This causal interrelationship is the *peculiar character of sociocultural causality—one that differentiates it fundamentally from the causality of natural phenomena.* The latter is based on inherent—physical, chemical, or biological—qualities of the objects or variables.

The causality of sociocultural systems (but not congeries) is almost always a mixture of *meaningful plus causal interdependence. This interdependence is grounded, not in the physicochemical or biological properties of the vehicles or persons, but mainly in the fact that they serve the same system (or congeries) of meanings.* Causal interdependence in empirical cultural systems is due to the interdependence of the meanings that underlie the vehicles and agents and unites them into one interdependent whole.

This fundamental fact is frequently not realized by social scientists. Yet it is undeniable. Furthermore, it is actually employed (though inadequately) by all the scientists who are discussing and studying causal dependence and interdependence in sociocultural phenomena, including even those who will refuse to accept these statements and who regard causal relationships in sociocultural phenomena as identical with those in natural phenomena.

Now, between precisely which variables or factors or phenomena have the social scientists been trying to discover the causal relationships? Is it not between *science and religion, science and art, science and economic phenomena, religion and law, religion and political phenomena, economics and politics, economics and philosophy of religion, economic factors and music, Protestantism and capitalism, ethical systems and literature, technology and economics, crime and economic, political, and educational factors, educational systems and democracy, war and revolution, war and economic factors, the family and crime, and so on?*

What are these factors, or phenomena? Is each of them a mere causal class in the sense of the natural sciences, composed of objects and other phenomena with the same physical, chemical, or biological properties, and therefore, by virtue of these properties, a member of the same species, manifesting causal dependence? Emphatically not. Religion or economics, Protestantism or capitalism, law or music, and every other sociocultural variable and class is, from the standpoint of the material character of its components, an infinitely heterogeneous collection of objects, persons, events, and other phenomena, with the most diverse physical, chemical, or biological properties.

Religion, or the religious variable, consists (behavioristically) of buildings different in size, color, style, and material; of the most varied sculptures, ikons, and other symbols; and a bewildering miscellany of banners, ornaments, books, cups, dishes, lamps, candles, benches, tables, water, wine, ointments, brooms and vacuum cleaners, electricity and radios, organs, pulpits, and all the other objects commonly found in churches. It includes, moreover, the most fantastic diversity of actions (behavioristically considered): walking, standing, sitting, kneeling, making the sign of the cross, genuflexions, praying, preaching, confessing, and blessing, with all the paraphernalia of processions, ceremonies, and rituals. Finally, there is the still more diverse aggregation of persons: pope, bishops, priests, parishioners, and so on, with all their individual and group biological differences.

These and thousands of other objects, actions, events, and persons enter into the class or variable or factor of religion. Axiomatically, such an aggregation of diverse components cannot belong to one and the same class from the standpoint of physics, chemistry, or biology. The physical, chemical, or biological properties of the "material components of religion" are utterly incommensurate. These components represent virtually all the classes of physical phenomena (matter, light, sound, heat, electricity, etc.), and enormous number of classes of chemical phenomena (metals, coal, water, wood, paper, ointments, and so on); every variety of action and motion; and innumerable individuals of different age, sex, and race constitution.

What unity, uniformity, or causal relationships can be found in such a medley? In brief, *religion as a class, as a factor, as a causal system, as a variable, does not exist at all in the sense of a unity of natural physicochemical and biological phenomena.* Hence, it cannot be regarded as a class, factor, causal system, or variable. Yet all the investigators have so taken it and treated it. The only possible ground for such a procedure is the conception of *religion as a unified system of meanings* articulated through its vehicles and agents. There is certainly no basis for any unity or system in the physical, chemical, or biological properties of the components that it comprises. This means that these scholars, including those who contend that they do not recognize any meaningful unities, have been dealing with religion as a system of meanings objectified in empirical sociocultural reality. Unwittingly, they have been talking logico-meaningful prose while pretending that it was "natural-science poetry."

What has been said of religion is exactly applicable to art, romanticism, classicism, ethics, law, government, communism, capitalism, economics, banking, revolution, war, crime, and any other class of sociocultural phenomena. From the standpoint of the physical, chemical, or biological properties of the phenomena that make up these classes, each of them represents a fantastic medley, devoid of unity or uniformity, its constituents lacking any common characteristic and even any causal interrelationship.

If, nevertheless, such phenomena have been treated as a unity, factor, variable, class, or system, the only ground for that practice consists in the unity of the system of meanings that make economic, political, religious, artistic, scientific, juridical, ethical, and other phenomena classes, unities, systems, and so forth. Only as meaningful systems do they exist as unities, causal factors or variables, and the like. Neither in physics nor in chemistry, biology, or any other natural science can one find a "physics of religion" (like the physics of electricity or sound), or a "chemistry of classicism," or a "biological species of civil law." In fact, none of these classes is mentioned in any form whatsoever in the natural sciences. This means, then, that each of them is a meaningful class, and only as such can be conceived and dealt with. The same applies to any subsubsystem of these classes.[9]

Similarly, such unities and classes as *the family, the State, the Church, political associations, universities, academies of science, and labor unions are not to be regarded as pure causal unities.* No chemist, physicist, or biologist could give a chemical, physical, or biological formula for any of these social systems—particularly with regard to their differences. There is no "family chemical element" or "state chemical compound"; no "physics" of universities or labor unions (like the physics of sound, heat, and light); no biological constitution or species corresponding to Harvard University, the United States Steel Corporation, or a horticultural society. These social systems are but objectified or socialized systems of meanings, with their appropriate vehicles and agents. As such, they differ from one another; as such, each of them is a causal unity; as such, they are sociocultural realities. Whoever speaks of the family, the State, or the Roman Catholic Church speaks primarily in meaningful and then in causal terms. As pure causal systems, none of these institutions has existed, does exist, or ever will exist.

Still more conspicuous is the role of the meaningful system when it is "wedded to empirical vehicles" and, through that marriage, becomes also a causal system in the study of human interrelationships. From the standpoint of strictly physical, chemical, or biological qualities, no investigator can explain why millions of human beings sometimes exhibit enthusiastic reverence, admiration, respect, and obedience toward some individual—be he king, saint, pope, or hero—and do not experience these emotions with respect to other individuals; or why some individuals—kings, dictators, presidents, popes, generals, or captains of industry—exert a powerful influence over their fellows, and perhaps even decide the fate of millions in questions of war or peace, whereas other persons do not exert even a small fraction of such an influence. In all such cases, the difference in power and prestige between eminent leaders and the average man is so striking that no physicochemical or biological differences between them can account for it, the more so

[9] Hence the irony of the vociferous claims of social scientists who declare that they are strictly applying the causality of the natural sciences, relegating any meaningful unities to the limbo of metaphysics, and who then proceed to study the causal relationships between crime and education, crime and religion, religion and capitalism, propaganda and war, and so on.

since kings, presidents, popes, and dictators frequently fail to display any notable deviation in their inherent biological properties from common mortals and often are in themselves mediocrities. The enormous contrast between the common run of mortals and these executives of history as causative agents is due, then, to the systems of meanings of which they are instrumentalities or agents, as the heads of the State, or the Church, or the Army, or a big-business corporation, or other meaningful systems.

Only as an incarnation of such systems of meanings, as their central agents, do these individuals possess this relatively enormous power as causative agents. If they are divested of this role as the instrumentality of meanings, they lose their power and become ordinary human beings —as in the case of the deposal of kings, popes, and dictators—even though biologically and physically they remain unchanged. This demonstrates once again that, when objectified, a system of meanings becomes a power even in a purely empirical sense.[10]

The foregoing considerations show that, *among cultural phenomena, there exists hardly any purely causal relationship or system "unwedded" to meaningful relationships and systems, and based exclusively upon the inherent—physical, chemical, and biological—properties of the vehicles. Every sociocultural system is at the same time meaningful, and its "causativeness" is based mainly upon the system of meanings it incorporates.*

Purely causal relationships between physical or chemical objects do, of course, exist; for instance, H_2 and O give water (H_2O); under certain conditions iron rusts; ignited gas explodes; the volume of gas is in inverse ratio to the pressure; and so on, as regards all the uniformities of physics, chemistry, or biology. These factors operate in a cultural setting just as they do outside of it. However, *these natural causal relationships are not sociocultural phenomena, but solely physical, chemical, or biological, and as such are the proper subject matter of the respective natural sciences.* Insofar as they do not function as vehicles of meaning, but do function, so to speak, at their face value, they fail

---

[10] If one prefers the terminology of energetics, one may speak of the "logico-esthetic energy of meanings," as a powerful force quite different from other forms of energy. This energy, in the sociocultural world, seems to control the other forms of energy to a considerable extent. I prefer, however, not to use this terminology, which I regard as inadequate in many respects.

to constitute cultural factors, and do not properly come within the scope of sociology or of any of the social and humanistic sciences.

When natural phenomena form cultural elements, they become vehicles of meanings or values, such as a flag, a religious relic, a book on philosophy or chemistry, a record of a Beethoven sonata, an automobile, a spade, a radio station, a locomotive, even a sun-god or a thunder-god. *When they become vehicles, their natural properties and relationships are driven, so to speak, backstage, and the stage is occupied by the properties imputed to or superimposed upon them by the systems of meanings whose external agencies they have become.*

Under such conditions, as we have seen, space-time objects, inherently different, become identical; those that are identical become different; those existing naturally without any causal connections become interdependent parts of one system; and those otherwise united become disunited and devoid of any particular power. For instance, a mere piece of paper (appointing *A* to be commander in chief) and insignificant insignia confer upon an individual tremendous power; a biologically powerful person becomes entirely subordinated to and ruled by individuals who may be physically very weak (for example, millions of strong soldiers by their commander in chief); otherwise harmless energies, such as sound and noise (as in diplomatic altercations), produce the devastations of war; a simple group of sound syllables, such as the famous Christian *filioque,* splits the whole Christian world into Eastern and Western Christianity; a tiny black figure—the sign of the swastika or the hammer and scythe of the Soviets—becomes the most stimulating irritant or vitalizer, swaying vast masses of human beings.

In brief, *when an assortment of natural objects and other phenomena becomes linked with a system of meanings—becomes its vehicle—the natural properties of these objects undergo tangible modification.* Through such a union, they lose some of their natural qualities and acquire new ones. The system of meaning that unites them becomes in tangible fashion their "ruler," and this ruler may play havoc with their natural properties, as well as their natural causal relationships.

On the other hand, what is true in the most autocratic of literal marriages is true also in the "marriage" of a system of meanings to its external vehicles, namely, that the dominant partner is not entirely free from the influence of the controlled mate; some adjustment, some accommodation, some concession, has to be made to the weaker party. *If the meanings control the vehicles and play havoc with their natural attributes and relationships, the vehicles likewise impose some concessions, limitations, and modifications upon the pure system of meanings, once it has become grounded as a causal system in the empirical sociocultural world.*

Owing to the inadequacy of the language vehicle (oral, written, and otherwise), many complex systems of meanings cannot express themselves effectively through the language vehicle. As a result, they become infected by congeries, misunderstandings, contradictions, and other "sins" and imperfections. This is particularly true of the most complex and delicate systems of meanings—scientific, artistic, philosophical, religious, juridical, and so forth. Many systems of meanings that appear faultless in their pure estate—such as democracy, socialism, communism, the Epicurean or the Stoic system of ethics, the utilitarian system of the maximum of happiness for the maximum number of human beings, or the ethics of the categorical imperative—are transformed after their union with their respective vehicles and agents into something very different from their pristine perfection. They invariably become so infested with certain congeries and distortions that they often lose their original identity and degenerate, under the influence of the natural properties and relationships of their vehicles and human agents, into something distinctly different.

After being grounded in the empirical world, many a sublime utopian ideal is converted into something flat and prosaic. When such an exalted system of meanings as Christianity, Hinduism, or Buddhism was translated into a socialized causal system, much of its purity was sacrificed; vulgarized and distorted, it became but a pale reflection of its erstwhile meaningful form. When such a system as the Darwinian theory of evolution became socialized among large masses of the population, it was reduced to the bald formula: "Man is descended from a monkey." And so it is with almost any complex and delicate system of meanings when it passes into the empirical world of culture and becomes linked with external vehicles and human agents.

Space-time vehicles, including human agents, have their own natural (physicochemical and biological) properties and relationships; and these properties and relationships, though transformed and often neutralized by the system of meanings, are rarely obliterated entirely. By virtue of these qualities and relations, the vehicles enjoy their own "natural or immanent course." When wedded to meanings, their natural attributes tend to persist; persisting, they press upon the meanings, now annulling some of their important elements, and thus preventing their full realization; now vitiating them with certain congeries; now actually transforming them into something very different.

Thus, if the systems of meanings, when socialized, transform the properties of their vehicles and agents and dominate them, the vehicles, in their turn, inhibit, modify, or distort the systems of meanings when these become empirically grounded. The influence is thus reciprocal. As to which of the two parties exerts the greater influence, no general answer can be given. The situation varies according to the system of meaning and the nature of the vehicles.

The foregoing analysis may be summarized as follows:

(1) There are purely causal and purely meaningful systems, as well as purely causal and purely meaningful congeries.

(2) Purely causal systems, in contradistinction to meaningful systems, are virtually nonexistent among sociocultural phenomena as such.

(3) A union of these two systems makes an empirical sociocultural system. Such a union leads to a transformation of the natural properties of the vehicles and agents and of their natural relationships; on the other hand, it produces a modification of the pure systems of meanings by their vehicles and agents.

PROPERTIES OF EMPIRICAL SOCIOCULTURAL SYSTEMS

The essential properties of any sociocultural system comprise the following:[11]

(1) The meaningful-causal nature of the interdependence between the parts and the whole. In this respect, the system differs fundamentally from purely causal and purely meaningful systems.

(2) The three-componential structure, embracing meaning, vehicle, and agent. The absence of the meaning component renders a system nonsociocultural—merely physical or biological. Absence of the vehicle and agent components makes a system purely meaningful, as distin-

---

[11] The following enumeration is an abstract of a more detailed analysis of these properties presented in Sorokin, *Dynamics*, Vol. IV, chap. ii.

guished from empirical sociocultural reality. Absence of the human-agent component produces a defunct sociocultural system.

(3) A sociocultural system is characterized by a general and differential interdependence or conductivity. All its important parts, as well as the whole, are tangibly interdependent; but the degree of interdependence is not the same among all its parts, being more intense between the vital elements and less intense between the secondary and minor elements.

(4) A sociocultural system is a reality possessed of individuality, from the structural, functional, and meaningful standpoints.

(5) A sociocultural system functions as a whole, and all its important components vary together as a meaningful-causal unit.

(6) The emergence of a sociocultural system exhibits three phases: (a) mental conception, where two or more meanings are fused in one consistent unity; (b) objectification, in which the system of meanings is clothed in a material vehicle and thus becomes capable of being transmitted to other human beings; and (c) socialization, when it recruits its human agents, as the bearers and operators of the system.

(7) These three phases usually exhibit a time sequence. In exceptional instances, they may be virtually synchronous; in other cases, the time span between these phases is considerable, sometimes amounting to decades or even centuries.

(8) In the process of change in togetherness, the component of meanings tends, as a rule, to vary earlier than do the other components (vehicles and agents).

(9) Every sociocultural system is selective in appropriating new elements and rejecting others.

(10) It has a margin of autonomy vis-à-vis the external forces amidst which it functions.

(11) It is a self-directing unity insofar as its modifications are concerned. The essential forms of its future development are implicit in the system itself, as its potentialities. Hence its development consists essentially in unfolding its potentialities and in translating them into actualities. The principal role of the external factors is to accelerate or retard, facilitate, or hinder the unfolding of these potentialities; sometimes, however, they destroy the system itself.

(12) A sociocultural system is marked by alternate periods of growth and decline. Sometimes it becomes extinct, and in rare cases it is resurrected.

INADEQUACY AND LIMITED APPLICABILITY OF THE METHODS AND PRINCIPLES OF THE NATURAL SCIENCES IN THE STUDY OF SOCIOCULTURAL PHENOMENA

The preceding concise analysis shows the fundamental difference between sociocultural phenomena and systems and physicochemical and biological phenomena and systems. The component of meanings in sociocultural phenomena makes this difference almost unbridgeable —in any case, basic.

This disparity makes it impossible to employ identical methods and principles in the study of physicobiological and sociocultural phenomena. More specifically, the methods and principles of the physicochemical and biological sciences cannot be applied in their entirety to, and are insufficient for, a study of sociocultural phenomena. Even among the natural sciences, each has its own peculiar methods, principles, and techniques: those of physics are not exactly the same as those of chemistry; those of macrophysics differ from those of microphysics; and those of physics and chemistry are quite distinct from those of biology. Because of the fundamental difference between sociocultural phenomena and physicochemical and biological phenomena, the sociocultural sciences require in even greater degree their own peculiar methods, principles, and techniques. In this sense, sociology and the social sciences necessarily constitute a group of sciences *sui generis,* distinct in logical and epistemological structure from the natural sciences. In this sense, they depend as little upon the natural sciences as these depend upon the sociocultural sciences.

It should now be clear why all efforts to apply the same methods, principles, and techniques to the two fields have invariably failed and must continue to fail. Without exception, they have resulted in a distortion of the principles of the natural sciences; in a distortion of logic; and, finally, in the complete destruction of the identity of sociocultural phenomena as such. The net result has thus always been negative.

A few examples will give an idea of these blunders perpetrated by the blind imitators of the natural sciences. We are pompously told that "consciousness is an electron-proton aggregation" (A. P. Weiss);

that consciousness is a "complex integration and succession of bodily activities which are closely related to or involve the verbal and gestural mechanisms, and hence most frequently come to social expression" (K. S. Lashley[12]); that emotion is "a particular stimulus-response relationship" (W. S. Hunter[13]).

If I had not put at the beginning of these definitions the words "consciousness" and "emotions," nobody would have guessed that these formulas were the definitions of consciousness and emotions. To such an extent they are poor, inadequate and "deaf-mute." Furthermore, my table is also an electron-proton aggregation. Does this mean that it is "consciousness"? A frog exhibits "a complex integration and succession of bodily activities which involve the vocal and gestural mechanisms." Does this mean that the frog is "consciousness"? A snake certainly shows "a particular stimulus-response relationship." Shall we conclude that the snake is "emotion"? These remarks show that these "scientific" formulas are, in fact, the worst kind of metaphysics.[14]

The same may be said of hundreds of similar "behavioristic" and "operational" analyses of practically any sociocultural and meaningful phenomenon undertaken by the partisans of "natural-science sociology" or "natural-science psychology." For instance, a certain mental phenomenon is defined as the "behavior of an object of specified characteristics reacting to a stimulus of specified characteristics within the specified field of forces."[15] The reader can hardly guess what is actually defined by this behavioristically operational definition, and least of all can he guess that it is a scientific definition of "fear." In fact, the definition may mean anything or nothing, suggesting no specific characteristic of fear or of anything whatsoever.

The same is to be said of such definitions as "cessation of crying; gurgling, cooing, and many other undetermined (reactions). Predomination of visceral factors shown by changes in circulation and respiration, erection of penis."[16] This is supposed to be a scientific definition of "love-behavior," while "stiffening of the whole body, screaming, temporary cessation of breathing, reddening of face, changing to blueness of face" is given as a scientific definition of "rage-

[12] K. S. Lashley, "The Behavioristic Interpretation of Consciousness," *Psychological Review*, XXX (1923), 327 and 329.

[13] W. S. Hunter, "The Problem of Consciousness," *Psychological Review*, XXX (1924), 1-31; and "Psychology and Anthroponomy," *Psychologies of 1925*, p. 91.

[14] Sorokin, *Sociological Theories*, p. 622.   [15] Lundberg, *op. cit.*, pp. 12-14.

[16] J. B. Watson, "Experimental Studies of the Growth of the Emotions," *Psychologies of 1925*, pp. 49-50.

behavior." Dr. Watson seems never to have observed that many people do not scream when in a rage, nor become blue in the face. On the other hand, these bodily changes associated with rage may be easily applied to "fear-behavior," which he defines as "checking of breathing, jump or start of the whole body, crying, often defecation and urination."[17]

What is most important is that these definitions in no way even touch fear, rage, love, or any other psychological and meaningful experience. Even as a description of overt fear, love, or rage behavior, they are a thousand times more inaccurate and vague than the description of such behavior as given by great novelists in sociocultural terms. Without exception, all such attempts to catch meaningful phenomena in a strictly scientific behavioristic or operational net have failed to catch any sociocultural fish at all. Instead, they have landed only logical and factual monsters.[18]

No better are the results of the interpretation of sociocultural phenomena in terms of physics, mechanics, and other natural sciences. They represent merely either a transcription of formulas of mechanics in application to sociocultural phenomena or utterly meaningless statements. The assertion that "an increase of kinetic energy of an individual is equivalent to a decrease of his potential energy," or that "the total energy of a social group in regard to its action at a given moment (Ti) is equivalent to the total energy of the group which it had at an initial moment (To) plus the total amount of the work which during this period of time $(Ti-To)$ has been done by all forces external to the group," or that "the total energy of an individual in the field of forces remains constant throughout all its modifications,"[19] is nothing more than a simplified transcription of a proposition of physical mechanics transferred to the field of the social sciences, and as such both irrelevant and meaningless.

In order that such propositions may possess real significance and may be applied to sociocultural phenomena, we must know, first, what the authors mean by "kinetic and potential force or energy" in relation

[17] *Loc. cit.*

[18] For a further criticism of these procedures, cf. Sorokin, *Sociological Theories*, pp. 623-627.

[19] For similar propositions, cf. S. C. Haret, *Mécanique sociale* (Paris and Bucharest, 1910), and A. P. y Barceló, *Essais de mécanique sociale* (Paris, 1925). For further references, cf. Sorokin, *Sociological Theories*, chap. i and subsequent chapters of this volume.

to man, society, and culture; second, what the unit of this force is in this connection; and, third, how we can measure with this unit the various forms of sociocultural force or energy.

In physical mechanics, as applied to material points or bodies and their motions, the problems relative to force and energy, their unit, the methods of measuring of the relationship of forces, and so on, are excellently defined. But in the sociocultural field, the imitators of mechanics have hardly ever even raised these problems. They certainly have never offered a working definition of sociocultural energy or force, of its unit, or of the method of measurement by means of such a unit. They have never demonstrated how such formulas can be applied to the individual or group or to sociocultural phenomena generally. Hence their propositions are utterly empty insofar as they concern man and sociocultural phenomena. Nay, more; the authors in question submit no evidence—observational, experimental, statistical, or otherwise—to prove that, for instance, "the total energy of an individual in the field of forces remains constant throughout all its modifications," or "that an increase of kinetic energy of an individual is equivalent to a decrease of his potential energy."

Finally, if the procedure actually proved successful, it would serve merely to demonstrate the futility and superfluity of the social sciences! The aforesaid transcriptions are based upon the assumption that man is a "material point" or "material body," that his milieu is "the field of forces," that human activities and sociocultural events are but "motions of material points or bodies." If the assumption is correct, then the need for such transcriptions and of "social physics," "social mechanics," and the social sciences in general disappears, since the phenomena in question are the proper concern of the physical and mechanical sciences.

The laws of physical mechanics do not say that they are applied to all material bodies with the exception of human bodies. They are applied to human bodies and to all other social things so far as their material and physical character is concerned. Therefore there is no reason to insist on, or to create, a special theory of "social gravitation" or "social inertia," or a "law of social entropy," or any special law of physical mechanics. The "mechanists" try to break with violence into a room whose doors are wide open.[20]

[20] Sorokin, *Sociological Theories*, pp. 31-32.

On the other hand,

Trying to interpret man and social phenomena in the light of the principles of mechanics or general energetics, they disregard a series of specific characteristics of social phenomena which belong only to the human world, and which do not belong to other physical, chemical, or biological phenomena. As a result of the mechanistic school's "equalization" of sociocultural and physical phenomena, the theories ascribe to physical phenomena a series of human characteristics (anthropomorphism), and take off from sociocultural phenomena a series of their specific traits. Because of this the laws of mechanics are disfigured, their "nature" is made "anthropomorphic," and the essentials of sociocultural phenomena are passed over, without even touching them.

It may be true that social instinct is but a variety of physical gravitation; yet, can we say that each phenomenon of gravitation, for instance, of the earth and the moon, is a "social instinct"? It may be true, as Voronoff (and other imitators of mechanics) say, that "the social phenomena of association and coöperation are nothing but those of addition and multiplication of forces"; but does this mean that each case of addition and multiplication of forces in physical mechanics is a social phenomenon of coöperation and association? Evidently not. If not, then what is the difference between social coöperation and other cases of addition and multiplication of forces studied by mechanics?

This shows that the imitators of mechanics and physics study sociocultural phenomena only as purely physical manifestations. All that is specific in sociocultural facts, and all that differentiates them from inorganic phenomena, is factually excluded from the study. Human beings are simply transformed into a mere physical mass; facts of social life, human conduct, heroism, love, hatred, struggle, coöperation, ethics, religion, fine arts, science, literature, and so on—all these are transformed into a mere "physical mass," and a study is made of its transformation and its "motion." In this way, all that is specific in sociocultural phenomena is lost, being passed over and left without any analysis whatsoever. This means that all these social physics and social mechanics are useless, because they do not study sociocultural phenomena at all, as distinct from the "mass of material bodies" and their "motion." They are useless also because human beings, as a physical mass, are studied by physics, chemistry, and mechanics; and as a mere organism by the biological sciences.[21]

To repeat, there is no adequate reason for the existence of an amateurish "social physics" and "social mechanics" side by side with an authentic system of physics, chemistry, and mechanics capable of a

[21] *Ibid.*, pp. 33-34; also chap. i *et passim*, for a survey of numerous theories of the imitators of mechanics, physics, chemistry, and biology, and for a more substantial criticism of the fallacies of such theories.

more competent investigation of the same phenomena. Similarly, there is no excuse for a dilettantish "social biology" side by side with an authentic biology which is much more competent to deal with human beings as pure organisms. The fundamentally different character of sociocultural phenomena, as compared with physicochemical or biological phenomena, makes it impractical to treat them simply as a variety of physicochemical and biological phenomena or to apply to them the basic referential principles of physics, chemistry, and biology, as these are applied to the natural sciences.

Since the component of meaning of sociocultural phenomena excludes physical space, physical time, and the causality of natural science, and since meanings lack material mass, volume, color, sound, chemical composition, and other physicochemical properties, the principles of the natural sciences are much more inapplicable to meanings, and to sociocultural phenomena of which meanings are components, than to the "microscopic physicochemical phenomena" of wave mechanics to which, according to the natural scientists themselves, neither space, causality, nor other principles of macrophysics are applicable.[22]

[22] "It is absolutely meaningless from the point of view of physical operations . . . to talk about the *space inside* an electron. . . . Since 'inside' is a spatial term, we might as well admit that 'inside of the electron' is itself a meaningless combination." "The electron as a whole is outside the range of the spatial concept." Likewise, the concepts of time and causality, and several others, are inapplicable in the field of subatomic physics. See P. W. Bridgman, *op. cit.*, pp. 30-35 ff.

"Since all experiments are subjected to the laws of Quantum Mechanics, and thus to the equation (Δ p. Δ q $\div$ h = 6.55.10⁻²⁷ erg x second) the failure or nonvalidity of the Causality Law is definitely established by the Quantum Mechanics." See W. Heisenberg, "Über den anschaulichen Inhalt der quantentheoretischen Kinematik und Mechanik," *Zeitschrift f. Physik*, XLIII (1927), 172-198. See also his *Physical Principle of the Quantum Theory* (1930), chaps. i-iii; and *Wandlungen in den Grundlagen der Naturwissenschaft* (Leipzig, 1935).

In the field of microphysics, "we have found out that the mechanical laws are breaking down," and "philosophic determinism . . . is now shown by experimental physics to be a false generalization." R. A. Millikan, "Time," *Time and Its Mysteries* (New York, 1936), pp. 17-19. See also L. de Broglie, "Continuité et Individualité dans la physique moderne," *Cahiers de la nouvelle journée*, XV (1929), 73; and P. A. M. Dirac, *The Principles of Quantum Mechanics* (Oxford, 1935).

Other eminent mathematicians and physicists—such as E. Schroedinger, A. Eddington, P. Jordan, and M. Born—find that the principle of causality, as well as that of space and several other categories, is inapplicable to the field of subatomic physics and must be replaced by a different set of principles, such as that of "indeterminacy" and the like.

Since the physicists themselves find a set of the principles of macrophysics inapplicable to subatomic physical phenomena, it is amusing to see certain social scientists trying to apply to sociocultural phenomena concepts of macrophysics which are inapplicable even to a set of physical phenomena themselves. Such attempts are due: (1) to a lack of any real knowledge of these principles of physics on the part of such social scientists,

Since meanings do not have any of the properties of physicochemical phenomena, and since meanings are the most important component of sociocultural phenomena, none of the physicochemical principles are applicable to them in the form in which they operate in the physicochemical sciences. This syllogism is practically unimpeachable. Hence the absurdity of the claim that sociology and social sciences must be an *alter ego* of the physicochemical sciences. These considerations are quite sufficient to refute all such pretensions.[23]

If the nature of sociocultural phenomena is fundamentally different from that of the physicochemical and biological phenomena, and if the principles of these natural sciences are inapplicable to a considerable degree to the cognition of sociocultural reality, it follows that their

---

who replace them by a homemade distortion of these principles; and (2) to a similar lack of understanding of what sociocultural phenomena really are. It is but natural that this double distortion should produce atrocious results for the physicochemical sciences as well as for the social sciences.

For the inapplicability of causality, Euclidian space, and other principles of macrophysics to subatomic physics, see also A. Eddington, *Philosophy of the Physical Science* (New York, 1940), pp. 90, 180-184, and 221; M. Born, *Moderne Physik* (Berlin, 1933); E. Schroedinger, *Über Indeterminismus in der Physik* (Leipzig, 1932); A. Boutaric, *Les Conceptions actuelles de la physique* (Paris, 1936); L. Silberstein, *Causality* (London, 1933); P. Jordan, "Die Erfahrungsgrundlagen der Quantentheorie," *Die Naturwissenschaften* (Berlin, 1929), 17; H. Weyl, *Philosophie der Mathematik und Naturwissenschaft* (München—Berlin, 1927); H. Weyl, *The Open World* (New Haven, 1932); F. Christmann, *Biologische Kausalität* (Tübingen, 1928); L. de Broglie, *La Physique nouvelle et les quanta* (Paris, Flammarion, n. d.); F. Oppenheimer, *Der Kausalbegriff in der neuesten Physik* (Leipzig, 1931); E. Meyerson, *Identité et realité* (Paris, 1912); and *Du cheminement de la pensée* (Paris, 1931), Vol. I, *passim;* P. Frank, *Les Principes de causalité et ses limites* (Paris, Flammarion, n. d.); and M. Taube, *Causation, Freedom, and Determinism* (London, 1936).

It is instructive to note that the eminent physicists themselves, such as M. Planck, quite definitely state that the field of sociocultural phenomena—especially the field of the "ego" and "free will"—is exempt from causation. See M. Planck, *Where Science Is Going* (New York, 1932), pp. 145-169; and M. Bohr, "Causality and Complementarity," *Philosophy of Science* (1937), pp. 289-290.

Our pseudosocial scientists appear to be *plus royaliste que le roi même!* From this standpoint, W. C. Reckless, T. E. Kuczma, and a few other social scientists are right in stating that "the concept of causation [in its macrophysical sense] is, after all, rather inapplicable to the study of social behavior." See W. C. Reckless, *Criminal Behavior* (New York, 1940), p. 2; and T. E. Kuczma, *The Genetic Approach to Crime* (Poznan, 1939). Unfortunately, these scholars do not go far enough in this direction, and take the contemporary probabilistic-externalistic "multiple causation" as a substitute for the deterministic causality of macrophysics. The new "adopted child" is hardly better fitted for a study of the intra- and inter-system relationships among sociocultural phenomena than the rejected child of the deterministic causality. The reasons for this statement are given in the next chapter.

[23] For other absurdities of the respective theories, cf. Sorokin, *Sociological Theories,* chap. i.

methods as such are also to a certain extent inapplicable. Hence the *necessity for sociology and other social sciences to have their own framework of referential principles and methods.* The most important contributions to our understanding of sociocultural phenomena made by such thinkers as Plato and Aristotle, Saint Augustine and the Scholastics, Ibn-Khaldun and Vico, Machiavelli and Montesquieu, Herbert Spencer and Auguste Comte, were made, not through imitative transference of the concepts, principles, and methods of the natural sciences, but through a direct study of sociocultural reality, with a set of principles and methods suited to its nature and adequate for such a task.

In part, the framework of the principles and methods of the socio-cultural sciences may run parallel to those of the natural sciences and be in a sense homological to these, though profoundly different. In part, also, the referential principles of the sociocultural and natural sciences are mutually incompatible and are essentially heterogeneous. The following list gives an idea of what is meant by homological principles with reference to both classes of sciences.

HOMOLOGICAL REFERENTIAL PRINCIPLES

The Natural Sciences	*The Sociocultural Sciences*
(1) Two-componential structure of the phenomena: *(a)* physicochemical; *(b)* vital, or biological.	(1) Three-componential structure of the phenomena: *(a)* immaterial meanings; *(b)* biological; *(c)* physicochemical.
(2) Physicochemical and biological systems as causally interdependent systems.	(2) Sociocultural systems as meaningfully and causally interdependent systems.
(3) Causal relationship between the phenomena.	(3) Meaningful-causal relationship between the phenomena.
(4) Chance relationship between the phenomena (lack of causal relationship).	(4) Congeries relationship between the phenomena (lack of meaningful-causal relationship).
(5) Space.	(5) Sociocultural space.
(6) Time.	(6) Sociocultural time.
(7) Motion.	(7) Quantitative and, especially, qualitative change.
(8) Velocity.	(8) Sociocultural tempo.
(9) Mechanistic periodicity.	(9) Sociocultural (conventional) periodicity.
(10) Rhythm.	(10) Sociocultural rhythm.

(11) Observational, dialectic, and intuitional methods of study applied exclusively to "objective," or external, properties, and relationships.

(11) Observational, dialectic, and intuitional methods of study applied to the inner meanings as well as to the external vehicles of the sociocultural phenomena, properties, and relationships.

As has been said, while these and several other principles of the two classes of science run parallel and are homological, each principle nevertheless remains profoundly different from its analogue. With reference to causality, time, and space, this difference will be shown in subsequent chapters. With reference to tempo, periodicity, equilibrium, and causal and meaningful-causal systems, the difference has been demonstrated elsewhere.[24]

For the present, it is enough to say in illustration of the point that, when a social scientist speaks of "social movements," he does not mean physical motion; and conversely, that physical motion is not social movement. City workers during the "rush hour" exhibit a plenitude of physical motion, but this motion does not constitute a social movement. Conversely, there is many a social movement that does not manifest itself in any increase of physical motion. When we speak of the tempo, or velocity, of change in sociocultural phenomena—for instance, from capitalism to communism, or from the Gothic to the Baroque—we do not mean the units of physical space divided by the units of physical time, as in the physical sciences. When sociocultural sciences study the phenomena of wealth and talk of the "mass of wealth," they do not envisage a mass of matter in contradistinction to its absence. A socially "powerful" person or group does not necessarily mean either the world's heavyweight champion or a group which has at its disposal the maximum of physical force. Solidarity does not mean the physical gravitation of one man to another or a physical coming together; otherwise two regiments of enemies deadlocked in mortal combat would represent the maximum of solidarity. "Social rapprochement" is not a shortening of the physical space between the respective persons or groups. Meaningful consistency has little to do with, say, either uniform and rectilinear motion or the operation of two or more mechanical forces of the same direction and sense. Sociocul-

---

[24] Cf. Sorokin, *Dynamics,* Vol. IV, chaps. i, ii, ix, x, xiii, xiv, *et passim.* In these chapters, the nature of sociocultural rhythms, periodicities, equilibrium, and tempo are analyzed in considerable detail.

tural equilibrium (if it means anything at all) has nothing to do with the equilibrium of mechanics.[25] And so on.

Even more marked is the difference in the case of those principles which are nonhomological and which must be applied exclusively to either physicochemical and biological phenomena or to sociocultural phenomena. For instance, *anything concerning the component of meaning—such as thought, mentality, aims or purposes, values, solidarity, hatred, and the like—is inapplicable to physicochemical phenomena;* otherwise there results an atrocious anthropomorphization, and hence distortion of the respective physicochemical phenomena. On the other hand, *the categories and concepts related to meaning and its derivatives are absolutely indispensable in the study of sociocultural phenomena.* There has never been any history of sociocultural phenomena—economics, political science, sociology, or psychology—which has not been obliged to deal with aims and purposes; with values; with religious, esthetic, philosophical, and scientific meanings; and with all the infinite range of beliefs, ideas, emotions, feelings, volitions, and other derivatives of the category of meaning. This category, together with its derivatives, is a fundamental prerequisite of the sociocultural sciences. Its indispensability for these sciences and its complete inapplicability to the natural sciences determine hundreds of other differences characterizing the respective procedures and disciplines.

It is futile for a sociocultural scientist to speak in terms of "atoms," "the electron-proton," "mass," "velocity," "gravitation," "entropy," and other elements of the natural sciences in an analysis, description, and classification of sociocultural phenomena. Conversely, a natural scientist who indulged in loose talk about the "purposes of atoms," the "mentality of electrons," the "religious beliefs of amoebae or paramecia," the "esthetic emotions of material bodies moving uniformly and rectilinearly," the "passionate love or hatred of molecules," the "ethical norms of gravitating bodies," and the like, is obviously ignorant both of logic and of the natural sciences. Any attempt to transfer to another group the principles indispensable to either the natural or the sociocultural sciences and applicable only to one group invariably leads merely to logical and factual aberrations.

This explains, furthermore, the differences in the *uniformities of*

[25] *Ibid.,* IV, 669-693.

the natural and the sociocultural sciences. Leaving aside several external discrepancies,[26] the content of these uniformities is radically different in the two cases. For instance, the statement that organized social groups originate mainly in two ways—spontaneously or deliberately—is a proposition that formulates two types of very general uniformities in the genesis of such groups. These two types virtually exhaust their modes of origin. In this sense, the proposition is a genuine formula of sociocultural uniformity. It is evident, however, that no natural scientist can properly apply it to a group of electrons, atoms, or molecules, or even to herds of "societies" of fish, ants, bees, wasps, or monkeys. Similarly, in describing how two or more persons meet, the social scientist can state that "they meet by agreement, or appointment, or by the order of authority." Each form of meeting embraces a large number of cases, and thus represents a general type and hence a fairly general uniformity. But such a formula of uniformity is evidently inapplicable to the "meeting" of electrons, atoms, molecules, or even of most of the biological organisms.

With the proper modification, the same may be said of almost all the other uniformities in the natural and sociocultural sciences: they are disparate in their nature and content. This disparity, together with the fashionable notion that only the uniformities of the natural sciences are genuine, is responsible for the widely diffused opinion that the social sciences possess few, if any, uniformities, whereas the natural sciences are replete with them. When carefully considered, this theory is found to be entirely without foundation. In reality, both fields of inquiry exhibit a large number of appropriate formulae of uniformities, despite the difference in their character and content. Likewise, in the discovery and formulation of uniformities the respective sciences have their own peculiar advantages and disadvantages. The widely prevalent notion that all the advantages are on the side of the natural sciences is distinctly fallacious.

The foregoing discussion gives some idea of the homological and nonhomological referential principles of the natural and sociocultural sciences. It indicates also the need of the sociocultural sciences for their own framework of referential principles. In subsequent chapters, the profound differences between even the homological principles of these fields of inquiry will be analyzed in some detail with respect to the three cardinal principles of causality, time, and space.

[26] Cf. *ibid.,* IV, 97-199.

CHAPTER II

SOCIOCULTURAL CAUSALITY

THE CONTEMPORARY CONCEPTION OF THE STABLE AND UNSTABLE ASSOCIATION OF VARIABLES

It is not the purpose of this study to survey the innumerable definitions of causality and of its derivatives. Suffice it to say that, aside from numerous secondary differences between these definitions, there have been three fundamentally heterogeneous conceptions of causality: ideational, idealistic, and sensate.[1] From another standpoint, these fall into two distinct classes: one conceives causality as a *necessary* relationship, either objectively sustained by the variables or subjectively imposed by our minds as an a priori category; the other postulates no *necessity* in such a relationship, viewing it as an empirical stable association of two or more variables—in the terms of David Hume,[2] a mere recurrent empirical "contiguity and succession" of *A* and *B*. Each of these conceptions involves hundreds of variations of the meaning of causality. It is enough to cite W. K. Clifford's observation that "the word represented by 'cause' has sixty-four meanings in Plato and forty-eight in Aristotle."

These were men who liked to know as near as might be what they meant; but how many meanings it has had in the writings of the myriads of people who have not tried to know what they meant by it will, I hope, never be counted.[3]

Nor am I going to discuss the enormous number of implications of causality. My task is simpler, consisting on the one hand in an indication of the limitations and fallacies of the prevalent conceptions and use of this principle in contemporary sociology and social science, and on the other in constructive suggestions for its improvement.

The prevalent character of the causal-factorial relationship between the sociocultural phenomena is so peculiar that it is difficult to characterize it adequately. Its initial principle is supposedly simple: if two

---

[1] Cf. P. A. Sorokin, *Social and Cultural Dynamics,* Vol. II, chap. xi.

[2] Cf. David Hume, *Treatise on Human Nature,* I, 80 ff.

[3] W. K. Clifford, "On Aims and Instruments of Scientific Thought," *Lectures and Essays* (London, 1886), pp. 85-109.

variables, A and B, are in such a relationship that each time A is given B is also given, and whenever A varies B varies, such a relationship is causal. Its characteristic is the inseparability of A and B. A is the cause, or factor, or "the independent variable"; B is the effect, or "dependent variable."[4] The relationship remains causal and functional if this inseparability is mutual, and instead of one-sided dependence of the effect upon the cause, we have mutual interdependence of the two variables. But as soon as we try to apply it to sociocultural phenomena, we are confronted with the almost complete absence of any such inseparable relationship between the objective and material sociocultural variables. We find hardly any relationship between an objective sociocultural A and B which displays this inseparability in its strict sense. Instead, we have a situation in which A and B here and there appear together and seem to vary together; but sometimes A (or what seems to be A) is not followed by B (or what seems to be B), and B (or what seems to be B) is not preceded by A (or what seems to be A). Such is the relationship we find in ninety-nine, if not one hundred, per cent of the cases of causal relationship between the objective sociocultural variables. Their relationship appears to be not strictly causal but a "stochastic," or chance, relationship.[5]

Hence the difficulties of "causal-factorial" analysis in the social sciences. If A and B were always found in conjunction, and if other sociocultural variables exhibited similar indissoluble "conjugal" ties, the analysis would be a simple operation. All that we should have to do would be to observe which variable is uniformly and indissolubly wedded to which; to pick out such pairs; and to formulate the respective laws, or uniformities, of their causal union. Since, however, few, if any, of the sociocultural variables behave in this way, and since most, if not all, of them are "promiscuous," appearing in the company now of A, now of B, now of C, the hunt for the indissoluble causal "marriages" becomes impossible.

Impossible, likewise, is the application of the strict conception of

---

[4] "The concept of causal connection means that the cause and effect are inseparably connected with each other: if A is the cause of A', the effect A' follows always and everywhere the cause A, and A' cannot be found anywhere where A is not present." See A. A. Tschuprow, *Grundbegriffe und Grundprobleme der Korrelationstheorie* (Leipzig and Berlin, 1925), p. 12.

[5] For the nature of the stochastic relationship, cf. *ibid.*, pp. 20 ff. See also J. Bernoulli, *Ars Conjectandi* (Basileae, 1713), p. 213; and L. von Bortkiewicz, *Die Iterationen* (Berlin, 1917), p. 3.

causality. Since there are no duly registered certificates of "causal marriage" of the variables, all that we can do under such circumstances is to find out which "liaisons" between the variables are comparatively stable and which are entirely accidental; which pairs of variables frequently keep pace with one another and which are entirely promiscuous. The whole matter is thus thrown into the field of chance, and (since there are no "registered marriages") we must rely upon purely detective work—that of spying out the more or less stable and the more or less promiscuous associations of the variables. Hence the *replacement of strictly causal relationships by probable (or chance) associations of the variables in contemporary social science.* The objective of "causal-factorial" analysis now aims, not so much to discover the permanent monogamous marriages ("necessary relationships") between the variables, as to determine just which variables are associated more regularly and which are entirely independent. Cause and effect are displaced by the variables (mutually or one-sidedly dependent). The cause becomes an independent variable; the effect, a dependent variable. This replacement requires a corresponding modification of the detective technique.

Having become probabilistic, the contemporary search for a comparatively stable association of the variables has become also mechanistic and externalistic. If the liaisons between the more or less promiscuous variables are chance liaisons, devoid of the inner ties of the duly registered causal marriage, and therefore of the inner obligation to live and function together, which of the liaisons are stable and which are entirely promiscuous can evidently be detected only through externalistic observation of the pairs of variables; for the detective scientist cannot go to the marriage registry to find whether the variables are married or not. All that he can do is to spy out the behavior of the variables and, on this basis, report which are more and which are less promiscuous.

Hence the *externalistic* character of the contemporary study of the associations of variables—a consequence of the assumed principle of probability. It is externalistic in three senses:

(1) The study is concerned with a chance relationship, devoid of any inner (necessary) ties.

(2) The variables are externalistic, transsubjective, material (space-time) phenomena that can be observed by a detective external to them.

Variables cannot be something immaterial, like meanings or ideas. Being immaterial, pure meanings cannot be discovered at all by an external observer. He can perhaps grasp something of the meanings when they are objectified in material vehicles. But as this appears to him subjective and unverifiable, he prefers to be *an unbiased external observer of objectively given material variables,* such as the amount of pig iron produced; the number of shares exchanged on the stock market; the number of buildings erected; the number of marriages, births, and deaths registered; the number of icecream cones eaten; and the like. Here he feels certain of his data and on solid ground. Such variables are observable objectively; the observation of one observer can be checked by that of the others.

(3) The dependent variable (the effect) is often considered to be a passive victim of the independent variable (the cause or factor), which, by "pressing," "pushing," or "pulling," "forces" the variable effect to behave as it does. In some cases of so-called "multiple causation," the dependent variable is regarded as the victim of a whole gang of factors or causes. In the case of the interdependence of the variables, each is considered to be the "victim" of the other, without whose pressure it could not be what it is and could not do what it does.

Hence the *externalistic, objectivistic, and somewhat materialistic character of the prevailing conception of the association of variables.*

This has led, further, to a *mechanistic technique* for detecting the comparative stability of the liaisons of variables. Since there are no inner (necessary) ties between them; since the strictly inductive methods of identity, difference, concomitant variation, and residues are rarely, if ever, applicable to the study of sociocultural phenomena, because the other conditions (even if we are aware of them) are hardly ever constant or under our strict control; and since there is scarcely any possibility for the variables solemnly to vary (according to the rules of induction) in the presence of a solemn company of witnesses (conditions) who remain constant—for these reasons the detective-explorer is forced to observe them as frequently as he can in all circumstances and to register in his notebook how many times they appeared together, how many times they appeared separately or with other companions, and what is the ratio of the cases of variables which keep pace with one another to the total number of observed cases. Hence the *statistical technique* of the study of such associations, with all its paraphernalia and dogmatic prescriptions. In other cases, our detective-explorer may use different techniques—experimental (though a strictly experimental situation is seldom available for sociocultural variables, and so-called "experimental" and "inductive" studies in the social sciences are but pretentious misnomers), roughly observational, clinical, and so forth. However, all these techniques remain essentially externalistic and mechanistic.

Such are the characteristics of the present-day social-science conception of the relationship of variables and the procedure for detecting its comparative stability or instability.

It is hardly necessary to add that, in this substitution of the concept of probabilistic, externalistic association for that of strict causality, the social sciences have proceeded hand in hand with the natural sciences, which, during the twentieth century, have made a similar shift from rigid causality to chance association.[6]

What shall we say about this conception of the relationship between the variables and of the procedure used for the detection of its stability or instability? Shall we regard all this as "the last word of science," destined to stand forever? How well suited is it to the study of the relationship between sociocultural variables, and how fruitful has it been in such a study? How reliable are the results obtained?

---

[6] The conception of causality in the natural and social sciences from the sixteenth to the nineteenth century, inclusive, was predominantly deterministic and causal. Not only natural phenomena but also social phenomena were regarded as being tied together by rigidly causal relationships, as "the necessary relationships arising from the nature of things" (Montesquieu's famous definition). They were considered as immutable and invariable; therefore strictly uniform. "Social phenomena are under the domination of unvarying law in precisely the same sense that astronomical phenomena are." See Lester Ward, *Dynamic Sociology* (New York, 1907), I, 458-460 and 511-512, and II, 602-603 *et passim*.

In the twentieth century, the natural and social sciences have replaced this strict causality by that of chance relationships. At the present time, the law of chance is "the most fundamental and indispensable of all physical laws," and all the predictions in the physical sciences are based upon "the assumption of noncorrelation of the behavior of individual particles, which is derived from the law of chance." See Sir Arthur Eddington, *The Philosophy of Physical Science*, pp. 61, 89-90, 181-184, and 221; R. A. Millikan, "Time," *Time and Its Mysteries*, quoted, pp. 17-19; and L. Silberstein, *Causality*. Cf. also the works of W. Heisenberg, N. Bohr, L. de Broglie, and others quoted in Chapter I.

A similar rightabout-face has occurred in the social sciences. Cf. Sorokin, *Dynamics*, Vol. II, chaps. xi and ix, which discuss the data, names, and nature of the change.

The Ordinary Limitations and Fallacies of the Prevalent Conception of the Causal-associational Relationships between Sociocultural Variables

Since the contemporary conception of the association between sociocultural variables is based on probability, for this reason alone no conclusion obtained can ever be certain; at best, it can only be roughly approximate and more or less probable. Its very nature makes it also temporary and "provincial" in its probable validity—not eternal and universal. Since there is no inner necessity even in comparatively stable associations, and since the explorer can never investigate all the past, present, and future relationships between his variables A and B, he does not have any ground to consider his findings as perennially and universally valid. Chance may tomorrow produce a combination of A and B quite different from what he has observed. Thus the probabilistic conception of the association makes it inevitably somewhat uncertain and limited in its uniformity. Insofar as valid and universal certainty is the main objective of scientific research, the discussed probabilistic conception aims only at a second-class, "provincial," and temporary validity of an inferior kind, rather than the certainty and validity that would be implicit in strictly causal relationships if these were actually exhibited by sociocultural phenomena. Such is the first handicap due to the shift from the belief in the existence of causal relationships to that of chance relationships.

However, this is not the only drawback. Even the relative validity of the conclusions reached through the above probabilistic analysis of the more and less stable association of the variables becomes still more questionable—often entirely unreliable—when the ideal conditions essential for the success of the study are lacking or are not carried through.

The results become highly uncertain when the number of the total observed cases of A and B is only a fraction of all possible cases of the association under investigation, no matter how large may be the absolute number of cases observed, or how high may be the coefficient of correlation or association. If we investigated, say, ten thousand cases of murder, and in all these instances we found that all the ten thousand murderers were dolichocephali and blondes, we should not thereby be entitled to conclude that the cause or factor of murder is dolichocephalism and blondness. One reason is that ten thousand murders are but a negligible percentage of the total of past, present, and future murders committed among all peoples. Another reason is the possible "mistaken identity" of the "factor villain": we can never be sure that out of *millions of possible factors* amid which murders occur we have chosen the right "villain." In this particular case, the mistaken identity of the factor is evident; for murders are committed also by brachy-cephali, mesocephali, and brunettes.

Likewise, the validity of a conclusion is impaired when the ratio of the cases of association of *A* and *B* observed is very low in proportion to the total number of observed cases of *A* and *B* where one variable is not followed by the other.

Again, the result is highly uncertain where the totality of the conditions in which *X* occurs is exceedingly large and diverse. In all such cases, the probability of identifying the right villain as a factor or associated variable among possible millions is rather low, and the probability of choosing the wrong villain is rather high. The point is that a discovery of the real cause of a comparatively simple phenomenon—such as the variation of the temperature at which water boils—is a much more difficult task than many think. Usually, the process of such a discovery is depicted as a simple application of an inductive method, especially of the rule of concomitant variation and of difference.

But the real procedure is very different, says A. A. Tschuprow.

The experimenter heats water to 100 degrees Celsius; the water begins to boil. Does he have the right to start his causal analysis with the assumption that the complex of causes of this observed result consists of the form, material, and size of the water-container and of the temperature reached? What happens if he begins to vary the conditions of his experiment (according to the principle of concomitant variation) in order to find out whether the temperature at which water boils sustains a causal relationship to the material and form of the water-container? To what conclusions would he be led by the strictest application of the rules of induction if he did not include in the relevant conditions the barometric pressure? Repeating the experiment in the same container, he would see that, according to the barometric pressure, water boils now at 99 degrees (Celsius), now at 101 degrees. On the other hand, at any of these temperatures, water will now boil, now will not boil, in a brass or iron or glass container, and so on. In brief, the experiment cannot come to any definite conclusion if the barometer remains constant during the experiments. Under less favorable conditions, the experimenter risks arriving at a wrong conclusion, in spite of the most rigorous application of the methods of induction. The water is heated in a small container and boils at 100 degrees. The next day it is heated in a large-sized container and boils at 99 degrees, owing to decreased barometric pressure. If barometric pressure is not included in the relevant conditions of A, B, and C, the method of difference will yield the conclusion that the temperature of boiling water is causally connected with the size of the container. Meanwhile, if he did not know in advance that the boiling temperature stands in a causal relationship with the atmospheric pressure, our experimenter would hardly think to record the barometric indicators. This means that working experimentally in an unfamiliar field, where the causal relationship remains to be discovered, the investigator can hardly apply the inductive methods, and, when he does, cannot have any guarantee against mistakes.[7]

Still greater is the danger of picking up a wrong factor as a real cause in the study of sociocultural causal relationships. That this is true is demonstrated by the whole history of causal-factorial research in the social sciences. This history is an ever-expanding graveyard of wrongly chosen causes, factors, and causal connections. Further testimony to the same effect is furnished by the immense variety of causal factors, or "independent variables," claimed by different investigators with reference to the same sociocultural "dependent variable" whether it be war, revolution, crime, the cycle of economic prosperity and depression, democracy, the triumph of Christianity, an art style, the fall of Rome, the decline of civilization, a certain form of the family, or a factor of birth, death, and marriage rates. I know of hardly any single sociocultural phenomenon whose cause or factor is the same according to all the existing theories. On the contrary, for practically any sociocultural phenomenon, from business depression to the fall of Rome, the theories regarding its causation or association are widely divergent.[8] If the villain factor were correctly chosen, such a discrepancy could not exist. If it exists and is, indeed, the rule, it follows that most of the theories are fallacious.

The foregoing discussion indicates the typical situations where the

---

[7] A. A. Tschuprow, *Ocherki po teorii statistiki (Studies in Statistical Theory)* (St. Petersburg, 1909), pp. 111 ff. These pages present a detailed and brilliant analysis of the difficulties in question.

[8] An example of this disparity of causal-factorial diagnoses is furnished by the enumeration of existing causes of war given in P. A. Sorokin, "A Neglected Factor of War," *American Sociological Review* (August, 1938), 475-486. What is said of the list of causal factors of war may be said of almost any sociocultural phenomenon. For other conflicting theories respecting the causation of all the important sociocultural phenomena, see Sorokin, *Contemporary Sociological Theories, passim.*

conclusions are highly uncertain and turn out in the majority of cases to be wrong. Meanwhile, the above conditions of uncertainty are the actual conditions under which the outlined type of causal-factorial (or associational) analysis is made. An overwhelming majority of "causal-factorial" studies are made under conditions in which: (1) a given phenomenon, X, occurs in thousands of different circumstances; (2) the total observed number of cases is but a small fraction of the total past and present number of occurrences of X; (3) the ratio of probability, or the coefficient of correlation, in this limited number of observed cases is far from being perfect or even high. The results of such studies are bound to remain completely uncertain. This is the reason, not only for the expansion of the "graveyard" of mistaken theories and for the bewildering variety of causal factors of the same phenomenon, X, offered by different investigators, but also for the increasing trouble with the coefficients of correlation and their statistical substitutes encountered at the present time.

When the first statistical studies of chance associations appeared and the first coefficients of correlation were devised, we viewed them as a kind of a magic key with which to unlock the exact measure of the causal relationship (or chance association) between the variables studied. When eventually the correlation technique became common, and a series of coefficients of correlation between *the same* variables was worked out, evidences of their incompatibility began to multiply. In some studies, the coefficient was found to be high, in others low; in some positive, in others negative. The net result is that, amidst such discordance, we know about the causal relationship of the variables (or their connection) as little as before. Such is exactly the situation that prevails in most of the relationships studied statistically. This growing disparity in the results of the statistical studies of the relationship between the same variables is a further evidence of the uncertainty of the results,[9] as well as of the dubiousness of the procedure.

[9] Needless to say, such statistical devices as "representativeness of the sample," "standard deviation," and especially "the probable error" are, for the most part, purely technical fictions which in no way measure or indicate the presence or absence of a real error in the conclusions. All that they really mean is a conventional device for measuring the conventional degree of the technical error in regard to the technical amount of the data, "processed according to the conventional technique." In many cases, not only is the formula for computing the "probable error" erroneous, but the whole material, data, and procedure, as well as the conclusions, are fallacious. These devices often represent nothing but "a misleading exactness." "We must beware of confounding the degree of precision with the certainty of science itself. The certainty of science and our pre-

If we have truly experimental conditions, with a real constancy of all the conditions except the studied variables, and can vary these as we need, according to the canons of true induction, all the foregoing uncertainties will disappear. By applying the strictly inductive methods of difference or agreement, or of concomitant variation, we enjoy a much better chance of arriving at more valid conclusions.[10] Unfortunately, in a study of sociocultural associational or causal relationships, we hardly ever encounter such conditions, and can hardly ever apply the actual experimental-inductive method. Virtually all so-called "experimental" studies in the social sciences are pseudoexperimental: they hardly ever exhibit the "constancy of all the other conditions"; they can seldom vary their variable as it needs to be varied; their "constancy" actually amounts merely to keeping all the variables constant on paper; their "control groups" are not control groups in the real inductive sense. In short, I know of scarcely any really inductive and experimental study in the social sciences. And the more complex and important the problem, the more impossible becomes its experimental investigation.

So-called Multiple Causation. To lessen the difficulties, the investigators of the causal-factorial relationship in sociocultural phenomena often turn to the principle of so-called "multiple causation." They state that a given X (such as war, revolution, business depression, increase of crime, marriage, the blossoming of the arts, or a change in the nature of the family or of the political regime) is the effect, or dependent variable, not of one "cause" or "factor," Y, but of a function of several factors, $Y, N, M. \ldots$ The statement assumes the form of the equation $X = f(Y, N, M \ldots)$. On paper, this procedure looks perfectly reasonable; but in reality it is not at all sound. Let us take, for example, the theories of multiple causation of war as advanced by most of the investigators of the phenomenon:[11]

---

cision in the knowledge of it are two very different things (often confounded). A very absurd proposition may be very precise (for instance, the sum of the angles of a triangle is equal to three right angles), . . . and a very certain proposition may be wanting in precision in our statement of it, as for instance, when we assert that every man will die." See Auguste Comte, *Positive Philosophy*, trans. Martineau (New York, 1855), I, 30.

    This sound distinction is often forgotten nowadays. We cultivate mainly "precise absurdities" or "exact uncertainties."

[10] Though even there, as the quotation from Tschuprow on pages 44-45 shows, the possibility of an erroneous conclusion is enormous.

[11] Subsequent quotations are taken from Sorokin, "A Neglected Factor of War." Cf. also his *Dynamics*, Vol. III, chaps. ix-xi.

A typical example is Dean Inge's enumeration of the factors of war: pugnacity, plus artificial stimulation, plus pressure of the population, plus machinations of the government to distract attention from internal affairs and to stop a revolution at home, plus aggressive imperialism, plus fear, plus a drive for unification, plus something else.[12] Aldous Huxley's multiple causation is as follows: geographic and climatic conditions, racial factors, economic factors, passions, wicked rulers, plus a series of psychoanalytical factors which he stresses as the most important.[13] Sir Josiah Stamp agrees that wars are caused by a "collection of conditions" among which he particularly mentions economic penetration, economic inequality, and differentiated population.[14] Professor James Ford enumerates the following elements of the multiple causation of war: economic factors, the private manufacture of armaments, dictatorships and totalitarian regimes, misguided education, mob psychology, anger and emotionalism, wrong attitudes, ambition, avariciousness, and so forth.[15] Sir Arthur Salter cites religious, dynastic, political, and economic causes, each consisting of several subclasses.[16] G. A. Johnston mentions specifically, among many other causes, social injustice, the monotony of industrial life, the artificial stimulation of consumption, and unemployment.[17]

The slogan of multiple causation is very popular nowadays. We use it all the time as something quite definite, sound, and unquestionable. As a matter of fact, the problem of multiple causation is neither clear nor unquestionable, nor is it free from serious logical and factual difficulties. One or two applications of the principle used in the above formulas of the multiple causation of war need to be mentioned specifically, as particularly fallacious. First, consider the form in which factors which are incommensurable and which belong to profoundly different planes of phenomena are combined or even juxtaposed in accordance with the multiple principle. Suppose we take as the formula of multiple causation of war the following: the universal law of the struggle for existence, the herd instinct, the instinct of pugnacity, fear, lust for power, the existence of wicked rulers, the division of mankind into different nations, sunspots, and certain religious and economic factors. One can see that these factors belong to fundamentally different planes of reality, and as such are neither commensurable nor comparable, nor are they generally capable of being united into any real unity. How is it possible to compare and commeasure the role of sunspots and that of fear or lust; the weight of fear and that of the universal law of the struggle for existence; the weight of these and of the division of mankind into nations or of the religious factors? It is evident that they cannot be measured, or even roughly appraised in any comparative way;

---

[12] Dean Inge, in *The Causes of War*, ed. H. J. Stenning (London, 1935), pp. 15-19.
[13] *Ibid.*, pp. 47-58.   [14] *Ibid.*, pp. 83-95.
[15] James Ford and K. M. Ford, *The Abolition of Poverty* (New York, 1937), p. 259.
[16] A. Porritt (ed.), *The Causes of War* (New York, 1932), pp. 1-25.
[17] *Ibid.*, pp. 26-62.

there is no measuring stick applicable to all of these. The very attempt to set up a classification of that type is one of the gravest of logical errors. It is a cloak that hides a profound ignorance, that prevents any understanding of the causes of war or of any other phenomenon treated in the same way. In brief, such a use of multiple causation is logically impermissible.[18]

Furthermore, even when they are free from this error, the formulas of multiple causation do not give *per se* any criterion for choice of the real causes out of millions of circumstances under which a war breaks out. Suppose we take the first World War as an illustration. Here are a few out of millions of attendant circumstances: the shot at Sarajevo; Viscount Grey's psychology; the bad influence of Rasputin upon the Czarina; the economic imperialism of Germany; the vast territory of Russia; the low birth rate in France; Hegel's and Nietzsche's philosophy; the private manufacture of armaments in England; German "fear" of the Russian rearmament; the popular reception of President Poincaré in Russia in the summer of 1914; Polish aspirations for independence; the desire of the military class to increase its prestige; the departure of Emperor William II for a sea trip a few days before the opening of the war; the supposed backward culture of Russia and her Slavophile policy; heavy rains in parts of Austria in the summer of 1914.

All of these conditions were indeed present immediately before and at the beginning of the war; but shall we take them all as causes just because they were existing before and at the beginning of the war? If so, we must consider millions of other conditions existing then as part of our multiple causation. There is no end to the enumeration of conditions present before and at the opening of the war. If we exclude all these millions of conditions, then what reasons can we give for retaining only those enumerated above? We have no valid criterion for judging that the enumerated conditions are more important than those not enumerated. Even if we ignore this difficulty, the above conglomeration of the factors of our "multiple causation" is still nothing but an enumeration of a few incidental conditions chosen haphazardly or arbitrarily and mistaken for the causes. Evidently such a catalogue neither is a causal formula nor has any cognitive value.

Hence the neat formula $X = f(Y, N, M \ldots)$ is null and void in all theories of multiple causation such as the above theories of war. The part $f(Y, N, M \ldots)$ is utterly meaningless in that it lumps together a series of incidental, incommensurable, and incomparable

---

[18] In P. Horst's *The Prediction of Personal Adjustment* (New York, 1941) one can find all the criticized shortcomings incorporated under the name of "scientific method." See my criticism of this work in the *American Journal of Sociology* (July, 1942). In S. C. Dodd's *Dimensions of Society* (New York, 1942) the prevalent mechanistic methods are pushed to obvious absurdity and nonsense.

factors. It is also void as a series of incidentally picked variables *(Y, N, M . . .)* out of millions of other variables surrounding the phenomenon *X* (all the wars of the past and the present).

Finally, it is still more useless for a reason similar to W. Heisenberg's principle of indeterminacy. If even in the region of subatomic physics it is impossible to determine precisely the relationship between comparable and commensurable variables—the velocity, position, and time-moment of the electron[19]—, still less possible is it to determine the value of each of the incommensurable factors *(Y, N, M . . .)* of *X*.

What is said respecting war may be said of virtually all the other applications of the principle of multiple causation to the analysis of sociocultural phenomena where their factors *Y, N, M . . .* are incommensurable. For the reasons indicated, they are practically all void.

Further diminution of the validity of the results of this prevalent conception of factorial analysis is imposed by the *principle of limit*. As a rule, a causal or associational relationship between two variables *A* and *B* holds good for only a limited range of the values of *A* and *B*. Beyond this limit, it either disappears or else undergoes a fundamental transformation. For instance, the harder one strikes a piano key, the louder the resulting sound. However, beyond a certain limit, an increase in the force of the stroke will result, not in a louder sound, but in a broken piano. Arsenic, when taken in certain quantities, is poisonous; but in smaller amounts it is not lethal. The physicochemical sciences clearly indicate such limits in a causal relationship by stating that there is a "stability limit" (Knorr and others), a "critical temperature," a "critical pressure," a "critical concentration," and the like, beyond which the causal relationship either ceases to exist or undergoes a change, the system of equilibrium is destroyed, and so forth. "Chemical reactions do not take place completely in one direction but proceed only to a certain point and there make a halt."[20]

Social scientists usually forget to state the limits beyond which the

[19] The principle of indeterminacy means that two "canonically conjugate" variables q (the position of a particle) and p (the corresponding momentum) cannot both be precisely determined beyond Planck's constant, or "the quantum of action" ($h = 6.55.10^{-27}$ erg x second). The more exactly we determine one of these variables, say q (the position of the particle), the less precise becomes p (the momentum) and the velocity of the particle. Even when one of these variables is precisely determined, the other remains entirely undetermined.

[20] Alexander Findlay, *The Phase Rule and Its Application* (London, 1904), pp. 7, 21, 22, 96, 200, and 234.

assumed causal relationship between their variables ceases to exist or radically changes. We have thousands of formulas that postulate the existence of causal relationships but that state no bounds to their validity. For instance, many contend that there exists a positive or negative association between the following phenomena:

(1) Business depression and criminality.
(2) Business depression and mortality.
(3) Business revival and birth rate.
(4) Poverty and marriage rate.
(5) Divorce and suicide.
(6) Urbanization and mental disease.
(7) Education and suggestibility.
(8) Population density and fertility.

Granted . . . that in all these and thousands of other formulas the evidences offered are satisfactory, shall we conclude that the positive or negative relationship found is likely to hold whatever value the variables may assume? By no means. We know that within certain limits improved nutrition tends to accelerate growth and increase stature, but beyond a certain point no additional improvement, quantitative or qualitative, in food will be followed by a further increase in stature. Poverty, below the physiological minimum, has an adverse effect on fertility, but above this line comparative poverty does not necessarily have the same result. At some point, compared with a state of relative comfort, it may serve as a stimulus or be associated with increased fertility.

Similar statements may be made regarding the relations between poverty and criminality, urbanization and mental disease, marriage and suicide. Mobility within certain limits is a factor in demoralization, but in other degrees facilitates morality. We may conclude similarly as regards prosperity. Density of population within certain limits can be a positive and, within other limits, a negative factor in fertility.

There is no need to multiply the instances further. With a reasonable degree of probability, we can conclude that there is scarcely any causal tie between societal variables which holds for all values given to them.[21]

If the investigator fails to indicate the limit of the values of A and B within which the relationship holds, or if he assumes that it holds for any value of A and B, he renders his formula still more indeterminate; for the majority, if not all, of the causal or associational relationships there is a limit for the values of the variables beyond which the discovered relationship does not hold. Indication of such a limit is ordinarily lacking in the prevalent causal-factorial analyses; therefore they become either quite indeterminate or misleading.

[21] Sorokin, *Dynamics*, IV, 698.

Such are the ordinary defects of the prevalent conception and procedure relating to the causal-factorial-associational analysis of the relationship of sociocultural phenomena. These defects are sufficient to invalidate most of the findings of the analysis. No wonder therefore that, in spite of the persistent efforts to discover the actual causal relationships between sociocultural variables, contemporary social science possesses scarcely any rigid and precisely defined causal formula. Instead, we have a vast forest of fallacious causal uniformities and of vague, conditional, temporary, local uniformities roughly valid for only a specific set of variables placed in a given constellation of circumstances and for a limited incidental range of values. Apart from this local and temporary validity, we do not know how valid they are; and we have no basis for accepting them as universally valid formula.

Thus the probabilistic conception of "associational causality," though convenient, has robbed the social sciences of practically all rigid, certain, and universal formula. It has reduced these disciplines to a mere storehouse of a multitude of facts and pseudoformulas, none of which is reliable and unquestionably valid. It has transformed the sociocultural world into a nebulous realm peopled by a host of shadowy phenomena attended by the ghosts of causal connections. As soon as we attempt to grasp any of these connections, they vanish like ghosts into thin air. Such is the nemesis of yielding to the specious allurements of the probabilistic conception!

Still More Serious Fallacies of the Prevalent Causal-factorial Analysis in the Social Sciences

The enumerated defects of the contemporary conception of causal-associational relationships between sociocultural variables, though serious, are not fatal. But the prevalent mode of causal-factorial analysis in the social sciences—a procedure largely motivated by an imitation of the natural sciences—reveals much graver fallacies. These are so serious that, in many cases, they entirely invalidate the results obtained and render the probabilistic conception inapplicable to an enormous number of cases involving the major part of the relationships between various sociocultural phenomena.

Fallacies Resulting from a Misconception of the Componential Structure of Sociocultural Phenomena. The first *of these fatal defects is due to a misconception of the structure of sociocultural phenomena, especially of the three components of which they consist.* The investigators of the causal-associational relationship between the variables hardly ever ask themselves precisely what kind of variables exhibit the stable or unstable relationship for which they are looking. When, for instance, they investigate the relationship between religion and economic factors, or between technology and political organization, or between familistic and legal forms, just what do they mean by these variables, and precisely what do they seek to accomplish?

Are they studying the relationship between the *meaning components* of these variables—namely, between the meanings of religion and economic factors, of technology and political organization, and so on? If so, they are on the wrong track, because pure meanings lack both stable and unstable associations, both causal and noncausal relationships. In regard to one another such meanings may stand either in a logically and expressively consistent or inconsistent relationship. They may be meaningfully independent or dependent upon one another; but no causal relationship is applicable to meanings.[22]

The relations between the theorems of geometry, between Kant's philosophical propositions, between the premises and the conclusion of a syllogism, and between any other sets of meanings is neither causal nor noncausal, neither stable nor accidental. These concepts are even more unsuited to characterize the relationship between meanings than to indicate the subatomic relations of physical phenomena. Hence the pure meaning component of the variables cannot be employed for purposes of causal-factorial-associational study.

Do, then, the investigators take the *vehicle component* of sociocultural phenomena for the variables whose relationship they are trying to uncover? In our example, the vehicles would embrace church buildings, prayer books, ceremonial vestments, crosses, rosaries, ikons, and an enormous number of other symbols of the religious system of meanings; factories, machinery, business office buildings, banks, money, railroads, merchant ships, real estate, and other vehicles of the economic system of meanings; and so forth. If investigators take the vehicles externalistically, without consideration of their meanings and human agents, the results are bound, in most cases, to be either insignificant or utterly absurd. If the vehicles are taken as purely physicochemical or

[22] See Chapter I of this book and esp. Sorokin, *Dynamics,* Vol. IV, chaps. i, ii, *et passim.*

biological phenomena, "externally and objectively" given, without consideration of their meanings, the sociological study of their relationships as physical objects is unnecessary, because the physicochemical and biological sciences furnish all that can be known of their relationships as physicochemical and biological variables.

Such an investigation, disregarding the fundamental property of the variables as the vehicles of meanings, ceases to be an examination of religious and economic variables, because it deals merely with objects as such—objects endowed with certain physical and chemical properties, and devoid of any religious or economic properties. They are religious or economic phenomena only insofar as they are vehicles of the respective systems of meanings. Stripped of this role, they are simply physicochemical phenomena, neither economic nor religious. Since part of the externalistic studies treat the vehicle variables in this sense, the futility of the procedure is quite clear.

If the vehicle variables are taken as some sort of cultural phenomena, but without a clear realization that they are but the vehicles of meanings borne by human agents, the result is likewise deplorable. As has been said, a physicochemical or biological phenomenon becomes a sociocultural vehicle only through its functioning as an objectifying agency of meanings. We know also that the connection between a certain meaning and its vehicles is, as a rule, comparatively loose; the same meaning may have several different vehicles, and the same physicochemical phenomenon may be a vehicle for many different meanings. Rarely does one find a given meaning objectified by only one vehicle or a given material phenomenon that serves but one meaning (see above, Chapter I).

It is thus impossible to take a certain vehicle variable as such and study it without reference to the system of meanings it objectifies. If this is done, no one—not even the investigator himself—knows the sort of variables whose mutual relations he is attempting to study; he does not know whether the variables are to be regarded as purely physicochemical phenomena or as vehicles, and if the latter, what kind of meanings and systems these vehicles serve or with what kind of agents they are connected. The whole setting of the study becomes indeterminate, because the same material variable—for instance, money, a book, a building, or an automobile—may be a vehicle of quite different sociocultural systems. It plays a different role and has different properties in different systems. An airplane may be an instrument now of charity, now of destruction. A lady's veil is an object of beauty in one system; a protective appliance (against dust and insects) in another; a customary requisite of decency in Mohammedan countries; and so forth. A sociological study of a veil, a book, a dollar, or an airplane as such, in an effort to find out the relationships of the vehicle to some other variables, is a futile undertaking, because the object in question (X), when it serves different systems of meanings, represents a series of different variables (X, Y, Z . . .). If it is considered as one and the same thing in all the various systems in which it functions as a vehicle, this means an erroneous identification (as X) of things which, in reality, are different in each of the respective systems—now X, now N, now M, now Z. No valid results can be expected from a study of the relationships of different things mistaken for one and the same variable.

If, finally, the investigator should take these variables as simply vehicles of systems of meanings (economic, religious, artistic or otherwise), it would mean, first, the abandonment of his vaunted "objectivistic, externalistic, and probabilistic" position. Second, he would not be entitled to take any single group of vehicles as adequate representatives of the systems and, from the relationship of the vehicles, to infer the relationship of the systems. We know well that each single vehicle —for instance, a church building or a bank building—is but one of millions of vehicles of the respective religious or economic system; that the vehicle variable taken is not necessarily the most important one among these millions; that the religious or economic system in other periods and countries may not exhibit this particular variable among its vehicles; and so on. The conclusions reached, therefore, would again be of little value and quite indeterminate.

The indeterminancy and mystery of any result obtained in such a study are especially striking when the sociocultural systems represented by such vehicles are complex, such as the variables of economics and religion, education and democracy, war and business depression, urbanization and internal disturbances, the fine arts and sciences, ethics and politics, law and business. These and hundreds of other variables are very complex systems of meanings and are objectified in thousands of different vehicles. Can we take any single one or a few of these vehicles—say, the number of unemployed or the amount of pig iron produced—as the adequate vehicle for the economic variable, and the figures for church attendance or the number of church buildings as the adequate vehicle for the religious variable? Certainly not. Furthermore, either one of the vehicles may mean a very different thing in different societies and cultural constellations. Hence, by studying the relationships between these objective variables without full consideration of the systems of meanings they stand for in a given meaningful system, as well as of the agents of the systems, we cannot arrive at any definite, valid conclusion, regardless of what may be the actual results —positive or negative, a high or a low index of association, and so on.

In brief, when certain material phenomena are examined as variables, we get nowhere if they are taken simply as physicochemical or biological phenomena, or if they are taken as a species of cultural phenomena but without a full apprehension of the variables as mere vehicles for meanings, operating in a certain constellation of meanings, vehicles, and agents. On the other hand, if the investigator gives full consideration to all three components—meanings, vehicles, and agents —he must abandon his externalistic, objective, probabilistic platform and become a "logico-meaningful" investigator in the sense of the theory expounded in this work and especially in my *Social and Cultural Dynamics*.

The same objection applies to the third component of sociocultural phenomena: human agents. When human beings or groups *qua* variables are investigated as mere biological organisms, a study of their mutual relations is nothing but an amateurish and superfluous reiteration of the biological knowledge already available in that field. If, in such a study, the sociocultural properties of the variables are entirely disregarded, the results are inevitably misleading. If human beings are regarded in some indefinite way as sociocultural phenomena, no valid study of their relations is possible without full consideration of all the important systems and congeries of meanings of which they are the bearers, and of all the important vehicles of these meanings employed by the bearers. If these various factors are fully considered, then the human beings cannot be viewed as purely externalistic or behavioristic phenomena; then all the important systems of meanings they bear come into play; then the study ceases to be objective and external in the above sense of the term.

The foregoing defects, however, do not exhaust the fallacies that arise from a disregard of the structure and components of the sociocultural variables.

Owing to their unawareness of the componential structure of sociocultural phenomena, our "externalistic-probabilistic" explorers frequently select as their variables *different components of different sociocultural systems or congeries* and painstakingly investigate their relationships. The component of meanings in one system is confronted with that of the vehicles or human agents in other systems; the component of vehicles in one system is confronted with the other two components in other systems. Such a procedure is as absurd as an investigation of the causal-factorial relationship between the anatomy of a fish's tail, the respiration of a horse, and the digestion of a bird— different elements of separate biological systems. In this concrete case, the absurdity is obvious.

Unfortunately, in the social sciences, such "researches" are being constantly undertaken. When a researcher attempts to establish the causal-factorial relationship between religious beliefs (as a system of meanings) and economic conditions (as the system of vehicles and agents of an economic system), he is guilty of precisely the same fallacy. When one seriously investigates the influence of technology (as a system of vehicles) upon law (as a system of meanings), he attempts the same futile juxtaposition of incommensurate variables. A vast array of studies, dealing with such problems as the influence of the density of the population upon the equalitarian ideology, the influence upon the capitalist system of the Protestant belief in predestination, or the effect of economic factors upon ideologies frequently presents just such impermissible constellations of variables. We are so accustomed to studies of this kind that we often fail to notice their fatuousness.

This incongruous setting of variables is responsible for the constant fruitless strife in the social sciences between the partisans of different "main factors." The Marxian theory of economic determinism and Max Weber's somewhat opposed theory of the relationship between ethicoreligious and economic phenomena furnish a good example. When Karl Marx—and especially the less intellectual Marxians—triumphantly claim that the economic factor of the means and instruments of production determines the rest of the sociocultural phenomena—and particularly the forms of religion, philosophy, art, and law— and when Max Weber no less confidently contends that it is religion

and (closely associated with it) *Wirtschaftsethik* that really determine
the forms of economic organization in a given society, they are proceeding along the line of the above-mentioned study of the causal relationship between the tail of a fish, the respiration of a horse, and the
digestion of a bird. They take the meaning component in the ethicoreligious system and a quite different component—that of vehicles—
in the economic system, compare the "efficiency" of these incommensurable components, and then present us with almost diametrically
opposite conclusions. No wonder! Since the variables are incommensurable, no valid conclusion is possible; therefore any arbitrary
conclusion—according to the bias of the investigator—can be inferred,
without the possibility of either proving or disproving its validity.

Let us substantiate a little this rather severe criticism. When Marx
states that "the *material* power of production" and "the mode of production in *material* life determine the general character of the social,
political, and spiritual processes of life," that "the *material* transformation of the economic conditions of production" determines "the legal,
political, religious, aesthetic, or philosophic—in short, ideological—
forms," and that "it is not the consciousness of men that determines"
the economic system but the fact that "this consciousness must, rather,
be explained by the contradictions of *material* life, by the existing conflict between the social forces of production and the relations of
production,"[23] he takes the component of *material vehicles and agents*
of economic systems (and, implicitly, of many other systems) and confronts it with the components of *meanings* in the legal, political, religious, scientific, philosophic, esthetic, and other "ideological" systems.
Having done so, he triumphantly concludes that these "ideological"
forms ("ideologies," "consciousness," "spiritual processes," and the
like) are all determined by the economic factor.[24]

Continuing this tradition, many contemporary sociologists commit
the same mistake. They analyze culture into "material and nonmaterial" (W. Ogburn and others), "technological and ideological"

---

[23] Karl Marx, *A Contribution to the Critique of Political Economy*, trans. Stone
(New York, 1904), pp. 11-13.

[24] Incidentally, it is to be noted that a series of contemporary interpretations reduce
Marxism to a sort of nonmaterialistic, almost idealistic, sociological system. Such interpretations, however, have no serious basis in the works of Marx, representing the
theories of the interpreters themselves rather than of Marx. An example of such an interpretation of a dematerialized and "de-Marxized" Marx is given by Talcott Parsons in
his *Structure of Social Action* (New York, 1937), pp. 488-495.

(A. Coste, L. Weber, T. Veblen, and others), and "civilization and culture" (M. Tugan-Baranovsky, A. Weber, R. MacIver, and others). They hold that the "material, technological, civilizational" aspect dominates in periods of a change, whereas the "nonmaterial, ideological, cultural" aspect lags behind; that the "material, technological, civilizational" part diffuses universally, whereas nonmaterial culture diffuses only within its own parochial limits; that the "material, technological, civilizational" part is accumulative and becomes better and better, whereas the "nonmaterial, ideological" part is not cumulative and changes erratically. These theories, in a slightly modified form, do essentially what Marx did: they take the vehicle components of many a cultural system—science, in the form of its objectifying vehicles (tools, machines, and technological inventions in general), economics, in the form of its materialized vehicles of production (trade, commerce, and so on), and other sociocultural systems—and confront these with the component of meanings in the same and (especially) in other sociocultural systems, such as religious beliefs, scientific theories, political theories, esthetic systems of meanings, and ethical and juridical norms. Thereupon, like Marx, they conclude that the "material, technological, civilizational" phase of culture dominates and determines the "nonmaterial, ideological, cultural" phase of sociocultural phenomena.[25]

If all these scholars had clearly realized the three-componential structure of sociocultural phenomena, they would hardly have ventured to formulate such fallacious theories. The actual situation is very different. All sociocultural systems have their own nonmaterial, ideological component, or system of meanings, and their material component, the objectifying vehicles and human agents. Science, as a sociocultural system, consists of a body of theories (meanings) and a vast array of vehicles (schools and universities, laboratories, libraries, endowment funds, and so forth). Religion consists of a system of beliefs as the component of meanings and of a multiplicity of material vehicles (from chalice and church building up to its property and funds). Esthetic systems likewise have their system of meanings and their system of material vehicles (museums, concert halls, opera houses, financial endowments, and the like). Law is a complex of immaterial

[25] A detailed critical analysis of all these dichotomic theories is given in Sorokin, *Dynamics*, Vol. IV, chaps. iii-vii.

norms and a huge array of material vehicles (statute books, court buildings, police, prisons, electric chairs, and the like). And so it is with any sociocultural system. It is, accordingly, impermissible to take the component of vehicles in one set of systems and the component of meanings in another set, to confront them, and then to conclude that the given component of vehicles generally dominates the given component of meanings.

Equally unsound is the confrontation of the technological or technical with the ideological sociocultural phenomena. Every sociocultural system has both its technical and its nontechnical aspects. An economic system has its own business technique of production, distribution, and even of consumption—a technique derived in part from those of science, law, religion, and ethics. A religious system, likewise, has its special and complicated technique of religious rituals and ceremonies, prayers, and musical performances. The fine arts, in turn, have their characteristic techniques of musical composition and playing, of painting and sculpture, of poetic and dramatic composition, of theatrical production, of architectural creation. Science, again, has its individual technique of research and teaching, as well as the technique of inventions incorporated in the applied sciences (such as medicine, agronomy, technology, and economics).[26]

The total sociocultural field exhibits many different systems, each of which is composed of three basic components. Schematically, the situation is as follows:

(1) Scientific systems, consisting of meanings plus vehicles plus human agents.

(2) Religious systems, consisting of meanings plus vehicles plus human agents.

(3) Ethicojuridical systems, consisting of meanings plus vehicles plus human agents.

(4) Economic systems, consisting of meanings plus vehicles plus human agents; etc.

The erroneous theories we have been considering take the component of meanings—the nonmaterial, or ideological, variable—from one system, and the component of vehicles—the material, or technological, variable—from another. They then hypostatize and generalize each of these components into a universal category, as two independent

[26] Cf. the detailed analysis of this point in *ibid.*, Vol. IV, chaps. iii-vii.

classes of sociocultural phenomena, and conclude that the material, or technological, variable is more powerful than the nonmaterial, or ideological.

In other cases, as we shall see, these theories take the components of meanings and of vehicles from the *same system* and confront the factor of vehicles with the ideological meanings. However, they treat the vehicles, not as components of the same system, but as independent entities, existing by themselves. Having cut out the heart or a leg of an organism and assumed that it exists by itself as an independent variable, they dogmatically announce that this material vehicle definitely determines the rest of the system in its structure and its dynamic functions. Thus they derive the conclusion that the material variable of science or religion determines the immaterial variable of scientific or religious meanings; that the factor of economic vehicles determines the immaterial factor of economic meanings; and so on. In line with this logic, one could easily prove that any part of an organism (lungs, glands, heart, or what not) determines, as an independent variable, the organism as a whole, including its functions and changes.

The aforesaid conclusion would, of course, be indisputable if a leg or a heart could actually exist outside of the respective organism as an independent variable. Fortunately or not, such a phenomenon is unknown to contemporary science, except in the case of amputated legs or hearts preserved in special containers, and these do not determine or control any organism whatsoever. Similarly, the nonexistence of the "material and technological vehicles" of science, religion, business, or any other sociocultural system independently of the rest of the components (particularly that of meanings) inexorably refutes the "indisputable" conclusions of such misguided theories.

The situation, indeed, is even worse than this. None of these dichotomists succeeds in actually excluding from his "material, technological, civilizational" variable the elements of the "nonmaterial, ideological, cultural" variable. In spite of the vagueness of Marx's definition of his economic factor and the nebulous definitions of the "material, technological, civilizational" factor offered by other dichotomists, they all introduce into their dominant variable, by a back door, theoretical science and the norms of law and ethics.

Economic systems are determined by the legal norms of a given society. They define property and theft, and determine which economic activities and relationships are lawful and which are to be prohibited. In this sense, law inevitably enters an economic system as its formative and most important element.[27] But as law is inseparably connected with the prevalent ethics of a given society, and both with the prevalent religion, elements of ethics and religion also enter the economic or technological system. Furthermore, the forces of production, as well as productive technology, are determined decisively by the existing body of technological inventions; and these, in turn, always represent an applied form of science. Thus science also is one of the most important elements of the "material, technological, civilizational" variable of economics.

In other words, if we take the Marxian and the dichotomists' economic, "material, technological, civilizational" variable, it turns out to be a composite derivative, consisting of the elements of science, law, ethics, religion, and even the fine arts. X ("material, technological, civilizational" economic) variable $= f$ (science $+$ law $+$ ethics $+$ religion $+$ fine arts $+$ something else). When then they confront it with the "nonmaterial, cultural, ideological" variable (science, religion, philosophy, the fine arts, ethics, law, "consciousness," and "spiritual life") and conclude that the first variable controls and determines the second, they violate all the fundamental laws of logic, confronting as different factors what—in part, at least—is identical—science with science, law with law, religion with religion—and making identical what is profoundly different—putting into the same class, labeled "material, civilizational, technological factor," such heterogeneous elements as scientific, religious, esthetic, and other meanings, together with a fantastic medley of material vehicles of these systems. Each of the two variables thus becomes a hash which only omniscient God could resolve into its elements. We need, indeed, a new Swift to write a new chapter on contemporary social scientists in a new *Gulliver's Travels!*

In a little different—and better—form, the same mistakes are made by Max Weber and other "idealistic" social scientists. Weber takes religion as his independent variable and, assuming that it plays the

---

[27] R. Stammler and L. Petrajitsky have brilliantly demonstrated that legal norms are the "form," or determining principle, of economic systems and that no economic system is thinkable without the legal norms that define its nature. Cf. R. Stammler, *Wirtschaft und Recht* (5th ed., Leipzig, 1924), and L. Petrajitsky, *Lehre vom Einkommen* (Leipzig, 1893); also J. Commons, *Legal Foundations of Capitalism* (New York, 1924).

decisive role in what he calls *Wirtschaftsethik* (practical ways of conduct), investigates the influence of religion upon the economic organization and processes. His examination leads him to the conclusion that the economic variable is tangibly conditioned by the religious factor through the medium of the *Wirtschaftsethik*, and, as a specific case, he cites Protestantism as the preponderant factor in the emergence and growth of the modern capitalist economic system.[28]

[28] Cf. Weber, *Gesammelte Aufsätze zur Religionssoziologie* (3 vols., Tübingen, 1922-23). A comprehensive analysis and criticism of his theory is given in Sorokin, *Sociological Theories*, pp. 673-696; also in his *Dynamics*, II, 500. At the present time, a considerable part of the conclusions of Weber, especially concerning the relationship between Protestantism and capitalism, and other effects ascribed by him to Protestantism, are untenable. Capitalism, utilitarianism, rationality, the development of science, technology, rational management, and many other phenomena attributed by him to the influence of Protestantism appeared approximately two hundred years before the emergence of Protestantism. And after the Reformation, all these alleged effects of Protestantism were equally evident in Protestant and in Catholic and other non-Protestant countries. Protestantism and a host of other phenomena—such as the emergence and growth of capitalist economy, utilitarian ethics, the visual and other sensate forms of the fine arts, the progress of the natural sciences and technological inventions, and the Renaissance—were the consequence of a more fundamental and general reason—namely, the transformation of the medieval dominant ideational culture into a sensate culture. The transformation began roughly at the end of the twelfth century in most of the compartments of Western culture. Protestantism itself was only one of the consequences of this transformation, and a comparatively late one at that. Hence, to take it as a "preponderant factor" of these phenomena, is as reasonable as to regard the growth of a moustache as the preponderant cause of all the numerous anatomical, physiological, and psychological changes undergone by a person between childhood and the age of puberty.

For these simple and undeniable reasons, the thesis of Weber concerning especially the relationship between Protestantism and capitalism is, as has been said, untenable. The attempts of the all too enthusiastic followers of this eminent scholar to defend it have resulted only in self-contradictions, in a series of factual historical errors, and, finally, in depriving Weber's theory of its originality. A pertinent example of such an unsuccessful defense is furnished by the writings of T. Parsons. When he outlines Weber's theory and stresses its originality, he declares that, in a study of the functional relationship between Protestantism and capitalism, Weber demonstrated the *"preponderant causal rôle* of the system of religious attitudes" in the emergence and growth of capitalism. See Parsons, *op. cit.,* p. 512.

When critics of Weber press him to acknowledge that most of the effects ascribed to Protestantism appeared at an earlier period and were equally evident in Protestant and non-Protestant countries, and point out that there is no ground to claim a preponderant causal role for Protestantism in these respects, he radically shifts the ground of his defense and seeks to take refuge in the statement that "Weber has not established and never meant to establish that *other than religious elements have not to a highly important degree* been involved both in the concrete process of development of a religious ethic itself, and in that of its influence on concrete social affairs" (including the development of capitalism). See *ibid.,* p. 576.

Thus on page 512 of Parsons' book Protestantism is a "preponderant factor." On page 576 its preponderancy disappears and, instead, other factors are credited with a highly important role in conditioning, not only capitalism, but Protestantism itself. Either Protestantism was a preponderant factor or it was not. To say simply that it was

Again, Weber's statement of the conditions of the problem is very indeterminate. It is not clear whether he confronts the religious sociocultural system in its three-componential structure with the economic sociocultural system in its three-componential structure, or whether he is concerned only with their systems of meanings or with their vehicles and agents. When he analyzes the role of the meaning of Calvinistic predestination, he confronts one of the meanings of the Protestant religion with the economic vehicles and agents with their practical ways of conduct. Elsewhere, he confronts the Protestant system of meanings with the economic system of meanings—namely, when he compares the *Wirtschaftsethik* of Protestantism with the ethic of capitalism. In still other places, he treats each of the systems—religious and economic—as a whole. On account of this shifting of the constellation of components, the whole analysis is vitiated.

This indeterminacy is still further increased by Weber's interpretation of the *Wirtschaftsethik*. On the one hand, he takes it mainly as a religious product, sometimes exclusively as such. On the other hand, he repeatedly stresses the fact that the *Wirtschaftsethik* is conditioned, not alone by its religious factors, but also by cosmic, geographical, historical, political, and other factors.

This shows that the *Wirtschaftsethik* (X) is in no way a product of the religious factor only (A), and neither Weber nor we know what its relative importance is among the other factors (B, C, D, E, F) which shape it. For this reason, granting that Weber's analysis of the effects of the *Wirtschaftsethik* on economic life is accurate, we in no way can ascribe these effects to

---

one of the factors is to rob Weber of the originality of his theory; for what social scientist has *not* attributed some role, and often a very important one, to religion in economic and social affairs?

R. K. Merton's effort to support Weber by assembling a series of data supposedly confirming Weber's doctrine is likewise futile. His somewhat haphazard and random compilation is entirely one-sided and can easily be confronted by a much more convincing array of facts tending to show that, as has already been observed, utilitarian ethics, rationality, scientific discoveries and inventions, and all the other phenomena mentioned by Merton, emerged and rapidly developed as early as the thirteenth century—prior to the rise of Protestantism—and that they subsequently played an equally important role in Protestant and non-Protestant countries. See R. K. Merton, *Science, Technology, and Society in Seventeenth Century England* (Osin's, 1938), Vol. IV, Pt. 2, chaps. iv-vi.

For a fuller and more systematic enumeration of the facts mentioned by Merton— and several additional ones—cf. Sorokin, *Dynamics, passim*. P. A. Sorokin, *Social Mobility* (New York, 1927), and Sorokin, Zimmerman, and Galpin, *Systematic Source Book in Rural Sociology* (3 vols., Minneapolis, 1930-32), presents an even more complete series of data concerning the men of talent and genius so one-sidedly cited by Merton.

religion *(A)* only, because the factor of the *Wirtschaftsethik* is a complex embodiment of numerous and various factors *(B, C, D, E, F)* which shape it. . . . If Weber's conclusions concerning the effects of the *Wirtschaftsethik* were true, he would have proven only that a series of factors, *A, B, C, D, E, F,* . . . exert such and such effects on the economic life, but in no way could he be thought to have proved that these effects are that of religion (of *A*), as Weber often states, or that the religious factor is the most important among these *A, B, C, D, E, F.* . . . Even more, Weber's analysis does not show even tentatively what the share of the religious factor is in molding the *Wirtschaftsethik*, and, correspondingly, its share in conditioning the effects of the *Wirtschaftsethik* in the field of economic phenomena. . . . After Weber's work, we are as ignorant about the degree of efficiency of the religious factor as we were before.[29]

In addition, the whole matter is vitiated by the sin of the multiple causation (discussed above). When Weber treats the *Wirtschaftsethik* as a result of many factors (cosmic, geographical, historical, political, and the like), he puts into the single bag of multiple causation the most heterogeneous and incommensurable phenomena. The result is that we really do not know precisely what the *Wirtschaftsethik* itself is (one X), what role religion plays in molding it (another X), what effects the *Wirtschaftsethik* has upon economic life (third X), or the net role of religion in these effects (fourth X). Thus, instead of grasping the nature of the causal relationship between the religious and economic phenomena, we obtain merely a series of unknowns which leave us about where we were before. Certain only, to repeat, is the nemesis of careless stating the conditions of the problem and of failing to realize the three-componental structure of sociocultural phenomena. Weber's conclusion—one almost opposite to that of Marx— turns out to be equally arbitrary.

These examples, taken from the works of the most eminent sociologists of the nineteenth and twentieth centuries, sufficiently illustrate the fallacy in question. It is unnecessary to add that, in the works of less distinguished social scientists, this fallacy assumes the most absurd and flagrant forms.

Because of his unawareness of the three-componental structure of sociocultural phenomena, many an investigator fails to detect any relationship or connection between the components of the same system when these are treated as separate variables. No wonder! If one cuts out the

[29] Sorokin, *Sociological Theories*, pp. 690-691.

heart and lungs from a living organism, one can hardly hope to discover any causal interdependence between these variables.

Whether or not a research worker finds any correlation or association between the variables in such an impermissible setting, the
results are equally absurd. One species may properly be compared with
another, or the breathing of one species with that of another; the
breathing and flying of a given organism may be studied in their
relationships in the living organism. But to search for a stable or unstable relationship between a horse's breathing and a fish's tail is a
problem worthy only of a patient in an insane asylum! One sociocultural system (with its three components) may properly be compared or
confronted with another system (with its three components), and their
relationship may be studied. One may examine the relationship of
different components of the same system as they are given in that
living system.[30] But one cannot study the relationship of different
components of different systems, or that of the components of the same
system mistakenly regarded as separate variables, existing independently.

And yet, as has been said, such operations are carried on daily by a
crowd of social scientists who accept the prevalent notion of causal-
factorial-associational analysis. Is it any wonder that the results arrived
at by different investigators of the same variables are often opposites, or
at least erroneous and inconclusive? If they are not all entirely absurd
or misleading, this is due to the fact that, in spite of a wrong setting
of the problem, some investigators have actually studied the relationship between religious and economic *systems* (*qua* systems)—not between the vehicles of one system and the meanings of the other; or the
relationship between physicochemical systems (with their technological
vehicles) and religious systems—not between the vehicles or agents of
one and the meanings of the other. But when, in addition to a faulty
statement of the conditions of the problem, the investigation is carried
on in the framework of this wrong setting, the results are invariably
fallacious.

In summary, then, let us repeat that the causal-factorial studies in

---

[30] Contrary to the claims of the dichotomists, in a change undergone by *one and the
same system*, the component of meanings ordinarily leads the component of its vehicles
in the temporal order of the change. For the evidence, see Sorokin, *Dynamics*, IV,
377-385.

question become entirely indeterminate, unreliable, and fallacious, or else repudiate the probabilistic-externalistic platform professed and with it the prevalent conception of causality-association, whenever the investigator fails to keep clearly in mind the three-componential structure of sociocultural phenomena—particularly the component of meanings. Such studies can produce no valid results and are bound to be misleading in many ways.

Fallacies Due to the Neglect of the Principle of Immanent Change and of the Profound Difference between Sociocultural Systems and Congeries. Since the prevalent conception of causal-association relationship is probabilistic, based upon chance, it amounts to an assumption that all sociocultural phenomena stand to one another in the relation of congeries. Being, by definition, merely "chance companions," the variables do not have any deeper meaningful or necessary tie that keeps them "indissoluble."

Such a conception at once raises the difficulty of how and why some of the chance variables are associated more firmly than the others. If the variables were taken as purely physicochemical phenomena, then their more or less stable association could perhaps be explained by reference to their physicochemical affinity or lack of affinity. But we know that the variables—vehicles of the same system or congeries of meanings—are a medley of the most diverse physicochemical phenomena, between which there is no special and uniform physicochemical affinity (see above, Chapter I). Under such circumstances, belief in a possibility that some of the pairs of variables may be tied together more closely than the other pairs, or that A keeps pace with B more often than with C, N, and M, becomes a downright mystery. No comprehensible basis exists for such an expectation. On the assumption that all sociocultural phenomena are chance congeries vis-à-vis one another, the whole complicated technique (statistical, observational, and experimental) falls to the ground because of its violation of the "principle of sufficient reason." The results of such studies, no matter how meticulously exact they may be, are doomed to be conjectural, indeterminate, and purely accidental. Such is the first penalty for neglecting the profound difference between sociocultural systems and congeries.

Another fallacy of this conception is its erroneous *identification of*

*congeries and systems, which are subsumed under a single classifica-
tion: that of chance congeries.*[31]

A third fallacy follows from the second. As applied to congeries,
which both actually and by definition are "chance phenomena," the
technical procedure in question is more or less pertinent. But in its
application to a sociocultural system—to the intrasystem relationships
of its components and to the subordinated and co-ordinated intersystem
relationships—such a procedure is utterly misguided. A system is a
consistent whole, with meaningful-causal ties between its components
and between the subordinated and co-ordinated systems. Therefore *its
relationships are by no means mere chance phenomena.*

Similarly, the changes it undergoes are not chance phenomena and
are not governed exclusively or even mainly by an accidental complex
of fortuitous external factors, but by the immanent principle of self-
determination—by "the objective law of self-direction," as Eddington
puts it—and consist largely in the unfolding of its own potentialities.
In sociocultural systems, each antecedent phase determines each subsequent[32] phase, in accordance with the old conception of causality as
"the dependence of phenomena upon antecedents." To regard the
whole complex of sociocultural systems as mere chance congeries, and
to apply to it the procedure and technique of the investigation of
chance relationships between chance variables, constitutes a grave
error.[33] To rely upon the results of such a study is hence sheer
superstition.

[31] *Ibid.,* Vol. IV, chaps. i-iii *et passim.*

[32] For the principle of immanent change, cf. *ibid.,* Vol. IV, chaps. xii and xiii.

[33] It is to be noted that, unlike most of the social scientists, the eminent physical
scientists well understand and stress the fact that what we call sociocultural systems not
only are not chance phenomena but are not governed by the laws of chance. While in
the physical world "the law of chance is the most fundamental and indispensable of all
physical laws," an exception exists in the fields outside of physics, namely, "in the
manifestations of consciousness or life." Such phenomena are "governed by objective
law of direction instead of being wholly a field of chance." See Eddington, *op. cit.,* pp.
89-90, 181-184, and 221.

In different terms, the same point is stressed by Max Planck in his *Where Science Is
Going,* pp. 149-169, and Sir Frederick Gowland Hopkins, Charles E. Guye, and many
others. Cf. also L. du Noüy, *Biological Time* (London, 1936), pp. 24 ff. and 35. For
additional thinkers who stress the same difference, cf. Sorokin, *Dynamics,* Vol. IV,
chaps. xii and xiii; and Vol. II, chaps. xi and ix.

It is regrettable that the social scientists imitate the natural scientists where they
should not and fail to imitate them where they should.

It is likewise instructive to note the violent fluctuations of the causality fashion in the
social sciences. As we have seen, in earlier centuries they believed in universal rigid
causal relationships among all sociocultural phenomena. Now they believe in universal

Such being the nature of the fallacy in general, it induces a number of more specific errors in a survey of the structural and dynamic intra- and intersystem relationships. One of these is very frequently committed in investigations of *factors or independent variables of the structure, equilibrium, and changes of sociocultural phenomena.* It is, indeed, so common that it is advisable to consider it in some detail.

The prevalent "factorial analyses" fall into three main groups: (1) the purely *externalistic,* in which the factor is sought in an agency outside of the phenomenon studied; (2) the *internal,* in which the factor of a given phenomenon is taken from one of its elements but is treated as if it were external to it; (3) the *external-internal,* in which factors are derived partly from outside agencies and partly from the elements of the phenomenon itself.

Let us begin with the externalists. Whatever sociocultural phenomenon they investigate, they look for an explanation of its structure, "equilibrium," or "disequilibrium" (change) in external cosmic, biological, or sociocultural factors. Examples of such externalistic factorial analyses are furnished by the extreme geographic and biological interpretations of sociocultural phenomena, and by the theories that seek to explain everything in a system by external factors.[34] If all sociocultural phenomena were congeries, such a procedure might be more or less justifiable; for congeries do not change immanently, do not have antecedents, and do not bear in themselves the seeds of their future. Since they are passive, their status at a given moment—as well as their changes—is determined sometimes by sociocultural, sometimes by biological, and sometimes by cosmic agencies external to them. When, however, this procedure is applied to sociocultural systems, its fallacy at once becomes obvious.

No adequate external cause can be discovered for the immanent

---

chance relationship as governing all sociocultural variables. In the preceding period, sociocultural phenomena were conceived as systems; now they are regarded as chance congeries. Such violent shifts from one side to the other are in themselves an evidence of the inadequacy of both of these conceptions. The truth lies somewhere between the two extremities. Some sociocultural phenomena are chance congeries, whereas others are nonchance systems. Intercongeries relationships are chance relationships and can be studied along the lines of the probabilistic conception (properly modified). Intra- and inter-system relationships (in subordinated and co-ordinated systems) are chiefly non-chance relationships and cannot be studied in terms of the probabilistic conception and its procedure.

[34] Cf. Sorokin, *Sociological Theories,* chaps. i-vii; and his *Dynamics,* Vol. IV, chaps. xii-xiii.

disposition of an organism to undergo a series of changes between childhood and old age. If an investigator overlooks this property of the system and attempts to derive the factors of such changes exclusively from this or that external factor, his solution is bound to be either wholly or partly fallacious. The fallacy of the procedure is less obvious in the externalistic explanation of the structure and changes of "discrete sociocultural systems." Like organisms, such a system has its immanent properties, potentialities, modes, and phases of change independent of external agencies, which unfold themselves by virtue of the system's being a "going concern" immanently impelled to incessant change in a certain direction, each preceding status conditioning the next, with its own peculiar phases, rhythms, tempos, duration of existence, and so on.[35] When our externalistic-probabilistic research worker fails to consider this and fails to explore the "inner nature" of the system, its components, its potentialities, its status at a given moment, and the like, and instead looks for one or more externalistic factors to explain the structure and the changes of the system, he makes as flagrant a blunder as does the externalist in explaining the changes of organisms. Whether the sociocultural system be the family, the State, a religious, philosophical, ethical, or industrial system, or any other system, it first of all changes immanently, the direction of the phases and the forms of the change being implicit in the system itself since the moment of its emergence. Any attempt to reduce the structure or the change with its modes, direction, phases, and so forth, to the play of purely external (chance) factors is utterly futile.

This is what is usually done by the externalistic investigators in their "factorial" analyses. In so doing, they are guilty of a twofold blunder: (1) they ascribe the causation to an external factor, instead of looking for it in the system itself; and (2) in making this mistake, they select as the causative "villain" the wrong culprit, since the external factors are not the culprits that produce the *whole* change.

An apt illustration is afforded by the causal analysis of the phenomena of suicide. Before Durkheim's researches, many an important study ascribed the cause of suicide to climate, race, mental disease, poverty, poor health, or other factors external to social life and social organization as such. Durkheim has shown, however, that all such studies, without exception, reveal either "a mistaken identity" of the

[35] Cf. Sorokin, *Dynamics,* Vol. IV, chaps. xii, xiii, *et passim.*

real factors of suicide, which is ascribed to agencies that have little to do with it, or at least an unwarranted role of the factors external to the social system of which the individual is a member. Such factors possess some significance for certain secondary aspects of suicide, such as frequency distribution of suicide according to age, sex, mental disease, and poor health. But all the investigations overlooked the principal factors of suicide immanent in a given type of social system, such as excessive psychosocial isolation, excessive submergence of the individual in the collectivity, or anomic disorganization of the system. Durkheim and M. Halbwachs show that these are the indispensable "causes" of the phenomenon.[36]

The same may be said of thousands of other problems of the social sciences. If an investigator fails to keep in mind the principle and implications of immanent change and the difference between systems and congeries, and concentrates on external "factors" (of the fall of Rome, of the World War, of business depression, of the victory of communism or fascism, of criminality, of revolution, of the increase of divorce, of the decline of one religion and the ascendancy of another, of the success of a given fad or fashion, or some other factor), he inevitably commits the two blunders in question, no matter how "precise" his technique and how "complete" his data.

Other investigators of the *factor X* of a given sociocultural phenomenon (of its structure, equilibrium, or changes) *often choose for the factor X a variable that objectively is an element of the sociocultural system under consideration.* Not realizing, however, precisely what a sociocultural system is, and that the factor X is an element or component of the system in question, they treat X as an agency external to it. Although such investigators avoid the mistakes of the externalists, they commit even graver errors (including the aforesaid error of regarding a leg as determining the structure and changes of its respective organism). We are all acquainted with this type of factorial theory. When Marxians take the "economic factor" and make the whole sociocultural world a function (a dependent variable) of this factor, they follow the outlined procedure; for the "economic variable" is not outside the sociocultural world, but rather a part of it. They choose this part, forgetting that it is a component of the sociocultural field, treat it

[36] Cf. E. Durkheim, *Le Suicide* (Paris, 1911), and M. Halbwachs, *Les Causes du suicide* (Paris, 1930).

as an independent variable, and boldly write the familiar equation: "All sociocultural phenomena are a function of the economic factor" [*Sociocultural phenomena* $= f(E)$].

When Pareto makes his "residue-factor" one of the chief factors of practically all the "ideological" systems (religious, ethical, juridical, esthetic, economic, political, and so on), and of even the entire "social equilibrium" (undefined by him), he follows the same procedure. "Residues" are a property of human beings, members of these systems; and human beings are but one of the three components of each of these systems. Pareto takes residues as something external to the systems, makes them one of the basic factors, and then boldly writes the equation: "All or most of the sociocultural systems are mainly a function of residues."[37] A perfect example of the familiar argument is: "Organisms are largely a function of legs"!

When other investigators take religious beliefs, legal norms, political ideology, technological inventions, "mores," "ideas," or any other category of sociocultural phenomena and make them the dominant factor of the entire sociocultural world, or of an enormous number of sociocultural systems and congeries, they apply the same type of factorial analysis. The foregoing discussion of the material-nonmaterial, civilizational-cultural, technological-ideological interpretations of sociocultural life offers a few examples of such theories, whose number is legion. (Cf. my *Contemporary Sociological Theories,* Chapters VIII-XIII.)

Professor N. L. Sims's theory of factors may serve as an example of the *external-internal* variety of factorial analysis typical of most of the current procedures. He asks: "How does the social equilibrium become upset?" His answer is that the factors of sociocultural derangement and change are: (1) cosmic catastrophies (such as flood and drought); (2) subcultural (biological) agencies (such as the quantity

---

[37] As Professor Crane Brinton puts it: "For Pareto, a great deal of what Mr. Sorokin considers an essential part of the sociological process—much of the art, theology, philosophy, 'culture' of a society—is not in itself an important factor in social change, does not count heavily among the 'variables' which determine the conditions of a given society. . . . It is the 'residues' which the sociologist must take chiefly into consideration." C. Brinton, "Socio-astrology," *Southern Review,* III (Autumn, 1937), 255.

Dear Professor Brinton: If we exclude from "the conditions of a given society" its arts and sciences, religion, philosophy, law, and the like, what remains of its social and cultural conditions? Evidently nothing except a collection of biological organisms of the species *homo sapiens,* devoid of culture or sociocultural traits. Have a heart, and don't relegate the residues to the ranks of the unemployed or the W. P. A., deprived of *any* role in determining sociocultural conditions!

and quality of the population); (3) social factors (invasions, conquest, immigration, race conflicts, and class struggles); and (4) cultural factors (the accumulation of wealth, invention, mores, diffusion of culture, and so on).[38]

Here we have a sample of the familiar principle of "multiple causation," in which the incommensurable external and internal factors are combined into one set. We note also, that the internal and partly subcultural factors (population, invasion, mores, diffusion of culture, accumulation of wealth, invention, and so on) represent, in fact, a part of the sociocultural system itself, whose disequilibrium they produce. This means that population, invasions, mores, diffusion of culture, accumulation of wealth, and inventions, are the factors of changes in population, invasions, mores, diffusion of culture, accumulation of wealth, and inventions, as parts of the social system. Exquisite tautology, indeed—aggravated by violation of the logical laws of identity and difference!

It is hardly necessary to dwell at length upon the gravest errors of such factorial theories. They are guilty, first, of taking an element or component of a system, inseparable from it, and treating it as something external to it—as "an independent variable." Insofar as it is a part of a system, a component element cannot be a variable independent of the system. One cannot remove from a human organism its heart or lungs and treat these organs as "independent variables" in relation to the organism. If one did, he would have only a dead heart or lungs, quite different from the living organs—to say nothing of the fact that the rest of the organism would be equally dead. Both variables lose their identity when they are separated. Therefore a study of the relationship between the heart and organism in such a setting will be a study of the relationship between what *were* heart and organism and are no longer so. The conclusions derived from such an investigation are accordingly fallacious insofar as they pretend to be based on the relationships between a *living heart in its organism and the organism itself*.

The same is true of the separation of an element from its respective sociocultural system and its treatment as an independent variable or factor of the system. Whatever conclusions may be derived from such a study, they can have no bearing upon the relationship of this element

[38] N. L. Sims, *The Problem of Social Change* (New York, 1939), pp. 243-380.

in the system to the system itself. Pareto's "residues" are but one of the many elements in human beings, and these in turn are but one of the components of sociocultural systems. Since human beings are members of the systems, and since the residues are inseparable from this component of the systems, the residues are inseparable from the systems themselves. It is impossible to isolate the residues from human beings, and these from other components of the systems, and to treat them as "independent variables." If we were to do this, we should have merely dead pseudoresidues related to residueless pseudohuman beings who, like mummies, constituted a component of a society of mummies.

The same may be said of Marx's "economic factor" in its application to sociocultural systems and the whole sociocultural world, as well as of all other theories of factorial analysis of this type. In sociocultural systems, such a separation of one of its elements is impossible. If an element is to be examined in its relationship to the rest of the system and its other elements, it must be examined *in* the system, as one of its components—not as a pseudoexternal "independent variable." If someone should say that, methodologically, an investigator is entitled to take anything as its "independent variable," the answer is: A fool can certainly do this, but a scientist cannot assume that black is white and that what is an inseparable and dependent part is an "independent" factor.

A second and *still graver error consists in making a part—and sometimes a very small part—the "cause-factor-independent variable"* of the whole. This procedure represents, not only the old fallacy of the *pars pro toto,* but the still graver mistake of *making the part the cause of the whole.* In the case of concrete systems, such as an organism, the confusion is obvious. If somebody says that an eye, ear, finger, or heart is the factor that determines the structure and changes of the entire organism—that the organism is the effect, and the ear or heart is its cause—the fallacy is self-evident. In the case of discrete sociocultural systems, however, it is less apparent. If the residues are but elements of one of the components of the sociocultural systems, to take them for the main "cause-factor-independent variable" of the sociocultural systems is about as sound as to regard a finger as the cause of the whole organism. Within a system or organism, we can study the function of a residue or finger, and its relations to other elements and components of the system or organism; but under no circumstances can we make the residue or finger the factor or cause, and the system or organism the effect or dependent variable.

This applies equally to any "factor-cause-independent variable" which is a part or element of the system, whether it be the instruments of production, a technological, religious, political, or artistic factor, or what not. The very setting of such a factorial study is faulty, and nothing but fallacy can follow from it.[39]

When one surveys the factorial theories of Professor Sims's type, one notes that they exhibit all the sins of "multiple causation" indicated above, as well as all the vices of the theories that regard a part as a cause of the whole. Who except omniscient God could combine into one homogeneous unit all the multifarious incommensurable factors which Professor Sims puts into the basket of his "multiple causation"? What are his "social and cultural factors" but a vague and incomplete catalogue of certain of the elements, congeries, and systems of the total culture of a given society? In their incongruous totality, they are but a small fraction of the total culture of society, which is supposed to be conditioned and caused by this part; whereas the part, in its turn, is not conditioned by the whole to which it belongs. The doctrine is as sound as a theory of the factors determining the equilibrium of the solar system which enumerates the moon, the wind on the earth, solar eruptions, Jupiter, and the accumulation of carbon on Mars as the factors of the disequilibrium in the orderly revolutions of the system and of its members. In this sense, such theories are but abbreviated descriptive tautologies (explaining, through an enumeration of certain elements of the system, the system as a whole, including the elements

---

[39] From this standpoint, the above statement of C. Brinton on the residues and his acceptance of Pareto's claim are likewise nonsense. As has been said, "the conditions of a given society" are made up chiefly of its scientific, philosophical, religious, moral, juridical, cultural, political, and economic systems. If these are excluded as unimportant, then what remains? Hardly anything more than a horde of organisms, externally perhaps somewhat similar to human beings, with very strong residues (even instincts and reflexes)—certainly no cultural and social elements as superorganic phenomena. Such a horde might be largely controlled by its residues or instincts, but there would be few, if any, sociocultural phenomena to be controlled by this factor. If religious, scientific, philosophical, artistic, and other systems constitute the bulk of "the conditions of a given society," then the residues, as elements of the components of these social systems, certainly cannot be taken as their main independent variable or factor.

themselves). They make the part greater than the whole—a few factors more powerful than the whole that contains them.

The source of all such blunders is, among other things, the failure to distinguish between systems and congeries, and the treatment of systems as a mechanical complex of congeries from which, as from a dump, one can pick out one of the variables and, through it, explain the rest of the dump. Nowadays such errors are committed so often that we are somewhat accustomed to them and do not fully realize the unsoundness of the procedure. Is it surprising that, after centuries of preoccupation with such factorial theories, no unanimous conclusion has been reached concerning the factors of a given phenomenon; that the most diverse and contradictory doctrines continue to exist; and that we still know very little about the real causal-factorial-associational relationships of sociocultural systems and congeries?

A Concrete Case of the Theoretical and Practical Inapplicability of Natural-Science Causality to Crime. Finally, *the unfitness of the natural-science conception of causality or association to sociocultural phenomena is amply demonstrated by the invariable failure of all the persistent attempts to apply it practically and "operationally," especially in the field of criminal law.* Since the remote past, the application of natural-science causality has assumed a very concrete form, namely, in the punishment of criminals. A criminal is one who has committed a crime, who is the cause of the crime, as the legal causalists interpreted the term. Hence the problem arises: Who is the cause of a crime, and under what conditions and in what way?

This practical exigency called forth the analysis of the problem of crime causation in the criminal law and produced an enormous number of theories of "juridical causality." In spite of all the different concepts of causality offered by lawgivers, lawyers, judges, and theorizers in criminal law, none of them has met the test of judicial adequacy, without drastic correction, limitation, or even fundamental transformation, insofar as the concepts of juridical causality resemble those of natural-science causality (either of the earlier deterministic type or of the latter probabilistic type).

Already in the Middle Ages, Baldus, Bartolus, and the agencies concerned (judges, lawyers, and others) had to introduce a distinction between the *imputatio facti sive physica* and the *imputatio juris*—the factual, causal imputation of the crime to the perpetrator and the juridical imputation.[40] Not every physical causation of crime was regarded as juridical causation. Even physical causation was imputed only when the phenomenon of crime was a simple, immediate, and necessary effect of the action (or inaction) of the person in question, and when he either could foresee the consequences or was of legal age, possessed of a normal mind, and so on. On the other hand, in certain cases a crime was juridically imputed to one who physically had nothing to do with it, as, for instance, in the cases of "collective responsibility," "hostages," and the like. We already note the profound divergence between "physical" causation and "juridical" causation, and the impossibility of applying purely physical causation to the practical task of imposition or nonimposition of punishment upon the physical perpetrator.

Later on, especially after the beginning of the nineteenth century (and not without the influence of the natural sciences), the problem of juridical causality began to be studied intensively, particularly in Germany. Von Bury defined the cause as the totality of conditions necessary to produce the effect—the crime; but such a conception would render liable to punishment everyone who, directly or indirectly, was one of the conditions of the effect. If his parents had not produced the culprit, if a given merchant had not sold him the knife, if a given taxi driver had not driven him to the scene of the crime, and so on, the criminal would not have committed the crime. Hence, if such a conception were to be applied by the courts, an indefinite number of persons would have to be punished.

This conception was eventually replaced by Binding's interpretation of the cause as the factor that upsets "the equilibrium of forces"[41] and is the last condition in the chain of conditions of the disequilibration, resulting in crime. Since this concept likewise was unsuitable—partly because, from the standpoint of common sense and elementary justice, it led to the unwarranted punishment of those who did not deserve it and to the failure to punish those who did deserve it—it was supplanted by another series of theories of causality (Birkmeyer's, Bar's, Kries's,

---

[40] Cf. G. Dahm, Das Strafrecht Italiens im ausgehenden Mittelalter (Leipzig, 1931), pp. 180 ff.; and B. Furlan, Problem pravne kavzalnosti (Ljubljana, 1938), pp. 14 ff.

[41] This, by the way, indicates that the problem of social equilibrium had been analyzed, and that attempts had even been made to put the theory into operation long before Pareto and the contemporary "equilibrium" theorists in the field of the social sciences.

and others), which, after enjoying a brief heyday, in their turn were found inapplicable.[42]

In a word, from the purely operational and practical standpoint, all the concepts of causality derived from the natural sciences have proved unfit to indicate whom to regard as the adequate cause of a given crime, and hence upon whom to impose punishment. The juridical interpretation of causality—or, more specifically, of juridical responsibility and liability—has always applied norms very different from those of physical causation in the sense of the causality of the natural sciences. Many of the most important physical agencies of crime (such as children, the insane, and those acting without criminal intent, in the interest of self-defense, in emergency situations) are deemed guiltless and are therefore not punished; whereas many a person who has played no role as a physical causative agency in the perpetration of a crime is held responsible and penalized. The innumerable efforts to introduce the "scientific" concept of causality into the penal code as the basis for assessing responsibility and meting out punishment have invariably failed and will continue to do so. The reason is the impossibility of substituting causality of that type for sociocultural responsibility.[43]

The foregoing conclusions give some idea of the defects of the prevalent conception and procedure relative to causal-factorial-associational relationships. It is evident that the theory and technique in question have more than enough vices to invalidate most of the results of such studies. Let us turn now to a brief consideration of what constitutes an adequate conception and system of procedure in this field.

[42] Cf. the exposition and analysis of these theories in Furlan, *op. cit.;* R. von Hippel, *Deutsches Strafrecht* (Berlin, 1930), Vol. II; V. Solnar, "Le Rapport de la cause à l'effet et le droit positif," *Revue de droit pénal et de criminologie* (1937); and K. Binding, *Die Normen und ihre Übertretung* (Leipzig, 1914), Vol. II. For future references, cf. these works and P. A. Sorokin, "The Structure of the Contemporary Dogma of the Criminal Law," *Vestnik Psichologii i Krim. Antropologii* (1917), and "The Third School and the Dispute of the Classical and Sociological School in the Criminal Law," *Juridicheski Vestnik* (1915).

[43] "One theory of causality is piled upon another in the criminal law, but each of these theories borrows its reasons, not from the norms of the positive law, but outside of it, from the natural sciences. As a result, we witness distortions of the natural-science causality as well as that of the norms of the positive law, which autonomously determine whom they regard as responsible for crime and under what conditions, regardless of any physical causality." See Sorokin, "The Structure of the Contemporary Dogma of the Criminal Law," p. 59.

RULES GOVERNING THE INTEGRALIST[44] ANALYSIS OF MEANINGFUL-CAUSAL
AND CHANCE (OR CONGERIES) RELATIONSHIPS IN
SOCIOCULTURAL PHENOMENA

Separation of Systems from Congeries. Before undertaking a study
of the relations between sociocultural variables, we must ascertain, as
precisely as possible, whether the variables are systems or congeries.
There are three fundamental possibilities:

(1) Two or more variables may be isolated congeries, in which case
the study will be an investigation of intercongeries relationships.

(2) One or more of the variables may be systems, whereas the
others are isolated congeries.

(3) Two or more variables may be parts of the same system or may
be different systems, in which case the study will be an investigation
of intra- or inter-system relationships.

The methods, the technique, and the underlying principles must be
clearly differentiated in each of these three cases. If, for instance, the
variables are congeries, their relations can be assessed, to a considerable
extent, in terms of the contemporary procedure of causal-factorial-
associational analysis, without invoking the principles of immanent
change, of system, and so on. But even in this case, the investigator
has to keep in mind the three-componential structure of the congeries,
and particularly their meaning component. If one or more variables
are systems, then all the properties of systems—such as three-componential structure, immanent change, immanent phases, tempo,
rhythms, limits, relations with other systems,[45] and so on—must be
kept in mind in the study of the static and dynamic relationships of
the system or systems to other systems or variables. Without a consideration of these principles, the prevalent procedure of causal-factorial
analysis is bound to yield fallacies instead of valid results.

Meanings as the Main Clue. In order to discover whether the
variables chosen are systems or congeries, the investigator must remember that a system has a consistent set of meanings mutually dependent
upon one another, whereas congeries are only a dump of unrelated
meanings. *The meaning component gives us the first and most important clue as to whether the variable is a congeries or a system.*

---

[44] The term *integralist* denotes the author's system of sociology.
[45] A systematic theory of these principles is presented in Sorokin, *Dynamics,* Vol.
IV, *passim.*

In meaningful sociocultural phenomena, the meanings of the variables exhibit either consistency or inconsistency, dependence or unrelatedness. On the basis of the relatedness or unrelatedness of the meanings of the variables, there is a possibility of conjecture as to whether the given variables belong to one another and depend upon one another causally; whether they are likely to be parts of the same system of meanings; or whether they are independent of one another. It is the element of meaningfulness that permits us at once to grasp the correlation of the theorems of Euclid's geometry or of the articles of the Christian credo. The meaningful aspect of sociocultural phenomena permits logic and intuition to play a vastly greater role in ascertaining the existence of meaningful-causal relationships between the variables than is possible in the field of purely natural phenomena, which are devoid of meaningful components.[46] Without this meaningful aspect of sociocultural phenomena, we should not be able to apply much logic (or intuition) and should be enormously impoverished in our knowledge of their mutual relations. With only empirical observation at our disposal, we should not be able to grasp—especially in discrete and spatially dispersed sociocultural phenomena—any connections except congeries or chance relationships. Even the meaningful aspect of these can hardly be observed in a narrow sense of the term— that is, through the sense organs.

Strictly speaking, we cannot "observe" love or hatred, ambition or sacrifice, ecstasy, harmony or discord, consistency or inconsistency, or any inner experience of other men. What we can observe are only certain movements, gestures, contortions of the muscles, vascular changes, and the like. Still less observable are the "residues" of Pareto, the "interests" of Marx or Ratzenhofer, the "values" of the economists, or the wishes, drives, instincts, and attitudes discussed by the psychologists, sociologists, and social scientists. Likewise, we cannot observe

[46] Even in this field, logicomathematical deduction plays an important role, frequently leading to concrete discoveries like that of Neptune, by J. G. Galle, on the basis of the computations of Leverrier and J. G. Adams, or of certain new chemical elements on the basis of Mendelyeev's periodic system, and so on. But these deductions and computations are made, not on the basis of the relationships of the meanings of the phenomena in our sense, but on that of their structural or dynamic properties (motion, etc.) or their physicochemical or biological properties. It was not a meaningfully consistent or inconsistent relationship between Uranus and Neptune that led to the discovery of Neptune, but the *kind of physical motion* of Uranus, unaccounted for by the motion of any of the known planets.

such systems as nations, states, and empires, society and social classes, the community, or the Roman Catholic Church.

In brief, if we had only had empirical observation of "externalities" at our disposal, sociocultural reality would have been but a chaotic mass of congeries. Perhaps a few of the variables which frequently coexist or change together we should have been able to observe as somehow connected with one another. But they would have been very limited in number and confined to very narrow, concrete, material phenomena adjacent in space and in time. A vast proportion of sociocultural phenomena, particularly those separated by space and time, would never have been apprehended as "causally connected." But their meaningful aspect permits us to realize in millions of cases, dispersed over the whole planet, that there may be or actually is a connection between them—as, for instance, between the various activities of scattered Communist agents, since they represent the same meaningful system (the Communist party); between the sinkings of British or German ships on all of the seven seas; or between the blackouts in all the cities and villages of the belligerent countries.

Through purely empirical observation of external things and individuals, we could never apprehend the fact that demonstrations conducted by motley crowds consisting of individuals of both sexes, widely divergent in age and race, attired in the most diverse costumes, speaking a multitude of different languages, living under the most disparate climatic and geographic conditions, constituted a joint manifestation of protest on the part of the Roman Catholic Church against the persecution of Catholics. Nor could we guess that a bill introduced in Congress to sever diplomatic relationships with aggressive anti-Catholic governments, the visit of a diplomat to the Vatican, a Papal encyclical, the collection of money for victims of the persecution, and hosts of other externally heterogeneous phenomena were not chance phenomena vis-à-vis one another but articulations of one system, and therefore inwardly and causally connected with one another.

On the basis of purely inductive, empirical, external observation, we should certainly conclude that all such phenomena, separated as they are in space, were independent of one another; because they do not conform to the inductive laws of agreement, difference, concomitant variation, and "residue." Even if by chance we should suspect that they were connected, there would be no substantial reason for insisting upon their connection or uniformity; since, externally, they are so irregular, happen at such widely separated places, reveal so little uniformity of time, occur under such varying conditions, and involve such a diversity of individuals that they do not differ from purely accidental occurrences of unrelated phenomena. If, however, we know—and know with certainty—that they are connected, as manifestations of the functioning of the same system, through its vehicles and agents, this is due to our knowledge of the system as an objectified and socialized system of meanings. Knowing the system—its meanings, its vehicles, and its agencies—we throw a net of "meaningful-causal" relationship over thousands of discrete phenomena that look empirically independent of one another; and in most cases, our deductions are borne out by subsequent observations.

In brief, consideration of the meaningful aspect of sociocultural phenomena permits us, through intuition, logic, and then observation, to solve easily the problem whether a given variable is a congeries or a system, and whether the relationship between the variables is a congeries (or chance) relationship or is meaningful-causal. As a matter of fact, the overwhelmingly greater part of our knowledge of chance or meaningful-causal relationships between sociocultural phenomena is derived, not through strict observation, but through intuitive-logical inferences based upon the meaningful aspects of the phenomena and the relationships of the meanings to one another.

Having obtained our first—and most important—clue through analysis of the meanings of the variables, and knowing the three-componential structure of sociocultural phenomena, we must ascertain whether the given complex of meanings of the variables has its vehicles and agents; and, if so, what they are, and whether the three components of each variable show a tangible interdependence. If these tests suggest that a given variable is a system, we must ascertain, furthermore, whether it shows other properties of systems as enumerated above, in Chapter I, and as analyzed in detail in *Dynamics,* Volume IV, Chapters I and II. If it shows these properties, the investigator must determine the degree of interdependence between the three components of the system: Do the vehicles and agents objectify and socialize its system of meanings adequately, or do they perceptibly disfigure and distort it? How marked is the conductivity of the system from component to component? What are the physicochemical and biological properties of the vehicles and agents? By what physicochemical and biological forces are they, as purely physicochemical and biological entities, particularly influenced? And, under the pressure of these external forces, may their system of meanings in its empirical manifestation be influenced retrogressively?

To complete his preliminary study of the system, the investigator must ascertain precisely what is its system of meanings: Does it contain congeries? Is there an inner tension *(Spannung)* which is likely to lead to a split or modification of the system of meanings, by virtue of its implicit contradictions? Moreover, if the type of the system is known, what are its potentialities, the rhythms and phases of its existence, and the tempo of its changes, and at what stage or phase is it at the moment of investigation?[47] Finally, is the system a subsystem in a larger system, with what systems is it co-ordinated, and amidst what systems and congeries (in its sociocultural milieu) does it exist and function?

Finding Stable and Unstable Chance Relationships. The next problem is a study of the relationship between the variables. If, on the basis of this preliminary study, the variables are found to be congeries relative to one another, unrelated meaningfully, they are mere chance variables. As such, they possess no inner ties. However, through the play of incalculable chance forces, they may have acquired a certain amount of chance association. In order to discover whether they are quite independent or possess some degree of association, their relationships have to be studied along the lines of the prevalent probabilistic associational analysis. With certain modifications, this procedure is applicable to their examination and may disclose some association, though it always will be a chance association—highly tentative, localized, and temporary, incapable of being generalized as something certain, universal, and perennial.

For instance, statistical studies disclosed the fact that, in many regions of Russia, the years of bad crops were also the years of abnormal destruction of houses, forests, and other goods by fire. Meaningfully, bad crops and unusual loss of houses or forests through fire are congeries in their relations to one another. They are unrelated mean-

---

[47] An analysis of the rhythms, phases, periodicities, and tempo of sociocultural systems is given in Sorokin, *Dynamics*, Vol. IV.

ings. The positive association found is a chance association. Investigation has revealed how this chance association comes about. It is due to the common factor of strong winds. These winds cause droughts, and hence poor crops in dry localities; and they are also a factor in the prevalence of abnormal fires, facilitating their spread in the forests and in the villages with wooden houses. Through this external agency of strong winds influencing the crops and the spread of fires, the two variables happen to be indirectly connected. Hence the tangible association between the variables.[48] The association is, however, local and temporary. In localities where the soil has an abundance of moisture, and in villages with stone or brick houses, or that are well supplied with efficient fire-fighting apparatus and organization, the association would be lacking.

Similarly, a study may disclose a high correlation between, say, church attendance on Sundays in a given city and the number of cases of pneumonia in its population, but such an association (hypothetically assumed) can be only temporary and local, occasioned by the operation of some external common agency through "the vehicles and agents" of the variables. Meaningfully, the phenomena are unrelated.

In all such cases of intercongeries relationships, the prevalent method of causal-factorial analysis can be used, with the reservations and limitations specified above. Since congeries are chance phenomena, the probabilistic conception and technique is the proper method for investigating their relationships.

Study of Intersystem Relationships. Very different is the situation with respect to *intersystem relationships*. Here the technique of detecting meanings plays the most important part. This technique furnishes the chief clue to the nature of the relations between the variables. If their systems of meanings are found to be related, this creates an initial presumption of not only meaningful but causal interdependence of the variables; otherwise, it is to be assumed that the systems are congeries, unrelated meaningfully and causally.

The next step consists in determining whether the vehicles and agents of the systems are *in contact* with one another. If they are found not to be in contact (say, the economic systems of China and Australia, on the assumption that China and Australia are entirely isolated from one another), one concludes that the systems are either

---

[48] For a more detailed analysis of this association, cf. Tschuprow, *op. cit.*, pp. 116 ff.

completely independent congeries relative to one another (their mean-ings standing in the relation of congeries to one another) or empirical congeries (their meanings being logically interconnected, but there being no actual contact between their vehicles and agents). Hence they will display scarcely any causal interdependence.

On the other hand, if the meanings of the systems are related, and their vehicles and agents are found to be in contact with one another—either directly or indirectly—through a common supersystem of which the several systems are components, there is a reasonably certain ground for concluding that the systems are meaningfully and causally con-nected, and that, in their coexistence and changes, they will therefore probably display a substantial interdependence. All that remains is to check the validity of these conclusions observationally and, through more detailed study, to determine precisely the degree and nature of the interdependence.

It is accordingly clear that, *in exploring the interrelationships of systems, the meaning component and the "meaningful induction" are paramount.* Without them, we should be unable to grasp most of the meaningful-causal relations between the systems, and especially be-tween important variables. The reason is that the principal sociocul-tural systems are never identical, but differ from one another in respect to a series of secondary points even when they belong to the same class. Examples are afforded by the Christian, Hinduist, Confucianist, and Mohammedan religions; and by the Greco-Roman, medieval, and modern economic systems.

Since a given system is never repeated under identical conditions, the application of the rules of induction becomes exceedingly difficult—indeed, virtually impossible. This fact precludes discovery of the causal uniformities between systems. The difficulty is still greater in regard to the important sociocultural processes. Such processes as war, revolu-tion, prosperity, impoverishment, or the emergence, rise, and decline of certain religious, artistic, political, and philosophical systems, are sep-arated by considerable and unequal time intervals; they take place under the most diverse conditions; and they possess a vast number of characteristics which are unique for each occurrence. Anyone thor-oughly familiar with the inductive method will readily understand that, in these circumstances, it is hardly possible to detect any real relation-ships, and particularly the causal connections between such processes, by the technique of "objective observation" and induction. Not the method of difference, nor that of residue, nor that of concomitant variation, nor any other canonic inductive procedure will avail. If we had to rely solely upon the externalistic inductive procedure, most of the causal connections between sociocultural systems would inevitably escape us.

Fortunately, we have at our disposal the meaning component of the systems. As has been said, it comes to our aid where externalistic induction is inapplicable. It gives us the first clue and then steadily guides us in our orientation in the jungle of sociocultural causal and chance relationships. If the natural sciences have an advantage in that their phenomena are endlessly repeated under identical or comparatively similar conditions, permitting the natural scientist to apply the rules of induction in his experimental studies, sociologists have the unique advantage of "meaningful induction" and guidance. It permits us to discover quite validly which relationships among sociocultural systems are accidental and which are causal-meaningful. It enables us frequently to detect the causal interdependence between phenomena (systems and processes) which are repeated only a few times, appear quite dissimilar from the perceptional standpoint, occur under the most diverse conditions, and are scattered in space and time—in brief, among phenomena where any externalistic induction is utterly useless.

A pertinent example is the causal relationships between the heterogeneous phenomena in which the aforementioned protest of the Catholic Church manifests itself. Another, and perhaps much more significant, example is the discovery of the interdependence—static and dynamic— among the enormous number of systems and processes that constitute the ideational, idealistic, and sensate supersystems of culture, their rise and their decline. Perceptionally and objectively, there is certainly no resemblance between the impressionistic style of painting, materialistic philosophy, empirical epistemology, secular government, utilitarian ethic, nominalistic and singularistic mentality, the improvement of the material standard of living, and the contractual and compulsory character of social relations. Externalistically observed, these phenomena reveal no causal dependence or interdependence. A strict behaviorist and "operationalist" could not even surmise that a causal interdependence existed between such heterogeneous variables. My *Dynamics,* however, discloses the existence of very definite interdependence in the correlation of these and many other variables. As the articulation of the sensate supersystem of culture, they function and change together, each variable depending upon the other subsystem or parts of the sensate supersystem, each part depending upon the whole, and the whole supersystem depending upon its parts. The same is true of the vast number of subsystem variables that make up the ideational and idealistic supersystems. Only through the clue of the relationship of the meanings of each of these subsystems was it possible even to conceive of their possible interdependence.

Once discovered and empirically checked and tested, the meaningful-causal method permitted the detection of an entire nexus of causal interrelationships between the principal variables (systems), comprising a series of subnexuses of causal relationships between a multitude of important sociocultural variables. In their totality, these nexuses of causal-meaningful relations of the variables that make up the sensate, idealistic, and ideational supersystems of culture, and that determine their interdependent rise and decline, enable us to comprehend the structure and dynamics of a huge section of sociocultural life. They supply us with *a knowledge of static and dynamic meaningful-causal relationships unattainable through externalistic induction.* Let us elucidate this point a little further.

By static meaningful-causal relationship is meant the relationship: where A is given, B, C, D, are given, [provided] A, B, C, D, are meaningfully-causally connected. That is exactly what our theory of supersystems does in regard to an enormous number of systems and subsystems with their components—meanings, vehicles, and human agents. Knowing the essential character of our A, say, of the sensate supersystem (or the sensate phase in its dynamic aspects), we can say: if the sensate phase of the system (A) is given, then such and such B, C, D, E, . . . N will be given, because this A and these B, C, D, E, . . . N are meaningfully and causally connected. Concretely, if the sensate system (A) is given, then, with a reasonable degree of certainty, we can predict that its art will be predominantly visual (B), with all the essential characteristics of such an art (b, c, d, e, f) depicted in Volume I of *Dynamics;* that its system of truth (C) will be predominantly empirical, with concentration on the natural sciences and technological inventions, and other characteristics of such a system analyzed in Volume II of *Dynamics;* that supersensory religion will play a very modest part, while business and empirical science will have an enormous role in such a culture *(D);* that its ethics and law *(E)* will be predominantly utilitarian, hedonistic, expedient; that its government *(F)* will be secular, led by military, rich, or professional groups; that its literature *(G)* will be predominantly "realistic," sensual, in part erotic, with a common type of people as its main personages, mixed liberally with the "glamour girl," criminal, prostitute and other subsocial types; and . . . so forth, [down to the] minutest details, like the presence of quantitative colossalism, "progressivism," a "linear conception of historical process," and so on. The same is true of the ideational or idealistic systems. When either one of these is given, we can predict a large number of what forms would be assumed by its art, philosophy, religion, ethics, social organization, and so on, since this A and its $B, C, D, E, \ldots N$ are connected causally and meaningfully.

Thus we find ourselves in *the possession of a meaningful-causal relationship between an enormous number of most important sociocultural phenomena or variables,* which otherwise, being in "stochastic" relationship with one another, cannot be grasped if mechanically treated as mere "variables" or congeries. These meaningful-causal relationships concern, not only the relationship of A (supersystem) with its $B, C, D, \ldots N$, but also the relationship of B with $C, D, E, \ldots N$, and C with $B, D, E, \ldots N$ and N with B, C, D, E, and so on, if and when they are part of the supersystem. This means that these $B, C, D, E, \ldots N$ are also connected causally in the strictest sense of the static causal relationship: when B is given, $C, D, E, \ldots$ N are given; when N is given, B, C, D, E, are given.

So far as a discovery of causal relationship is possibly the supreme aim of any study, we find ourselves in possession of a large number of such relationships discovered through our "meaningful-organic" approach, guided by the meanings and through the method of system and supersystem, rhythm and superrhythm. From this standpoint, our method has all the predictable value which any genuine causal connection has: if A is given, $B, C, D, \ldots N$ will be there; if A is absent, $B, C, D, \ldots N$ will be absent. In addition, the meaningful-causal relationship here concerns, not merely two variables, but a nexus of many variables from all the main compartments of culture, and a large number of the variables within the same system (or compartment) of culture. Such a result is certainly one of the richest crops that any study can give.

Dynamic meaningful-causal relationship means the dynamic causal relationship between A and B, according to the formula: If A varies, B varies. In our case, it means, not only that if A varies B varies, but also that $C, D, E, \ldots N$ vary respectively and concomitantly (in togetherness). Viewed in this dynamic aspect, our superrhythm of domination of sensate-ideational-idealistic supersystems means: if the supersystem passes from, say, the ideational phase to the idealistic *(A),* then all the embraced rhythms and all their subrhythms also pass from the ideational to the idealistic phase. If someone states that, in such and such a culture, its ideational supersystem (or phase) begins to pass into the idealistic supersystem or phase, with this datum we can predict, with a reasonable degree of certainty, what kind of transformation will be undergone by the fine arts of the culture, by its system of truth-religion, philosophy, science; what trend will prevail in the movement of scientific discoveries and inventions; in law and ethics; in the economic well-being of the population, in the movement of war and revolutions, and in all the subsystems of the supersystem studied. More than that: knowing the kind of fundamental transformation experienced by B or C or N (when they are part of the supersystem), one can foresee with considerable probability the kind of transformation which D, E, and other embraced systems and their processes, with their rhythms and phases, will be undergoing. In other words, our formula discovers a complex net of dynamic relationships of interdependence, not only between the main process with its superrhythm (passage of the supersystem from phase A to B), but between all the embraced processes and their rhythms as well.

If we assume, for instance, that, at the present time, our culture entered the transition from its dominant sensate phase to the ideational phase, this datum is quite sufficient to predict hundreds of trends in our culture, such as an increase in war and revolutions in the transitory period—because, in such a period, war and revolution uniformly increase; a decrease in economic well-being, for the same reason; a progressively increasing depreciation of most of the sensate values, beginning with money and prestige of the rich classes as such; a slowing tempo of increase in scientific discoveries and inventions; a decline of contractual relationships; an increasing evaluation and role of supersensory religion; a decreasing empiricism, in all its varieties, and increasing mysticism, religious rationalism, fideism, and so on; a decline of utilitarian and hedonistic ethics; a transformation of law in the same direction; a decline of visual, sensate, sensual, and erotic forms and contents of arts, and so on. . . . All these trends will be given if the major premise is accurately diagnosed.[49]

The fruitfulness of this meaningful-causal method in the study of the relationship of systems, and the comparative sterility of those that attempt to study sociocultural phenomena mechanically, by mere application of poorly understood methods of physicochemical sciences, are comprehensible. When one approaches mechanically the study of the relationships between most of the sociocultural phenomena, and takes, for example, the relationship between the movement of quantitative nudity in pictures and of nominalism, treating them just as two variables, one can hardly find any relationship; one can hardly even guess that, in some way, they may be interdependent. Still less possible is it to find, through such a mechanical procedure, any relationships of interdependence between thousands of phe-

[49] Sorokin, *Dynamics*, IV, 430-433.

nomena meanings, vehicles, and human agents that make either a sensate or ideational supersystem and thousands of processes of which the life of the supersystem is made up. No inductive method in its mechanical application, no statistical correlation technique, can even be applied to such a task. If such methods are applied, they cannot give anything except blunders, for the same reason that they cannot find any relationship of interdependence between a piece of heart, a piece of lung, and a piece of gland all cut from the same organism. These dead variables, taken out of the system in which they were interdependent, and treated as just variables, cannot give any relationship which they had as parts of the same system and when within the system. Similarly, when this or that style of art and this or that philosophical current, plus the amount of pig iron produced, are taken mechanically, as mere variables, they can disclose as little interdependence as the above pieces of heart, lung, and gland. What is interdependent in a system is not so outside of it.[50]

Similarly, if one ignores the three-componential structure of sociocultural phenomena, viewing the variables as purely physical phenomena, one cannot hope to discover any causal relationship. We know that vehicles taken without regard to the meanings they articulate are mostly causal congeries in respect to one another. As such, they lack causal interdependence. The mechanical investigators, being "objectivists," take them at the face value of their chemical, physical, and biological properties. They either do not find—and justifiably so—any causal connections between such vehicle variables, or they find something fictitious. When such variables as the high frequency of prostitutes, gangsters, hypocrites, or glamour girls as the chief personages of fiction, the predominantly utilitarian character of legal and ethical codes, and the multiplicity of technological inventions are taken, and their relationships are studied mechanically through statistical or other techniques, obviously no genuine relationship of interdependence can be detected. Considered, not as embodiments of the same system, but as isolated variables, they cannot exhibit either positive or negative correlation; nor can they offer any other inductive basis that would suggest and support the existence of the relationship which, in fact, they possess as articulations of the same sensate system, and which, when grasped in that setting, is supported by the a posteriori inductive test. Viewed in a purely mechanical setting, they stand in the same congerial relationship as the dead heart, lungs, and glands referred to above.

[50] *Ibid.*, IV, 433-434.

Difference between the Integralist Conception of the Relationships of Sociocultural Phenomena and the Contemporary Probabilistic-externalistic Concept

The conception and procedure outlined differ markedly from the conception and technique criticized above.

1. The prevalent theory views all the relationships between sociocultural variables as chance, or congeries, relationships, some of the variables being associated somewhat stably, others being quite independent. The integralist conception, however, sharply divides the relations into two classes: (1) chance relationships between congeries, and (2) meaningful-causal relationships between the parts of the same system and between the respective systems.

By their very nature, the meaningful-causal relations are profoundly different from chance relations. In this sense, they are an excellent example of the law of sufficient reason, as the most adequate definition of the cause-and-effect relationships, formulated by Leibnitz. This law enunciates the integralist principle, in that it discloses both the chance and the nonchance relationships between sociocultural phenomena, and indicates clearly where each is to be found and in what form. Its proponents thus take sharp issue with the one-sided mechanical "causalists" and with the no less one-sided mechanical devotees of chance and contingency.

2. The prevalent probabilistic conception and procedure almost entirely neglects—at least in its *profession de foi*—the meaningful aspect of sociocultural phenomena and of their relationships. It seeks to imitate the natural sciences, whose phenomena lack the meaningful component and therefore naturally do not deal with their meaningful aspect. The integralist causal-factorial analysis of sociocultural phenomena, on the other hand, views the meaningful component as the most important specificum of a given phenomenon, and hence uses it as the most helpful and decisive clue for discovering whether the given variables are chance congeries or are tied together by meaningful-causal ties. Likewise, it views this clue as the only "inductive tool" that can demonstrate the existence of causal-meaningful relationships between a wide range of discrete, temporally and spatially dispersed, and infrequently repeated phenomena—the vehicles and agents of the same system of meanings—which, through purely externalistic observa-

tion, could never be identified as anything but chance congeries. Similarly, it uses the meaning component to detect a lack of association between phenomena which, according to the externalistic rules of induction, would be fallaciously interpreted as causally associated. Through its clue—the meanings and their relationships—it is able (as has been shown above) to connect a multitude of subsystems with their systems, and these with their supersystem; in other words, it can disclose a vast and complex network of meaningful-causal relationships entirely undiscoverable through the externalistic-probabilistic approach to the problem.

To be precise, the variables of the probabilistic approach have to be few in number, narrow in scope, and highly recurrent. Such comprehensive variables as economic systems, democracy, religion, ethical systems, and the fine arts—not to mention the supersystems as well as the relationships between such vast variables—are not amenable to study by this method. The integralist method, on the other hand, does not encounter any serious difficulties in its relational analysis. The same is true of the causal interdependence between a multitude of diverse vehicles and agents of the same system, such as the Roman Catholic demonstrations spoken of above. Externalistically, they would be overlooked as interdependent phenomena and, if noticed, would have to be put into the class of pure chance relationships. From the integralist standpoint, they are easily and validly grasped as interdependent articulations of the same system, in spite of their fantastic diversity.

In attaching such a diagnostic value to the meanings, the integralist analysis of factorial-causal problems does not dispense with the purely observational verification of the clues given by the meanings and of their relationships; but such a verification is always guided by the component of meanings. That the standpoint of the integralist sociology is sound is attested, among other things, by the uniform inconsistency of the externalists, who invariably employ this clue in their actual studies, contrary to their declarations. However, this use of the clue, being "unwilling" and incidental, usually has bad results.

3. Whereas the prevalent conception envisages only more or less stable or unstable chance relationships, the integralist conception looks for chance relationships between congeries, and for intimate meaningful-causal relationships between the components of a system and between subordinated and co-ordinated systems.

4. The prevalent method, if consistently carried out, lacks theoretically any guide in its tentative conjectures as to which variables exhibit stable mutual relationships and which do not. Since everything is regarded as a mere chance variable, it has to grope blindly among the variables and select them at random. This means an enormous waste of effort. At best, only after several trials and errors is such a procedure able to determine which variables possess which kind of relationships. In contradistinction to this "hit-and-miss" procedure, the integralist theory of causal-chance relationships is guided, at the start, by the relatedness or unrelatedness of the meaning components of the variables. This immediately suggests that most of the variables with unrelated meanings are probably chance variables, unrelated causally, and that most of the variables with related meanings are probably related also causally, provided their vehicles and agents are in contact. Such guidance permits one to rule out a number of unrelated variables at once and restricts the search for causal interdependence to the variables related meaningfully. In most cases, the validity of this procedure is proved by the observational test.

5. The prevalent method is obliged to treat congeries and systems in the same externalistic-probabilistic way. Such erroneous treatment, as we have seen, inevitably leads to fallacious, meaningless, or unreliable results. At best, they are only relatively valid for a given locality and period. The integralist method is free from these deficiencies.

6. Especially numerous and grave are the faults of the prevalent method in a study of the problems of change in sociocultural systems and in the analysis of the factors or causes of such change. The integralist method, per contra, with its principles of system, immanent change, rhythms and phases, limits, and so on, is exempt from these errors. Changes in congeries it views as chance phenomena, "caused" by chance external factors. Changes in systems it studies along quite different lines, giving due consideration to all the basic principles involved in such changes. Hence it is free from the fallacy of explaining everything in terms of external, incidentally picked factors, from the "mysteries" of multiple causation, from explaining the whole by its parts, and so forth.

7. By confusing congeries with systems, the prevalent method seeks uniformities in the chance relationships between chance variables. In selecting these chance variables, it often confronts as separately existing

variables inseparable components of the same system. In other cases, it takes as a unity (a single variable) what are in fact two or more unrelated and incommensurable congeries (for instance, the variable "material culture" or "nonmaterial culture," each of which is a complex of components of several systems).

The integralist procedure is very different. It looks for uniformities chiefly in the field of sociocultural systems and their relationships. Distinguishing systems from congeries, it does not unite into one variable a concoction of heterogeneous things; nor does it split into separate variables one unified system. This explains: (1) why my *Dynamics* deals with uniformities in the systems and in the intersystem relationships—not in accidentally chosen and grotesque variables; (2) why it rejects all of the dichotomists' theories of time uniformity exhibited by the lead and lag of two "concoctional" variables, substituting instead time uniformities of change in various compartments of *the same system,* of sequence of phases in the change of *the same system,* and of interdependent change of the components of the system and interconnected systems, as well as uniformity of relationship in the superrhythm, rhythms, subrhythms, and subsubrhythms of the subordinated systems. The same is true of tempo uniformities and the uniformities of spatial distribution of cultural values. All the volumes of *Dynamics* are dedicated to this logic and method, instead of to a hopeless quest for uniformities between accidentally chosen "concoctional variables" and their pseudorelationships.

8. Finally, even the technique of causal-factorial analysis employed by the integralist method is different from, and simpler and more reliable than, that of the externalistic-probabilistic analysis. The fundamental technique of the prevalent procedure is necessarily statistical. Purely experimental settings for the investigation of factorial-relational problems are hardly ever afforded by sociocultural phenomena; hence application of the strictly inductive rules is ruled out (except, perhaps, in some simplest and most obvious relationships). Mere observation in the form of clinical or "case-study" technique is clearly insufficient for any generalized conclusion respecting the observed relationships. Each case of a variable observed in its relationship to another variable presents different conditions, a different network of relationships, and is not a "causal" case but an instance of a "probabilistic, manifold, stochastic" variable. Accordingly, no conclusion derived from such a

case can be generalized and regarded as a uniformity. In these circumstances, only the statistical technique makes it at all feasible to attempt to unravel the uniformities in the relations of the variables in question. This requires the prevalent method to collect as many instances of the variables as possible (though the enumeration is rarely exhaustive or even representative or sufficient), and involves the complicated technique of their "processing," with all its arbitrary assumptions, and its uncertainties as to the validity of the results.

The integralist method, in its study of the relationships between congeries, sometimes has to adopt this technique (in a modified form). But in regard to inter- and intra-system relationships, it largely dispenses with this technique, or else uses it in a more economical way for posthypothesis verification. A study of the relationship of the meanings of variables, together with the subsequent investigation of the presence or absence of contact between their vehicles and agents, furnishes much more solid ground for a conclusion as to whether or not the empirically grounded systems are meaningfully and causally connected and interdependent than does the collection and "processing" of a large number of cases. This is especially true of the relations between such vast and complex system variables as the fine arts and religion, religion and political systems, science and philosophy, and science and economic systems, as well as the supersystems of the ideational, idealistic, and sensate type.

After arriving at conclusions in this way, one should make a statistical or observational test of their empirical validity. This test may be greatly simplified by choosing the relevant variables yielded by the analysis, instead of indiscriminately collecting every case that suggests the variable in question. If the foregoing technique is carefully followed through, along the lines outlined in this chapter, the empirical test seldom fails to support the conclusions.[51]

[51] This cautiousness is one of the reasons why, in the first three volumes of Sorokin's *Dynamics,* so much space is allotted to an empirical verification of the changes in the correlation of the systems of the sensate-idealistic-ideational supersystems, and why there are so many statistical tables and other empirical data. In spite of their copiousness, however, they give only the data that are crucial and relevant to the theory. I was reasonably certain that the conclusions arrived at would be confirmed by empirical verification. Another reason was to establish more precisely to what extent and at what period a rise or decline of each subsystem took place. The third reason was correctly surmised by Professor R. Park, who graciously observed: "He [Sorokin] is disposed to regard these statistics as something in the nature of a concession to the prevailing mentality and the contemporary system of truth. One suspects that at some time in the

Conclusion

The preceding analysis must have made it clear that the prevalent conception of causal-factorial relationships and the procedure for their discovery are inadequate in a number of respects. The present method has so many serious defects and is so unsuited for an examination of these relationships between sociocultural phenomena—particularly between the systems—that it must be abandoned and replaced by the integralist conception of chance relationships between congeries and meaningful-causal intra- and inter-system relationships. The essential features of the integralist theory are presented in this chapter and are uniformly applied throughout my *Dynamics*.

---

inception and planning of this project he must have said to himself, 'Well, if they want 'em, let's let 'em have 'em.' " See R. Park, in his review of Sorokin's *Dynamics,* in the *American Journal of Sociology* (March, 1938), 827.

When the mentality of social scientists changes and the contemporary system of truth, with its probabilistic-externalistic theory of the relationships of sociocultural phenomena, becomes somewhat sounder, there will be much less need for this kind of evidence and much more for evidence of the meaningful-causal type.

CHAPTER III

SOCIOCULTURAL SPACE

VARIOUS PHYSICOMATHEMATICAL, BIOLOGICAL, AND PSYCHOLOGICAL SPACES

JUST AS THE referential principle of causality of the physiochemical and biological sciences has been found to be inadequate for the cognition and ordering of sociocultural phenomena, similarly, the concept of space of the physical and biological sciences is also inadequate for either the location of sociocultural phenomena or the determination of the position of a given sociocultural phenomenon in the sociocultural universe; it is even more so for an adequate description of sociocultural change, movement, and displacement. For somewhat different reasons, this statement equally concerns the three-dimensional space of the classical mechanics—any kind of geometric space: Euclidian, Lobatchevsky's, Riemann's, the four-dimensional space-time continuum of Minkowski-Einstein, the n-dimensional space of G. Cantor's theory of group, or any other mathematicophysical or biological conception of space. The space concept of the classical mechanics is unfit, because of its inability to locate the position of a sociocultural phenomenon in the sociocultural universe and because of the very different structure of sociocultural space. The more general conceptions of space (of Riemann and others) are inadequate, partly because they are too general to be able to serve as the referential principle of sociocultural sciences and partly because they are more narrow than is necessary for an adequate conception of sociocultural space. They are too general in the sense that, like a net with too large meshes, they do not catch the sociocultural fish. They are too narrow in the sense that some of the "dimensions" of sociocultural space are not provided for in these conceptions of space.

In order to realize this inadequacy, let us glance at the properties of these various spaces and at the theories that try to apply them to sociocultural phenomena.

Space of the Classical Mechanics. Any displacement or motion studied by mechanics presupposes *space*, because, as Kirchhoff puts it:

98   SOCIOCULTURAL CAUSALITY, SPACE, TIME

"Motion is everywhere understood to mean change of position." Position is already a spatial concept. Without space, no displacement and no motion can be thought of or described. This makes it comprehensible why Lagrange styled kinematics, the science of motion, as "the Geometry of four dimensions, because in general it deals with four independent variables, namely the Time *(t)*, and the three Space co-ordinates, *x,* *y, z,* which fix the position of a particle."[1]

The space of the classical mechanics is that of the three dimensions. They are sufficient to locate the position of a particle or a material body in this physical universe. For a description of a movement (besides time), to these three dimensions, *x, y, z* (altitude, longitude, and latitude, usually in reference to the earth or a system of fixed stars) are added an indication of the origin, direction, and sense of the movement (vector), not to mention some other elements used in it. The space, further, is supposed to be uniform everywhere. Such are the essential traits of the space of the classical mechanics. Sir Isaac Newton's classical conception is as follows:

Absolute space, in its own nature and without regard to anything external, always remains similar and immovable.

Relative space is some movable dimension or measure of absolute space, which our senses determine by its position with respect to other bodies, and which is commonly taken for immovable (absolute) space. . . .

Absolute motion is the translation of a body from one absolute place to another absolute place: and relative motion, the translation from one relative place to another relative place.[2]

In the classical mechanics are accepted

as the facts of common sense, the reality of matter, that of space in which matter is situated and moving, and that of time without which the movement cannot be produced. . . . This universe presents itself to us as having the space of three dimensions, no more, no less. . . . The real space has not only the three dimensions but also the traits of isotropy and homogeneity. Its isotropy consists in that the directions which issue from the same point possess the identical properties; its homogeneity in that nothing distinguishes its points one from another. In a word, it is uniform and is everywhere the same.[3]

[1] H. Crew and K. K. Smith, *Mechanics for Students of Physics and Engineering* (New York, 1930), p. 85.

[2] I. Newton, *Philosophiae naturalis principia mathematica* (London, 1686); Definitiones, VIII, Scholium.

[3] Léon Lecornu, *La Mécanique* (Paris, 1918), pp. 6-8. See also J. C. Maxwell, *Matter and Motion* (London, 1882), p. 20; P. Appel and S. Dautheville, *Précis de mécanique*

This isotropic and homogeneous space in which the material point or body is located and is moving cannot by itself determine its position or its motion. Position and motion are determined through reference to the other material points or bodies. Which of these bodies is taken to serve as a frame of reference depends largely upon arbitrary choice. Usually, the earth or a fixed system of stars is taken as such point of reference. With the help of the three-dimensional system of co-ordinates based upon these frames of reference, mechanics describes either the position or the movement of the material bodies. For such a description, furthermore, a unit of space (length) is necessary. Such a unit is again somewhat conditional. It may be either a meter or a yard or some other unit of length used by various peoples.

A somewhat more detailed elucidation of these statements follows.

It is impossible to imagine an empty space. Whoever talks of the absolute space employs words devoid of meaning.[4]

Not only are we unable to know the absolute position of an object in space . . . and should talk only of its relative position in relation to other objects; but even the expressions: "the absolute size of the object" or "the absolute distance of two points" are devoid of any sense; one should talk only about the relation between two magnitudes and the relationship between two distances.[5]

In this, as well as in several other respects, the space of mechanics is very relative and conditional. It is relative also in the sense that it can have a meaning only when we have a unit for its measurement. And such a unit is again conditional. Without such an instrument of measurement, we cannot construct space and it loses its meaning.[6]

The position of a point (in space) can be determined but in relation to other points *arbitrarily* chosen as references. . . . In order to be able to refer to it it is necessary to measure certain distances. To measure means to take a meter and to cross (walk in) the space (along a straight line). Doing so, they assume that the meter does not change in its length during this displacement.[7]

Where is the particle? Such an inquiry has no meaning except when one asks for the position of the particle with reference to another position,

rationelle (Paris, 1924), chaps. i and ii; and E. Mach, *The Science of Mechanics* (Chicago, 1902), pp. 226 ff.

[4] H. Poincaré, *La Science et la méthode* (Paris, 1920), p. 95.

[5] H. Poincaré, *Dernières pensées* (Paris, 1913), pp. 38 ff.

[6] H. Poincaré, *Science et méthode*, pp. 96-104.

[7] Lecornu, *op. cit.*, p. 9.

which is known or is assumed to be known. For ordinary purposes one uses a frame fixed in the earth. (In other cases the frame is fixed in regard to certain stars.) In general, three specifications are necessary to describe the relative position of a particle: latitude, longitude, and altitude in regard to a certain point arbitrarily chosen, as the city of Rhodes was chosen by Eratosthenes, or any other point agreed upon.[8]

The above reminds us of the most important characteristics of the space of classical mechanics. It shows also that, without a concept of space, neither the position nor the motion of a material point or body is describable. It means also that no sociocultural movement or change, and no location of sociocultural phenomenon, is conceivable or can be described without a concept of space.

Other Physicomathematical Spaces. We know that the Euclidian space of the classical mechanics is not the only space constructed and used in mathematical and physicochemical sciences. There are several other—more generalized—conceptions of space, like the four-dimensional space-time continuum of Minkowski-Einstein, like the space concepts of Lobatchevsky, Riemann, G. Cantor, and several others. In these more generalized conceptions, space means generally a manifold of three, four, up to *n* dimensions in which *positional relationships* of any kind are described and determined, including the relationship of connection, position, and what not, provided that the determination is done logically and consistently. The relationships may be quantitative and metrical, or qualitative and nonmetrical, as in the topological spaces.[9]

Physiological and Psychological Spaces. There are not only several physicomathematical or geometrical spaces, but also several biological and psychological spaces, different from one another and from physicomathematical spaces. E. Mach's conception of the physicopsychological space gives an example of what is meant by such a space.

[8] Crew and Smith, *op. cit.,* pp. 3 ff. See also E. Mach, *op. cit.,* pp. 226 ff. and 234 ff.; and Appel and Dautheville, *op. cit.,* chaps. i and ii.

[9] See, for instance, B. Riemann, *Über die Hypothesen, welche der Geometrie zu Grunde liegen* (Berlin, 1923); M. Schlick, *Raum und Zeit in der gegenwärtigen Physik* (Berlin, 1920); A. Eddington, *Space, Time, and Gravitation* (Cambridge, 1935); A. Einstein, *Spezielle und allgemeine Relativitätstheorie* (Berlin, 1920); E. Borel, *L'espace et le temps* (Paris, 1933); H. Weyl, *Temps, espace, matière* (Paris, 1922); E. Meyerson, *Identité et realité* and *Du cheminement de la pensée,* three vols., quoted. For the nontechnical description of some of these spaces, insofar as they are applied to sociocultural phenomena, see the works of A. Portuendo y Barceló, S. Haret, P. Ferreira, P. de Miranda, M. Lins, K. Lewin, J. F. Brown, G. Lundberg, and others quoted further

The sensible space of our immediate perception, which we find ready at hand on awakening to full consciousness, is considerably different from geometric space. The space of the Euclidean geometry is everywhere and in all directions constituted alike; it is unbounded and it is infinite in extent. On the other hand, the space of sight, or "visual space" (and also the space of touch) is found to be neither constituted everywhere and in all directions alike, nor infinite in extent, nor unbounded.

The facts relating to the vision of forms . . . show that entirely different feelings are associated with "upness" and "downness," as well as with "nearness" and "farness." "Rightness" and "leftness" are likewise the expression of different feelings, although in this case the similarity, owing to considerations of physiological symmetry, is greater.[10]

The physiological space is of several varieties: the space of touch, of sight, and that of other organs of perception. What, for instance, are some of the properties of *visual space?* One of its qualities is an expansion and contraction of objects, according to whether we approach or go away from them.

The apparent augmentation of the stones at the entrance to a tunnel as we rapidly approach it in a railway train, the shrinkage of the same objects on the train's emerging from the tunnel, are exceptionally distinct cases of the fact of daily experience, that objects in visual space cannot be moved about without suffering expansion or contraction—so that the space of vision resembles in this respect more the space of the meta-geometricians than it does the space of Euclid.

[Furthermore, it is conical, bounded, and] at times it appears to have even very narrow boundaries. . . . A long cylindrical glass vessel tipped over the face, a walking-stick laid endwise against one of the eyebrows, appear strikingly conical in shape. . . . The oblateness of the celestial vault vertically—a phenomenon with which even Ptolemy was acquainted, and which Euler has discussed in modern times—is proof that our visual space is of unequal extent even in different directions. . . . Finally, visual space in its origin is in nowise metrical. The localities, the distances, etc., of visual space differ only in quality, not in quantity.[11]

The *space of touch* is again different from geometric and visual space.

The skin, which is a closed surface of complicated geometrical form, is an agency of spatial perception. Not only do we distinguish the quality of the irritation, but by some sort of a *supplementary* sensation we also distinguish its *locality.*

[10] E. Mach, *Space and Geometry in the Light of Physiological, Psychological and Physical Inquiry* (Chicago, 1906), pp. 5-6. See also his *Analysis of the Sensations* (Chicago, 1897), pp. 49 ff.   [11] Mach, *Space and Geometry,* pp. 6-7.

The space of touch has as little in common with metric space as has the space of vision. Like the latter, it also is anisotropic and nonhomogeneous. The cardinal directions of the organism, "forwards and backwards," "upwards and downwards," "right and left," are in both physiological spaces alike non-equivalent.[12]

Without continuing Mach's analysis, we can conclude with him that "physiological space, thus, has but few qualities in common with geometric space. Both spaces are threefold manifoldness." These spaces, though different from one another, at the same time are mutually corresponding or correlated. "They are related but not identical."[13] Each of these spaces (including the geometric one) is the result of biological adaptation. "Visual space forms the clearest, most precise and broadest system of space-sensations, but biologically, tactual space is perhaps more important."[14]

Physiological space is an adaptive result of the interaction of the elementary organs (of the same organism). Of cardinal and greatest importance to animals are the *parts of their own body* and their relations to one another. . . . *Geometric space* embraces only the relations of *physical bodies to one another,* and leaves the animal body in this connection altogether out of account.[15]

The above sketch gives an idea of the physiological space we deal with in our daily experience, indicating that it is possible to think of different kinds of geometric space and different kinds of physiological space. For this reason only it is conceivable to think of psychological and sociocultural spaces.

As an example of psychological space and distance, the conception of E. Bogardus and others can be mentioned. Its criteria of social distance are the feelings or the attitudes of sympathy and antipathy, solidarity and conflict, between two or more persons. The persons sympathetic to each other are psychologically near to each other; the persons with antagonistic feelings are separated psychologically. In this way, an elaborate concept of "psychological distance" is developed, and a technique for its measurement is established.[16]

One can set forth a number of psychological conceptions of space

[12] *Ibid.,* pp. 7-10.
[13] *Ibid.,* pp. 11-15.
[14] *Ibid.,* p. 19.
[15] *Ibid.,* p. 32.
[16] E. Bogardus and others call it "social distance." However, for the reasons indicated further, it is psychological rather than sociocultural distance and defines the psychological attitudes rather than the sociocultural positions of the persons. For further references and literature on this problem, see pages 139 ff.

and distance, as follows: There may be psychological spaces between the state of dreaming and in being awake; psychological distances between the state of being tired or fresh (the same geometric distance appears to be much longer to cross in the state of fatigue than in the state of freshness) or of being sober and being drunk; psychological space between the blind and the nonblind; and so on. Likewise, there are various psychological distances between individuals with an I. Q. of 150 and those with an I. Q. of 45; between brutal and soft persons; between introverts and extroverts; between farsighted and nearsighted persons; between good-looking and ugly ones; and so on and so forth. Many such distances (like those measured by "mental tests") are indeed established and—rightly or wrongly—measured, in various forms.[17]

APPLICATIONS OF VARIOUS PHYSICOGEOMETRIC CONCEPTIONS OF SPACE TO PSYCHOLOGICAL AND SOCIOCULTURAL PHENOMENA

Social Mechanics and Physics. Since psychological and sociocultural phenomena are continually occurring somewhere, and some of these have some locus, or position, and positional relationship to one another, it is but natural that spatial conceptions have always been used to determine their position and relationship in the sociocultural universe. Some of the investigators have tried to use the physicomathematical conceptions almost verbatim, transferring them into the sociocultural universe from geometry or mechanics or mathematics, without any serious modification of these conceptions. Others have tried to modify them to some extent, but without any fundamental change. As a result, we have had numerous attempts to create "social physics," "social geometry," "social and psychological topology," "social mechanics," "social energetics," and so on. Attempts of that kind are very old, and are found in ancient China, India, Greece, and Rome. In the sixteenth, seventeenth, and eighteenth centuries of our era, such attempts became systematic and led to the creation of the "social physics" of these cen-

---

[17] E. Thorndike's statement in regard to the measurement of intelligence is accurate: "Just what they measure is not known; how far it is proper to add, subtract, multiply, divide, and compute ratios with the measures obtained is not known; just what the measures obtained signify concerning the intellect is not known." See E. Thorndike, *The Measurement of Intelligence* (New York, 1927).

We shall see, further, that this pointed statement well applies to most of the applications of the physical space to the measurement and determination of the position of sociocultural phenomena in sociocultural space, not to mention an enormous number of other "measurements" of sociocultural phenomena.

turies, through the studies of Descartes, Hobbes, Spinoza, Malebranche, Leibnitz, Berkeley, Cumberland, and especially E. Weigel.[18]

These men all attempted either to use the space of Newtonian mechanics verbatim or to construct a somewhat homologous space for the determination of the position of sociocultural phenomena, their positional relationship, displacement, motion, and change. Unfortunately, the space of Newtonian mechanics too heavily weighed upon them to permit them to deviate from it as much as was necessary. Subsequently, the efforts to construct a kind of a sociocultural and psychological space were continued. But these efforts have again been confined to a rather analogous use of the geometric spaces, with very insignificant modifications. Of these recent attempts, the conceptions of A. Portuondo y Barceló, S. C. Haret, P. Ferreira, M. Lins, and some others can serve as typical examples. Let us glance at them:

Barceló uses, instead of space, the concept of *social position* of an individual or a group, in relation to a given psychological value:

> Nous appelerons *position* d'un individu ou groupement relativement à un phénomène donné à un instant donné: l'ensemble de tout ce qu'il y aura de psychique de quelque façon que soit, dans cet instant, chez l'individu ou dans le groupement et qui se rapporte au phénomène dont il s'agit.

This concept is "something analogous to the position of a material point or a system of points in space."[19]

> [However,] it is not space. Instead of space we have a *given relation* and that something psychological that we style position in a given relation is a psychological complex composed of all the residues of knowledge, sentiments, volitions, etc. of an individual or a group.[20]

Furthermore, in referring to G. Cantor's concept of "the arithmetic space of *n* dimensions," Barceló says that social relations which serve as the point of reference for defining the position of an individual or group is the "paramètre de *n* dimensions psychique," similar to the "arithmetic space of *n* dimensions," developed by Georg Cantor and some other mathematicians. By this arithmetic space, they mean

a complex number or figure of *n* real numbers or figures. These *n* real quantitative values $X_1, X_2 \ldots X_n$, which unite in the given complex value,

---

[18] See the history of such theories and their contemporary varieties in P. A. Sorokin, *Contemporary Sociological Theories*, chap. i, and his *Dynamics*, II, 428 ff.

[19] Antonio Portuondo y Barceló, *Essais de mécanique sociale* (Paris, 1925), pp. 7-8; also pp. 20-21 and 41-42.   [20] *Ibid.*, p. 41.

are expressed in relation to their corresponding divers units. Each value of the complex number defines the position of a point—as they style it—in the arithmetic space of n dimensions; and the values $X_1, X_2 \ldots X_n$, upon which the complex number depends, are n coordinates of this point.[21]

All this indicates that even Barceló, who perhaps tries to apply the principles of rational mechanics to social phenomena in the most straightforward way, is unable to use the concept of space of the classical mechanics and has to borrow G. Cantor's many-dimensional arithmetic space (his theory of group).

Unfortunately for him, in many other statements, Barceló does not escape a purely analogical use of the space of mechanics. As a result, we have a series of propositions devoid of any clear sense, in their application to sociocultural phenomena. Here are a few examples.

In the space of mechanics, a vector indicating a direction can have two "senses"—positive and negative. The author then states the same in regard to psychosocial movements; thus religious change, for example, can have only two "senses."[22] I, for one, do not see any sense in this statement, for a person can become an atheist, Christian, Confucianist, Buddhist, Judaist, and so on, so that to me there are, not two, but n "senses"—if we want to call each religious system by the term "sense."

Furthermore, the author talks of the "rectilinear" movement of an individual, of his inertia, of the velocity of his movement, of his being "at rest" or moving uniformly and rectilinearly, and so on.[23] All this has hardly any meaning, because the author does not talk of the physical motion of an individual or group, but of the psychosocial changes within an individual or group. I confess I fail to see how it is possible to talk of "the rectilinear change with a constant velocity at any given moment," or of the individual's being "at rest," or of the group and individual as being in an equilibrium in the sense of mechanics. When an individual is free and is at rest, and when he is influenced by many forces and these forces mutually annul each other, so that their final result is nil, then a free individual is at equilibrium. Such is the concept of this equilibrium. Here is my commentary on the matter: I am "at rest," standing at the middle of a street. At a given moment, two absolutely identical cars, with absolutely identical

[21] Ibid., pp. 199-200.
[22] Ibid., pp. 12-13.   [23] Ibid., pp. 111 ff. et passim.

force propelled in the opposite direction, bump me from the opposite sides. The forces (cars), being identical and driven in the opposite direction, mutually annul each other. But I wonder if I remain in equilibrium and "at rest." Unless it is the equilibrium and rest of death!

Or let us take the law of the equality of the action and reaction:

Each time as an individual receives a psychological action tending to change his status at rest, or in movement, this individual exerts, in his turn through reaction—another action equal and opposite and applied to the point whence the action emanates.[24]

Comments: I am recklessly driving my car. A policeman stops me and gives me a tag. This "sobers" me, and I drive less recklessly. My psychological status is changed by the action of the policeman. But I wonder through what mystery I exerted "equal and opposite" reaction upon him, and how it could be "equal and opposite," and who measured the actions and reactions and found them equal, and how this was done.[25]

The whole work is mainly a somewhat distorted transcription of the principles of mechanics with "individual" and "group" used instead of "material point," or "material body." From such a transcription, the principles of mechanics suffer, and nothing is added to our understanding of sociocultural phenomena. An individual or group, as a purely material point or body, is taken care of by the mechanics; therefore there is no need to create a social mechanics for that purpose. On the other hand, individuals or groups, as sociocultural phenomena, are not studied by mechanics; and the system of principles of mechanics is neither designed for such a study, nor can it serve as a frame of reference for it.

Haret's social space is somewhat different from the space of mechanics: "We mean by social status (*l'état social*) or social situation of an individual, the status defined by the three values which represent his economic, intellectual, and moral standing."[26] This shows that the author understands well the impossibility of utilizing geometric space for either the location of an individual or the description of his social status and change.

[24] *Ibid.*, p. 121.
[25] For a criticism of similar conceptions of equilibrium, see Sorokin, *Dynamics*, Vol. IV, chap. xiv.
[26] S. C. Haret, *Mécanique sociale* (Paris-Bucharest, 1910), p. 49.

Unfortunately, like Barceló, farther on Haret lapses into a series of statements where, contrary to his definition, he uses in the most analogous way the derivatives of the space of mechanics. Here are a few examples:

Haret gives a three-dimensional system of co-ordinates with the three axes, X, Y, Z—a mere replica of the system of mechanics. If there it has a full sense, one wonders what sense it can have here, since the point of the cross-section of these "axes" (economic, intellectual, and moral) is not a spatial point; since there is no possibility of giving any quantitative uniform value to the vectors and lengths of these axes; since there is no possibility of depicting by a line either the sense or the direction of these lines; and so on. For these reasons, the system of the vectors given by Haret is rather meaningless. And this is shown by the author when he says: "We accept as the origin of these co-ordinates the point at which the economic, intellectual and moral values *(avoir)* are nil."[27] This statement appears to me a mere collection of words framed along the corresponding proposition of mechanics. If it means that an individual does not have any economic, intellectual, and moral status, this signifies that he has no status at all; therefore his position or status remains undefined. If it means some scale of the economic, intellectual, and moral values, starting with zero, then the scale should be given; and it should be shown what it is, how it is constructed and measured, and how these three vectors are related to one another in defining the social position of the individual. Since this is not done, the proposition remains void.

Haret continues: "Every social force can be represented by a vector *MP* in social space."[28] Comment: If the system of the co-ordinates is meaningless, the term "vector," its direction and sense, becomes meaningless also.

When a force [acting on an individual] is constant in direction and when the initial impulse of the individual has the same direction as that of the force, under such conditions the individual's movement will be rectilinear.[29]

I confess I do not understand what "rectilinearity" means here. It certainly does not mean the physical motion of an individual along a straight line. If I am hungry (initial impulse), and if my friend per-

[27] *Ibid.*, p. 50.
[28] *Ibid.*, p. 51.　　　　　　　　　[29] *Ibid.*, p. 107.

sistently invites me to step into a lunchroom and have lunch (force constant in direction), I shall probably have the lunch. But I fail to see why my actions of stepping into a lunchroom, ordering the lunch, eating it, and so on, are to be styled "rectilinear" but not "circuitous." I fail also to see what the word "rectilinear" adds to the above description of my actions.

Still more mystical and meaningless are the concepts of the *mass* of an individual or groups, units of strength, concept of equilibrium of individual, that of virtual velocity, of inertia and so on, used by Haret.[30]

In brief, these works show how difficult it is to define the social location of individuals, groups, social phenomena, or to describe their "movements" in the terms of the space of mechanics and its derivatives. They illustrate also the fruitlessness of an analogical application of the principles of rational mechanics to sociocultural phenomena.

Generalized Topological Space. As an example of an application of the generalized Riemannian conception of space in its topological variety to psychological and sociocultural phenomena, the attempts of P. de Miranda, P. Ferreira, M. Lins, K. Lewin, and J. F. Brown can be mentioned.[31] For them, "space is a manifold in which positional relationships may be expressed."

Spaces may be constructed of any dimensions and properties, provided these are logically consistent. . . . In our definition of the psychological field as a space construct, space must be understood in its post-Riemannian sense.[32]

Starting with this post-Riemannian topological space, P. de Miranda, P. Ferreira, M. Lins, Lewin, Brown, and others try to apply it systematically to the field of psychology and sociology. Psychology is turned into "psychological field," "as a construct to which all psycho-

[30] *Ibid.,* pp. 102 ff. *et passim.*

[31] See Pontes de Miranda, *Introducção a sociologia geral* (Rio de Janeiro, 1927); Pinto Ferreira, *Teoria do espaço social* (Rio de Janeiro, 1939), and his *Von Wiese und die zeitgenössische Beziehungslehre* (Rio de Janeiro, 1941); M. Lins, *Espaço-Tempo e relações sociaes* (Rio de Janeiro, 1940); K. Lewin, *Principles of Topological Psychology* (New York, 1936); J. F. Brown, *Psychology and Social Order* (New York, 1936), and "On the Use of Mathematics in Psychological Theory," *Psychometrika* (1936), Vol. I, Nos. 1 and 2.

[32] Brown, "On the Use of Mathematics," quoted, pp. 79-80. See also G. Lundberg, *Foundations of Sociology,* pp. 131, 263, and 330. I am quoting the article by Brown because it very concisely sums up what others developed more substantially in their works.

logical activity (that is, behavior) may be ordered. It is spatial in the sense in which space has been defined above."[33] Having obtained their "spatial field," the authors proceed to transfer verbatim further specifications of the geometricotopological space, with its direction, vector, magnitude, distance, continuity or discontinuity, liberty or restriction; with its topological "path," "locomotion," "freedom," and all the other characteristics of the space of geometry, topology, or mechanics.

The space of Lewin-Brown differs from the rest only in that it is not always "metrical" and is n-dimensional. Otherwise, all their constructive work is but a mere transcription of the geometricotopological space, and a series of attempts to apply it to the "psychological field" for the location of the phenomena of behavior and determination of their characteristics. In other words, it is a purely analogical use of the concepts of space of physicomathematical sciences.[34]

Is the Lewin-Brown attempt fruitful? Does it give some cognitive advantage in the study of the psychological phenomena and their properties, in comparison with the "traditional" concepts and referential principles of the "traditional" nontopological psychology? The reader can judge for himself from a few facts used by the authors for demonstration of the fruitfulness of their borrowed concepts in the field of psychology. Like the space of mechanics, with its vector, direction, and magnitude,

The points in the psychological field are associated with both direction and magnitude but these may for the present only be nonmetrically defined. The behavior of an organism may be said to be directed towards a goal. The force behind the behavior may be said to have a magnitude. . . . Whenever an organism behaves psychologically, it may be said to be behaving in a psychological field. The goal which it is "trying" to find is to be ordered to a point within this psychological field. The force which is causing the behavior is ordered to a vector within this psychological field, as is its present position.[35]

Any thoughtful reader can hardly fail to see that the whole operation is a mere verbal preoccupation of "ordering of some phenomena of behavior" to the "psychological field" and rechristening some good and comprehensible terms of psychology with the terms "magnitude,"

---

[33] Brown, "On the Use of Mathematics," pp. 80-81.
[34] See the quoted works of Lewin and Brown.
[35] Brown, "On the Use of Mathematics," p. 81.

"force," "vector," "field," and the like, which not only do not add anything to our knowledge of the behavior "of a hungry rat trying to
get cheese" or "a man trying to clarify a psychological theory," but
only confuse this knowledge and distort the physicomechanical concepts of vector, force, magnitude, direction, and the rest. Such a useless
transcription of the terms would have some advantage and cognitive
value if the transported terms could be measured adequately or were
metrical, as they are in physicomathematical sciences. As P. Appel says
rightly:

> In mathematical formulae the letters designate numbers; these formulae
> can be applied only to the measurable quantities which can be expressed
> by numbers. In analytical geometry, x, y, z designate numbers. The para-
> meters x, y, z in the equations of mechanics are numbers.

Otherwise, where there are no units and numbers, all the formulas
and equations are void and meaningless.[36] Since these concepts in
psychology are declared to be nonmetrical,[37] this is sufficient to make
them perfectly useless in that field. The whole business of the importation of such concepts from physics and geometry becomes futile.
Here are a few more illustrations that show this still more clearly:

In the above case, an assumption that every organism in any motion
has a goal introduces a fallacy, if the term "goal" means what it means
in psychology—something identical with "purpose," "aim," "end," and
so on. We know that many of our actions are "goalless" (though not
causeless); still more true is this in regard to all other organisms. If
the term "goal" has no such meaning as cited, it becomes meaningless.
If it means something equivalent to the "spatial direction" in mechanics, then both "goal" and "spatial direction" become meaningless
or something distorted, because "spatial direction" in mechanics has
absolutely nothing to do with "goal"; and "goal," in any psychological
sense, has little to do with "spatial direction." For example, the goal
of Mr. X to become a millionaire, of Mr. Y to receive a Ph.D. degree
has no spatial direction. The whole translation of "goal" into "spatial
direction" is a most incorrect translation of a comparatively clear term
into a meaningless term.

The same can be said of "vectors," "magnitudes," and the other

---

[36] Quoted in Petre Trişça, *Prolégomènes à une mécanique sociale* (Paris, 1922), II,
169.

[37] Brown, "On the Use of Mathematics," p. 81.

terms used in the above quotation. Here are other still more instructive examples. We are told: "Every psychological activity may be ordered to a two-dimensional plane (surface) where organism and goal represent certain spatial regions within the surface."[38] I confess the statement is either meaningless or it tries to express in the most inaccurate —therefore unscientific—way some notions which are expressed more accurately in terms of the sociocultural sciences as, for example, that a hungry rat attempts to get the cheese put in its cage.

Psychological activity of all sorts will be ordered to a *path*, and may be said to represent a *locomotion* in the psychological field.[39]

At best, this statement is a mere disguised tautology that "psychological activity is psychological activity." Otherwise, it is either meaningless or the most barbarous translation of "psychological activity" by a very different and misleading term: "locomotion." Such a translation disfigures both terms: "psychological activity" (for instance, thought or daydreaming, which has no spatial properties of the topological space) and "locomotion," which means always a displacement of a material phenomenon or thing in geometrical space.

With still greater reason, this can be said of a very complex translation into a pseudomathematical *A, B, C, D* formula and into a series of several complex designs of such simple activities or phenomena as a football game between Harvard and Yale, or the desire of a freshman to join a fraternity. Such activities, as here described in these simplest of terms, are much more comprehensible to us than would be "the deaf-mute" description of them according to the purely analogical way of mechanics, with an *A, B, C, D* . . . formula and a series of various symbols and schematic diagrams. The *A, B, C, D* . . . formula and the diagrams do not help us to understand the simple description of these phenomena, but this simple description is absolutely necessary to the understanding of these "parasitic and superfluous" *A, B, C, D,* and diagrams. They are a mere liability, instead of being an asset in the cognitive sense.[40]

Still more true is this about further (very "scientific" sounding) "orderings" of the phenomena of social mobility (described elsewhere much more simply and accurately in the proper terms of sociocultural space and terminology)[41] to the "topological medium," with "fluidity,"

[38] *Ibid.,* p. 82.   [39] *Ibid.,* p. 84.   [40] *Ibid.,* pp. 85 ff.
[41] See P. A. Sorokin, *Social Mobility,* chaps. i-iii *et passim.*

"cohesiveness," "permeability," "hodological space," and the like. All this complicated "analogical fun" is neither necessary for a real analysis of the phenomena of social mobility nor can it help such an analysis; nor does it give us a scintilla of cognition of these phenomena, or represent any improvement in comparison with much simpler, less analogical, more adequate concepts actually used in the studies of these phenomena, without all these "pseudogeometrical" symbols.

To sum up: If the "post-Riemannian topological space" is somewhat congenial or analogous to what psychological or sociocultural space may be, a mere importation of the terms of mechanics, geometry, or topology into the sociocultural sciences, and a mere misleading translation of the adequate terms of sociocultural sciences into the terms of mechanics, or geometry, or topology is a perfectly futile occupation. It gives us only liabilities, but not assets. Here again we see the same that we have seen above in regard to causality, equilibrium, and other concepts of the mathematiconatural sciences indiscriminately imported and distortedly used in regard to sociocultural phenomena.[42]

The same, with a proper modification, can be said of a considerable number of somewhat similar attempts to make such a purely analogical application of the principles of mechanics, or geometry, or topology. Though made with different degrees of skill, competency, and fruitfulness, in some cases (for instance, in the specified works of Lins,

[42] An additional humorous characteristic of these, as well as many other "imitative studies," is their claim that any scientific definition is to be "operational" and that their definitions are "operational." Again, all such "operationalists" in the social sciences seem not to realize that this very old procedure of definition in the physical sciences is inapplicable to an overwhelming majority of sociocultural phenomena. Even in the physical sciences, it has its own weaknesses and limitations. See R. R. Lindsay, "A Critique of Operationalism in Physics," *Philosophy of Science* (October, 1937).

In the social sciences one cannot define "operationally" (in the sense of the physical sciences) neither music nor fine arts nor ethical systems nor religion nor even science. When one tries to do so, the result is a distortion of the operational definition in the physical-science sense, and pseudo-operational and inadequate definition of the respective sociocultural phenomena. The whole popularity of the term "operational definition" is but one of the superfluous fads that come and go in the social sciences. Professor P. W. Bridgman is the godfather of this term, and he excellently defined and applied it in physics as one of the eminent representatives of this discipline. But when he tried to extend its application to the sociocultural phenomena, he definitely failed, achieving, not a particularly scientific and "operational" sociology, but something far less scientific and "operational" than sociologies of the nonoperational sociologists. See P. Bridgman, *The Intelligent Individual and Society*, chap. ii *et passim*.

For a sound criticism of the social-science pseudo-operationalism, see H. Blumer, "The Problem of the Concept in Social Psychology," *American Journal of Sociology* (March, 1940); and G. W. Allport, "The Psychologists' Frame of Reference," *Psychological Bulletin* (January, 1940).

Ferreira, and others) with a full realization of the difficulties and with actual attempts to give a sociocultural content to the principles imported from mechanics, these attempts all suffer, in various degrees, from defects similar to those indicated above.[43]

Besides these analogical theories of psychological or sociocultural space there are nonanalogical theories, like the "ecological" conception of certain aspects of sociocultural phenomena, and the "social-distance" theories of psychosocial relationships or sympathy and antipathy and some others. These will be considered further, after the delineation of our concept of sociocultural space and its properties. For the present, let us see why all the varieties of physicogeometric-topographic space are inapplicable to sociocultural phenomena, and why they cannot determine their "position" in the sociocultural universe.

WHY THE SPACE OF MECHANICS, GEOMETRY, AND TOPOLOGY IS INADEQUATE IN APPLICATION TO THE SOCIOCULTURAL PHENOMENA

Such a space is inadequate in the field of sociocultural phenomena, first of all, because it does not permit a determination of the position of a large class of sociocultural phenomena in the sociocultural uni-

---

[43] Besides the works indicated in Sorokin's *Sociological Theories,* the following can be mentioned as the works which use, in some analogical way, the concepts of the post-Riemannian and Minkowski's geometry and mechanics, and try to apply them to sociocultural phenomena: M. Hauriou, *Leçons sur le mouvement sociale* (Paris, 1899); Charles Poirson, *Le Dynamisme absolut* (Paris, 1909); M. Lins, *op. cit.;* Pontes de Miranda, *op. cit.;* Pinto Ferreira, *op. cit.;* G. Devereux, "A Conceptual Scheme of Society," *American Journal of Sociology* (March, 1940); Gilberto Freyre, "Aspectos do Problema de Distancia Social em Sociologia," *Magazine Comercial* (January, 1936); G. Lundberg, *op. cit.;* and S. C. Dodd, *op. cit.*

In the field of social psychology and psychology, see L. L. Thurstone and E. J. Chave, *The Measurement of Attitudes* (Chicago, 1929); L. L. Thurstone, *Vectors of Mind* (Chicago, 1935); and A. Bentley, *Behavior, Knowledge, Fact* (Principia Press, 1935).

Least objectionable and more fruitful are the purely mathematical theories of study of social relationships exemplified by such works as N. Rashevsky, *Mathematical Biophysics* (Chicago, 1938); "Outline of a Mathematical Theory of Human Relations," *Philosophy of Science* (1935); "Further Contributions to the Mathematical Theory of Human Relations," *Psychometrika* (1938); and "Studies in Mathematical Theory of Human Relations," *Psychometrika* (1939). Such works do not use any analogies and are free from the mistakes of the "analogical" works. On the other hand, their deductions remain purely hypothetical until verified by an adequate study of the relevant empirical facts.

See a further criticism of such attempts in Sorokin, *Sociological Theories,* chap. i, and *Dynamics,* Vol. IV, chap. xiv; and Trisça, *op. cit.,* II, 137-152.

See also H. M. Johnson, "Pseudo-Mathematics in the Mental and Social Sciences," *American Journal of Psychology,* XLVIII (1936), 342-351; E. L. Thorndike, *op. cit.;* and P. H. Furfey and J. F. Daly, "A Criticism of Factor Analysis," *American Sociological Review* (April, 1937).

verse. Since it does not define the position, it does not determine the relationship of the phenomenon to other sociocultural phenomena and therefore does not allow us to describe and to understand adequately many forms of sociocultural change. Since these "services" are the necessary functions of any adequate conception of space, the failure to perform them explains why geometrical space of any kind is inadequate in our field.

Geometric Space Does Not Locate Sociocultural Phenomena. First of all, *any conception of geometric space does not permit us to locate or to determine the position or the properties and relationships of any kind of pure meaning.* Where is located the meaning of "two and two make four"; of Plato's philosophy; of Beethoven's symphony; of the Ten Commandments; of the Copernican system of cosmology; or of any concept whatsoever? These meanings are neither here nor there in the geometric space; they cannot be determined through any system of spatial co-ordinates of latitude, altitude, and longitude. Pure meanings are entirely outside any kind of geometrical space, be it the three-dimensional space of classical mechanics, or Lobatchevsky's, Riemann's, or any other space of mechanics, geometry, and topology. This is the reason why pure meanings are regarded as spaceless. Likewise, in the terms of geometrical space, they cannot be said to have any extension, size, volume, or dimension; they have no spatial form, whether rectilinear, circular, square, cubic, conical, or any other shape. Similarly, we cannot say which of them is larger or smaller, farther or nearer, higher or lower, to the right or to the left, and so on. No spatial characteristic of any kind is applicable to them because they have no extension. The net of the geometrical space is not designated to catch, and does not catch, any of the pure meanings; therefore, it cannot determine their position, location, relationships, or properties. Meanings just slip through its meshes.

If someone were to say that all meanings are located in the mind of the person who thinks a given meaning, the statement would not solve the problem. In that case, we would have to determine the location of the mind, which is also "spaceless." If someone were to say that the mind is located in the nervous system, he would have difficulty in determining where, at which point of the nervous system, the mind and the given meaning are located. Another difficulty would be to answer why and how, in the same nervous system, a given meaning is now supposedly present and a moment later is not present; why and how it is that there are millions of nervous systems that do not have an enormous number of meanings which some other nervous systems do have; why and how, in a state of activity, a particular nervous system has some meanings, while in a state of sleep it does not; how and why the same meaning is simultaneously present in an enormous number of nervous systems and absent in others; how and why all the meanings can be located in the same nervous system; and so on. All this signifies that neither mind nor meanings can be thought of as being located in the nervous system generally and at any one point specifically. No microscope, no chemical analysis, has found or can find any spot in the nervous system that contains an ingredient of meaning or any specified meaning.

If someone should say that "two and two make four" is located where the statement "two and two make four" is pronounced or written, that again does not give an adequate answer at all. The meanings of the mathematical proposition and of the musical composition remain the same, whether or not someone says the one or plays the other. If nobody in any way manifests the meaning of "two and two make four" or of the Beethoven symphony, these meanings, as pure meanings, still persist and remain the same, identical to themselves. The written, oral, or other objectification and manifestation of the meanings is one thing; the meanings as pure meanings are another. The statement discussed points out merely *the place of the vehicles and human agents of the meanings, but not the place of the meanings themselves.*

Not only the pure meanings, but even objectified and socialized meanings cannot be located in the geometric space of any kind. No geometric system of co-ordinates can definitely determine their position in the geometric space. Suppose we want to determine where the objectified and socialized table of multiplication is located. For that purpose, we have to enumerate all the books, papers, stones, records, and any other vehicle in which the table of multiplication is written, together with all the innumerable pages or sections of pages or other fragments of these vehicles and all the persons who, at a given moment, are either pronouncing, thinking, writing, computing, or otherwise occupied with multiplication. These "spatial points" are scattered everywhere. They are innumerable; their number is potentially unlimited. They change and shift all the time, because given persons are now manifesting or thinking the table and now cease to do so because some persons are now not busied with it and now they are. So also do the vehicles and their places shift and change incessantly: a given text of arithmetic is now here, now there; an old one is disappearing; a new one is being published.

The net conclusion of such a "location" of the objectified and socialized table of multiplication is that it is located somewhere and almost everywhere on this planet, among the places inhabited by man; and that is about all we can get in the way of the location of either the multiplication table or of an infinite number of other, quite different, objectified and socialized meanings. These meanings all seem to be "located" somewhere on this planet, in the places inhabited by man, and where human beings have lived, or live, or shall live. Now and then they appear where no human beings are living (for instance, in the remnants of a buried civilization); now and then they are absent, even where human beings live (as when they do not know the multiplication table or do not think of it). Such a "location" is evidently no location at all, and does not determine the position of a meaning in any even remotely definite way with regard to any "point of reference" of geometrical space. No latitude, longitude, or altitude of the table of multiplication can be established. Still less does the location define the position of each objectified and socialized meaning with regard to all other meanings and in the sociocultural universe. They are all simply thrown in a heap somewhere on the surface or under the surface or over the surface of this planet, and that is all that we can find out in that way.

Still less can we define any spatial characteristics of practically all the objectified and socialized meanings, because—as we already know —any meaning can and does have a most heterogeneous assortment of vehicles and human agents, with different physical, geometrical, chemical, and biological properties. For this reason, we cannot even ascribe to a given meaning any of the properties of one of its vehicles or agents. In addition, such a localization of the vehicles would not help us much, because their character and location are also changing. In brief, even any definite "localization" of the vehicles and agents of the objectified and socialized meanings becomes impossible, except, perhaps, that they are given somewhere on this planet in its inhabited areas. And still more impossible becomes the determination of the relative position of one sociocultural phenomenon to another in the sociocultural universe.

Geometric Space Does Not Define Social Position and Change. If we pass from sociocultural phenomena to social phenomena proper, we find the same impossibility of locating them in a geometric space. It is enough to ask such questions as: *"What is my social position?" "Where do I stand, in the sociocultural universe?" "What is my position in regard to war?"* in order to make this clear. The most meticulous geometric or geographic map cannot help at all to answer the questions. None of them, and no system of geometric space with any *n* dimensions, can indicate the spatial longitude, latitude, or altitude of the "social position" of any person, group, or "position" of anyone in regard to any sociocultural problem or situation, be it war, religion (remember Luther's: *"Here I stand* and I cannot do otherwise"), capitalism, or what not.

It is evident that a mere indication of the point of the geometric space where a given man or group or value is located does not determine at all his or its social position in the sociocultural universe. At the same geometric locus there may be, in the closest proximity, the master and his slave, the king and his valet, the dictator and his victim; and yet their social positions are as different as they can be. Furthermore, each of these persons can move incessantly in the geometric space and remain unchanged in his social position. And vice versa, each can remain at the same point of geometric space and enormously change his social position. Thus kings, like Louis XVI, Nicholas II, Alfonso of Spain, remain in the same palace and yet are demoted in their social position from that of king to that of criminal or plain citizen; while some of the slaves, criminals, or plain citizens ascend to the positions of dictator or king.

The same is true of the *sociocultural position of an objectified value.* Relics of kings or saints that were sacred yesterday become of negative value today, to be jeered at and insulted, without any serious displacement in the geometric space; and vice versa. On the other hand, an objectified value often remains the same, in spite of changing its location in geometric space enormously, as when a religious or other relic is moved from Jerusalem to Europe and yet retains its position unchanged in the world of the values. We see the same in the phenomena of *sociocultural displacement* in contradistinction to that in geometric space. The sociocultural phenomenon—be it an individual or a thing—can undergo a vast displacement in the sociocultural universe without changing its position in geometrical space; and vice versa, it may remain in the same sociocultural position in spite of changing enormously its position in the geometric space.

We talk of *social movements:* political, religious, ethical, esthetic, and so forth. Special courses are given under this name. Another common expression is *social stagnation.* Do these expressions really mean that, in the period of "great social movements," there is an enormous motion in geometric space; while in the period of "stagnation," no physical motion occurs, and all people and social activities are "at a motionless rest"? Of course not. So far as social movement is concerned, it has sometimes much less physical motion in geometric space than occurs during a big football or baseball game, or on a big racing day, or during the rush hour in a big city. And still neither football nor baseball game, neither racing nor rush hour, is styled "a social movement." The same is true of social stagnation. The amount of purely physical motion of the people in geometric space may be—and probably is—as great in the periods of social stagnation as in those of social movement. This means again that these terms really have no, or only a very remote, relation to a displacement or movement in geometric space. They seem to hint at some "space," but one quite different from geometric space and its derivatives.

The same is still more true of such expressions as: "the Spanish monarchy is *overthrown,*" "the country is in an unstable equilibrium," "the upper and lower classes," "social promotion and demotion," "Right and Left political party," "social climbing," "the very top of society," "at the very bottom of the social pyramid," "they are socially near," "all doors of society are open to him," "between X and Y there is a great social distance," "social position," "social ladder," and hundreds of similar "spatial" expressions with which we operate daily.

We talk and read daily that "prices are higher or lower," that "business is going uphill," that "the corner of the depression is turned," that "the birth rate is going down," that the "wholesale index of prices has an upward tendency," that "General Electric shares are climbing," and so on. Often these processes are depicted in the form of a curve fluctuating up and down on the page. "Uphill," "rising," "higher and lower," "climbing," "sliding downward," and similar phrases do not at all mean corresponding movements in geometric space. Prices, in their ups and downs, do not cross any geometric space in an upward or downward direction; the same is true of the oscillation of the birth-death-marriage rates and of the rise and fall of suicide, crime, invention, and other rates. All this has nothing to do with any displacement in geometric space, and the latter does not play any part in the description of these phenomena, which sounds as though they were physical movements in geometric space. Their real content has no relationship to geometric space. Even our "uptown and downtown" do not mean that uptown is situated higher in geometric space than downtown.

Likewise *social rapprochement* and *"social separation"* do not mean a rapprochement in a geometric space (in which case two enemies locked in a mortal fight would be the most conspicuous phenomenon of social rapprochement) and a departure in that space. Often social rapprochement manifests itself in an increasing geometric distance between the parties (as two parting lovers, the separation of persons in space as a sacrifice for the welfare of one or the other), and social separation in decreasing that distance.[44]

Any real sociocultural system functions and changes *in togetherness,* though its parts may be separated by enormous geometrical distances; and vice versa, the merely spatially adjacent objects and phenomena do not function and change in togetherness.[45] The system and its parts are one unity, though scattered in space; the congeries are a disunity and multitude, though they are in spatial proximity.

A person may be your spatial neighbor for years, and may yet remain a "stranger" to you; and a person may be separated from you for years by an enormous geometric distance, and yet remain your *"closest* friend." Social "intimacy" or "nearness" does not mean geometrical closeness, and vice versa.

Furthermore, if we take such social phenomena as "property rights," "the distribution of rights and duties," and the like, they are again undefinable in the terms of geometrical space. They are "here and there, everywhere and nowhere," in the geometrical space. The

---

[44] See L. von Wiese's main sociological interindividual categories of the social relationship: (1) toward each other (contact, approach, adaptation, union, solidarity); and (2) away from each other (competition, adaptation, conflict, antagonism) in his *System der allgemeinen Soziologie* (München, 1933); and L. von Wiese and H. Becker, *Systematic Sociology* (New York, 1932). See also Ferreira, *op. cit.*

[45] See Sorokin, *Dynamics,* Vol. IV, chaps. ii-iv *et passim.*

same thing can belong to a number of persons widely scattered. The same person can have a right to values widely separated and may be concerned with an indefinite number of most different "values," some of which do not have any spatial location. *Where* are the rights of the Pope, of the author, of the business corporation? Where is religion, law, the arts, ethics, science? Indeed, where is any cultural phenomenon?

Finally, *geometric space of any kind does not permit the proper orientation of a person or group in the sociocultural universe, nor adaptation to that universe.* If, according to E. Mach and others, various conceptions of geometric and physiological space originated, under the influence of either the cosmic or biological milieu, as an adaptive response to the agencies of these environments, it is but natural that the sociocultural milieu in which man is born and lives also required an adaptation to and an orientation in, and therefore led to some conception of, sociocultural space as the necessary means of adaptation and survival. When one considers that this environment was the nearest, the most immediate, and possibly the most important in the sense of conditioning man's actions, life, and death, such a supposition would appear even more than probable.

Primitive man, as well as contemporary man, had to know where and who were his friends and enemies; what kind of treatment he could expect from various persons and groups; what their power and influences were; what type of actions and conduct would assure his getting on in this mysterious universe of meanings, values, persons, groups; and what kind of conduct would lead him into trouble. In order to make such an orientation in this universe, he had to know something of its nature and structure, and its system of co-ordinates, which determined his own and other persons' and phenomena's positions; and to indicate which was which, and where in the sociocultural space each "which" was located.

A mere orientation in physical space is not sufficient for an adaptation to such a milieu. Man can know where this or that tribe is situated in the physical space; where this or that person is staying; where certain plants or animals are to be found. But if he does not know which of the tribes is "his own" and "friendly," and which is a mortal enemy, he is in danger. If he does not know that, of two persons sitting or standing side by side, one is a king or chief and the other is a valet or slave, he is headed for trouble. If he does not know that some of the sticks in a given territory are just sticks, while others —very similar—are "the sacred *churingas,*" he is again in trouble. If he does not know that some of the animals or plants of a given region are "totems" while others are not, he will find himself in difficulty. In other words, if a person is not oriented in the sociocultural universe, does not know its structure, its systems of meanings and values, its social differentiation and stratification, its distribution of rights and duties among the human agents—in brief, if he is entirely ignorant of this universe and its system of co-ordinates, which determine "who is who" and "which is which," his knowledge of physical space will not help him much. He will be lost, in trouble, and often even in danger of losing his life. This explains why an idea of the sociocultural space and of its system of co-ordinates appeared in the remotest past and, as we shall see further, was evident in at least a vague form in the most primitive societies.

The geometric conceptions of any kind do not help much in an orientation in, and adaptation to, this universe. Such an orientation requires that a person or group know the *qualities* of each sociocultural phenomenon and the *qualitative* sociocultural position of each person or group in contact. The mere statement that "this is the field of *a* dimension and this the field of *b* dimension," and all the other mathematicosymbolic letters and formulas do not give us the slightest idea what this *a* and *b* are—what their qualities are, where they are situated in the sociocultural space, what is their qualitative relationship to other sociocultural values, and so on. In brief, a person can be the greatest geometer or physical geographer, so far as the physical space is concerned, and yet he may be entirely ignorant of the sociocultural space, its structure and its system of co-ordinates. Therefore, he may be entirely lost and unoriented in that space. Geometric space, "bleached of all the sociocultural qualities," is not only not identical with sociocultural space but does not touch it at all. The whole sociocultural work slips through the meshes of the network of the co-ordinates of such a space.

Thus neither the location of sociocultural phenomena nor the determination of their positional relationship, neither a description of sociocultural displacement or social distance, remoteness, closeness, *rapprochement,* or separation, neither sociocultural movement and stagnation nor any static or dynamic property of sociocultural phenomena, can be adequately described and expressed, or grasped and studied, in terms of geometric space. Hence, the inapplicability of the conceptions of geometric space to an overwhelmingly greater part of the sociocultural phenomena.

On the other hand, the above analysis and the very expressions we use point out the advisability—even the necessity—of some sort of sociocultural space which will adequately permit us to locate sociocultural phenomena in their sociocultural universe, to determine their position in regard to one another, and to analyze their relationship, their change, and their properties in a manner somewhat homologous to geometric space in regard to physical phenomena. In brief, we need a category of sociocultural space as a fundamental referential principle as much as the physical sciences need a category of the geometric space of some sort. Without such a category, we are helpless in the study and description of the network of relationships among sociocultural phenomena. Hence the urgent need of the construction of a more or less adequate sociocultural space. The subsequent pages aim to give some suggestions as to what such a space is. The adequate definition of sociocultural space and of its properties is a task that exceeds the limited capacity of a single investigator. It is a task for the collective work of probably several generations of social scientists, unless meanwhile a social-science Newton appears among them.

What Is Sociocultural Space and How Are Sociocultural Phenomena Located in It?

In order to be adequate, sociocultural space must be able to determine the position of any sociocultural phenomenon among other sociocultural phenomena or in the sociocultural universe. As any sociocultural phenomenon consists of three components—meanings, vehicles, and human agents—sociocultural space must be able to indicate the position of each of these components, as well as that of the total sociocultural phenomena in the sociocultural universe. Next, the determination of the position and "positional relationships" of a given sociocultural phenomenon in this universe must be, not merely formal, but "essential," qualitative, giving us a knowledge of the nature and properties of the position and relationship. In this sense, sociocultural space must not be a mere imitation of the terminology and symbols of the geometrical or topological spaces.

All this means that the *position of meanings is determined when the place of the given meanings in the universe of meanings is determined. The place of vehicles is determined when a given set of vehicles is located in the universe of vehicles. The sociocultural position of an individual or group as socii or agents is determined when the individual or the group is located in the universe of human agents. Finally, when these determinations are made, the place of any empirical sociocultural phenomenon—be it a system or congeries—is determined in the sociocultural universe.*

Hence the *first characteristic of sociocultural space is that it represents a specific manifold, consisting of three fundamental planes or aspects: (1) the plane of meanings; (2) of vehicles; and (3) of human agents.* Any adequate determination of the position of any sociocultural phenomenon requires the determination of its "positional relationship" in these three respects. If this is not found, the position remains either completely or partially undetermined.

Before proceeding further, let us clarify what is meant by determination of the position of a given meaning, or vehicle, or human agent, in each of these planes or "dimensions."

The Location of Meanings in the Universe of Meanings. Let us ask: Where is the Newtonian law of gravitation, as a pure system of meanings, located? We know already that it is not located anywhere in any physical or geometric space. And yet it must be somewhere. The answer is: As a pure system of meanings, it is "located" in the system of mechanics. The system of mechanics is a part of physics; physics is a scientific discipline. Hence the conclusion that Newtonian law, as a pure system of meanings, is located in the "field" of science; more specifically, in the field of physics. Thus, roughly but definitely, its position in the universe of pure meanings is determined, and determined not fictitiously, in the purely analogical way of writing a's, b's, c's and other, simple or complex, mathematical symbols, but located "essentially" or "substantially," with its full content and properties.

Where is Bach's *Mass in B Minor,* as a system of pure meanings, located? Nowhere, so far as geometric space is concerned; in the "field of music," as one of the systems of the fine arts, so far as its position in the world of meanings is concerned. Again, the location is roughly definite and determined.

And so it is with any meaning, no matter what it is. The Christian credo is located in the "field of religion"; the Parthenon, in the "field of grand architecture," as a system of the fine arts; Napoleon's civil code, in the "field of law," more specifically the civil law, as a subsystem of the system of law; the "capitalist system," as a system of meanings, in the "field of socioeconomic systems of society"; and so on.

Thus all meanings, as pure meanings, find a definite location, not in the field of geometrical or sensory space, but in the universe of pure meanings. Their location gives us quite definite knowledge regarding their properties, and their relational position in regard to all other systems and congeries of meanings in the universe of meanings; knowledge as definite as the location of a physical object in the geometric universe. When we say that Bach's *Mass* is in the field of music, this at once excludes all the other fields of meanings (science, religion, law, and so forth); and if we want to specify its position still more precisely, we can easily do so through the further specification of exactly the kind of music to which it belongs.

Thus the location of a pure meaning of any kind is a determination of its position toward all the other meanings in the universe of meanings. Such is the first step of the determination of the relational position of meanings. Naturally, we must go farther and take a second step, namely, to inquire if there are in the universe of meanings some "points" that can be taken as convenient "points of reference," as a system of co-ordinates analogous to those in the geometric space.

In physical or geometric space, there existed and do exist many systems of referential points, different for different groups, cultures, and periods. A contemporary spatial reference point, be it the Greenwich meridian or a certain system of fixed stars, is only one of many forms, as we have seen. We have seen[46] and shall see again that the representations of physical space have varied greatly from period to period, from group to group. However, for practical purposes, the latest "standardized system of spatial reference," with its longitude, latitude, and altitude, seems to be most convenient for a cosmopolitan and international society. The referential spatial systems of many primitive and agricultural tribes (as "this village," "this tree," or "this

[46] *Ibid.*, II, 428 ff.

lake, shrine, city, or what not") are too local and parochial, too narrow and specific, to be a convenient medium for the international spatial system of reference points. Hence, the Greenwich meridian and a certain system of fixed stars are more adequate points of reference.

Similarly, in the world of meanings, very different meanings have been used as the "points of reference" for the location of meanings in the universe of meanings. Such meanings have been and still are: "God"—and particularly a specified God of this or that group—"Prosperity," "Efficiency," "Utility," "Happiness," *"Summum bonum,"* "Communism," "Mormonism," "Chosen People," "Democracy," "Totalitarianism," and any meaning which, for this or that reason, appears to be particularly important to a given person, group, or nation.[47]

Each of these meanings can indeed serve as such a point of reference. Taking "The God of Our Fathers" as a referential point, we can divide all the meanings, first, into positive and negative classes, from the standpoint of this "reference point," and then to indicate some further "relational positions" of the rest of the meanings to the point of reference. Such systems of location of meanings have indeed been used widely in the history of human thought. The Communist, by taking "Communism" for such a referential point, similarly establishes some relational positions of many meanings from the standpoint of his "point," dividing all the meanings into "Communist" or pro-Communist, and anti-Communist or "indifferent," and then making further specifications among each class. The totalitarian, Democrat, Puritan, American, Mexican, Christian, Kantian, Platonist, and so on will do likewise. Any specific meaning can be taken for the point of reference. The most diverse meanings have indeed been taken for such a point.[48]

Such a procedure and system of referential points permits us to locate some of the meanings to a certain extent. Having taken "Communism" as the referential point, we can say that such and such systems of meanings are in accordance with or sympathetic and congenial to Communism, and that such and such systems of religious, political, social, economic, artistic meanings are antagonistic or indifferent to it. We can proceed further and specify various types of the meanings in each class. In brief, some determination of the position of the meanings to the point of reference can be obtained.

[47] For a further discussion of this, see pages 141 ff.
[48] For a further discussion of this, see pages 141 ff.

However, all such systems of referential points are very inadequate. Like the local, tribal, parochial, referential points of physical space— such as "this tree," "that creek," "that barn," "the Jones' General Store," serviceable as a referential point of a given village—they do not permit us to locate an enormous part of the physical objects in physical space and respectively most of the meanings in the universe of meanings. Hence the necessity of a less local and parochial referential point of the universe of meanings that would permit us to locate all meanings. What system of referential points can serve such a purpose? The answer is: *an adequate classification of all the main sociocultural systems and of the supersystem of meanings; and the better the classification, the more precise the location of the meanings.*

If in the above case, instead of merely "Communism" or "Democracy" or "Americanism," we take the larger systems of meanings, such as "Science and Religion," we can locate in these reference systems a much larger number of meanings, and locate them more exactly, than through the use of mere "Communism" or "Puritanism." If we take a manifold of systems of meanings, such as *"Language-Science-Religion-Art-Ethics and Law," we can locate in such a manifold of the main cultural systems practically all the meanings.*[49] *These systems, together with the mixed and derivative system, embrace all types of meanings.* They are either scientific, religious, artistic, ethicojuridical, linguistic, philosophical, socioeconomic, political meanings, belonging to one of these "fields." There remains hardly any meaning that does not fall into or "belong" to one of these "fields." Through these systems of meanings as the main co-ordinates, each meaning can be definitely located in the universe of meanings, with all its properties and relationships. In this way, we obtain the "international," perennial system of the co-ordinates of meanings, which permits us to locate any meaning whatsoever in the universe of meanings.

Each of these five main and derivative systems has a large number of subclasses or, if one likes, "subco-ordinates." The system or co-ordinate of religion has such subsystems (or subco-ordinates) as Christianity, Taoism, Hinduism, Buddhism, Mohammedanism, Judaism, Confucianism, Zoroastrianism, and so on, down to Mormonism and hundreds of less important religious systems. Each of these subsystems of the religious system has again a number of subsubclasses or, if one

[49] See Sorokin, *Dynamics,* Vol. IV, chap. iii.

likes, "directions" and "senses." Thus Christianity includes Roman Catholicism, Greek and Russian Orthodox Catholicism, various Protestant denominations down to the smallest Christian sects.

The system of science has such subclasses or dimensions as mathematics, physics, chemistry, biology, social and humanistic sciences, and so on; and each of these subsystems of science has several subsubclasses, such as organic and inorganic chemistry, with their own further subdivisions; or the history of Greece, Rome, Egypt, Europe, and so on, with their further subdivisions. The same is true of language, the fine arts, ethics, and other main derivative systems of meanings. Each of these is divided into many classes, these into subclasses, and these again into subsubclasses.

However, when we know that a given system of meanings falls into the system (co-ordinate) of religion, knowing the main classes and subclasses of this system, we find no difficulty in putting a given "religious system" into the subclass into which it belongs. In this way we determine its position in the religious system and, through that, its position in the universe of meanings.

If we undertake a further step and find a supersystem which in some way embraces all these main systems of meanings into one unity, like our supersystem of ideational-idealistic-sensate-mixed forms, we obtain a still more universal, definite, convenient "referential principle" that permits us to locate almost all meanings in a way no less universal and precise than, for instance, the Greenwich meridian or one of the systems of the fixed stars. Only congeries perhaps would remain not located directly; but indirectly, even these are located, as the meaning congeries of such and such a kind, unrelated to this but related to that "field" of meaningful system. If even a portion of the meanings remains unlocated directly through the referential supersystem mentioned, this should not disturb us. Quite a considerable number of physical objects also cannot be located through the Greenwich meridian (practically all the remote stars and galaxies). For that purpose, astrophysics introduces another referential point—a certain system of the fixed stars; and even this system can be replaced, according to the necessity, by another system. If, therefore, the positions of absolutely all the meanings are not directly deteminable through our supersystem, as the reference point, this is in no way an objection against its serviceability as the most useful point of reference among all possible ones.

As has been shown in *Social and Cultural Dynamics,* the supersystem permits us (with the addition of the mixed class) to locate practically all the meanings, because it embraces all the main systems or fields of meaning. This, then, is the answer to our problem.

Thus, somewhat unexpectedly for many, we come to the conclusion that the *location of meanings in the universe of meanings consists in an adequate classification of the main systems of meanings, with the supersystem as a further step toward a convenient universal, cosmopolitan, referential principle for the determination of the relational positions of the meanings.* There is no other solution of the problem. As a matter of fact, exactly this method has always been used by practically all the investigators of meanings, no matter what classifications they have offered. The classifications of the systems of meanings may be different, but the method of classification of the main systems of meanings has invariably been the method of the determination of their position and relationship in the universe of meanings.

Many classifications of "referential points" of meanings, like the above "Puritanism," "Communism," and so on, were and are very inadequate and parochial, but they represent the same—only very inadequate—method of finding the "position" of meanings in the universe of meanings. Better and more adequate classifications are such, for instance, as De Roberty's classification of all the sociocultural meanings into the systems of science—religion and philosophy—fine arts—applied and technical systems of meanings like technology, medicine, agronomy, law, and ethics. It gives us the possibility of "locating" most of the meanings in this "four-dimensional system of co-ordinates of meanings." The discussed dichotomic "material-nonmaterial," "civilizational-cultural," "technologicoeconomical and ideological" system of meanings is again an example of a system of co-ordinates for the location of a large part of the meanings into one of these "super-classes of meanings." Any other classification of meanings does the same. The success and adequacy of the location depend upon the adequacy of the classification of the systems and supersystem of meanings; but the procedure remains identical, and is the only procedure for a location of the meanings in the universe of meanings. Only purely analogical preoccupations, busy with an importation of the paraphernalia of the system of physical space into the sociocultural world, do not use this method. But these attempts, as we have seen, hardly ever locate any meaning or value in any universe of meanings or values. All that they do is to transcribe from mathematics, geometry, or mechanics their x's, y's, z's and, according to the formulas, locate these among other letters and physicomathematical symbols. Such a preoccupation locates only these letters and symbols, without locating meaning anywhere.

The above analysis means that the *problem of sociocultural space and the task of location of meanings in the universe of meanings are not new, but very old. Indeed, they are as old as human thought.* In a very local and parochial form, they have been used since time immemorial. However crude and inadequate the classifications of meanings have often been, the societies and social thinkers who used this method have been on the right track, more sound, adequate, and even more serviceable than the way of the importers and imitators of the concept of the physicogeometrical space.[50]

To sum up: The determination of the position of any meaning in the universe of meanings means a placement of the meaning in that system of meanings to which it belongs. Finding its system, we can easily find the still larger system of which the first system is a sub-system. Ascending in this way, we find that the system of co-ordinates of meanings consists at least of the five main systems or co-ordinates: language-science-religion-fine arts-ethics.[51] These five co-ordinates (with their derivatives) permit us to locate practically any meaning in the universe of meanings. Using the supersystem, we can still further simplify the system of co-ordinates of meanings and easily determine the relational position of most of the meanings—systems and congeries —in the universe of meanings.

In such a system of co-ordinates of meanings, as an aspect of the sociocultural space, any meaning can be definitely located, and its

---

[50] Here again we see that the methods of the social thinkers of the previous centuries were in their general nature sound; that the problem of social space in its sound setting is not new; and that many an "importer" of geometrical space into the field of meanings does not have any basis on which to claim the discovery of the problem of social space or the right way for its construction. Our analysis shows also that the problem of classification of meanings, that has taken so much effort on the part of a legion of socio-philosophical scholars, is not a superfluous preoccupation of the "armchair philosophers," but one of the cardinal problems of the social and humanistic disciplines. Among other things it is the problem of sociocultural space, and of the determination of the position of the meanings in the meaningful plane of that space.

[51] Sorokin, *Dynamics*, Vol. IV, chap. iii.

position can be determined with a satisfactory degree of precision. So much, then, for the meaning dimension of sociocultural space.

The Location of Human Agents in the Universe of Human Agents of Meanings. Another component of sociocultural phenomena are the human bearers and agents of a given system or congeries of meanings. If the meanings are objectified, socialized, and grounded in empirical sociocultural reality, they have their human agents. Hence the second plane of sociocultural space is that of its human agents, and the problem of how they can be located in the sociocultural universe and specifically in the universe of all human agents of meanings.

We know already that human beings, as the agents of meanings and *socii,* cannot be located through the system of co-ordinates of physical or geometric space. Only as physicochemical objects and biological organisms (to a lesser extent) can they be located in the physical space, but not as sociocultural bearers and agents. How, then, can the sociocultural position of an individual be determined in sociocultural space, and what does such a determination mean?

Again, the old method of determining the sociocultural position of an individual or group—adequately or rudely—practiced in sociocultural life and sociocultural thought answers to a certain extent the question: "What do we do when we introduce someone to somebody else? What do the historians and biographers do, when they depict the biography of this or that person or group? The historian and biographer do a very definite thing, either in detail or in an abbreviated form: *they enumerate the main cultural and social systems to which a given individual has belonged and the specific position he has occupied in each of these sociocultural systems.* In this way, they determine his sociocultural position, and often very satisfactorily, if their enumeration of these items is accurate and complete.

When we say that "Mr. N., Jr., is a son of Mr. N., Sr.," we take a step toward the location of Mr. N. in the sociocultural universe. It is clear, however, that such a location is very indefinite and imperfect; it gives us only one of the co-ordinates of location (the family relation) toward one person, Mr. N., out of 1,800,000,000 persons in this human universe. It is as imperfect as a geometrical localization which says: "The tree is two miles from the hill." If such a location is to be satisfactory, we must know whether the hill is in Europe or in some other continent of the earth, and in what part of the continent, and under what degree; and if the tree is two miles to the north or south, east or west, from the hill. In brief, more or less sufficient geometrical location demands an indication of the relation of the located thing to the whole system of spatial co-ordinates of the geometrical universe. The same is true in regard to the "social location" of an individual (or social phenomenon).[52]

In order that the sociocultural location of N., Jr., be more precise, a number of other groups with which he is affiliated have to be indicated. This we often do in our "introductions."

The general formula of all such introductions runs as follows: "Let me introduce Mr. X (indication of the family system and sex group of X). Mr. X is an American (indication of the State and often the language system to which X belongs). He is a Protestant (indication of the religious system to which he belongs), a leading Republican (indication of the political party system to which he subscribes), an eminent and successful lawyer (indication of his occupational, economic, and scientific systems); president of the Board of the Trustees of the Fine Arts Museum (indication of the fine-arts system); a leader in the fight against corruption, bribery, slavery, exploitation (indication of a series of ethical systems); and so on." Though here the enumeration of the sociocultural systems to which X has belonged and of the positions he has occupied in each is incomplete and far from being systematic, nevertheless, through this inadequate enumeration, we have already obtained a rough idea of the sociocultural position of X in the universe of human bearers and agents of sociocultural meanings.

This is the form of our "introduction" of any X, and introductions are but an abbreviated or incomplete determination of the sociocultural position of the introduced persons for those who do not know it. Biographers and historians give a more complete enumeration of all the important sociocultural systems to which the personage they are discussing has belonged, and in this way furnish a more adequate determination of his sociocultural position and the changes in this position in the course of his life. If the work is done competently, we obtain an adequate knowledge of the positions in the human sociocultural universe which the person—be he Caesar, Saint Paul, George Washington, Madame Pompadour, or Rockefeller—has occupied. *If we know (1) all the sociocultural systems to which a given person has belonged, (2) the position of these systems in the universe of sociocultural systems, and (3) all the positions within each of these systems*

[52] Sorokin, *Social Mobility*, pp. 4-5.

he has occupied,[53] *then we know quite accurately the sociocultural position of the person and all the changes his position has undergone.*

There remains little, if anything, to be known in order to obtain a sufficiently accurate determination of the position of each individual or group as sociocultural agents and *socii.* No importation of the quasi-mathematical *a*'s, *b*'s, *c*'s, "vectors," "magnitudes," and other terms, and no quasimathematical formulas are necessary for the purpose. At best, these symbols and formulas add nothing to a determination of the person's position, and as a rule they do not determine it at all.

This age-old method of determining the position of human agents, though sound in principle, factually has often been parochial and local. For a primitive tribe or village, such a parochial variety of the method has often been satisfactory, since the human universe of such societies has been very limited and bounded by a few persons and groups. In such societies, a mere indication that "he is a son of *X*," or "he is an Arunta of a certain age and sex group," is sufficient. But with an extension and "internationalization of the human universe," such parochial "points of reference" have become insufficient.[54]

The need for a system of co-ordinates that could locate any man or

[53] Each sociocultural system has a differentiated and stratified structure generally; and in its components of the meanings (values) and human agents, the meanings (values) of the system make an hierarchy of the means and ends, beginning with the supreme end or meanings and ending with the lowest value, which is a means for all the other values. (See Sorokin, *Dynamics,* Vol. IV, chap. iv.) Likewise, the human agents of the system are also differentiated and stratified within the system, and do not occupy the same position within the system. The members or agents of the State sociocultural system are stratified in a long ladder of hierarchies and ranks, beginning with the king, or president, or dictator, and ending with the plain citizen and disfranchised criminals, with a large number of intermediary ranks between these highest and lowest strata. In the religious system, there is a similar hierarchy, beginning with a pope or patriarch, and ending with a common parishioner. In a business system, there is a similar grada-tion, beginning with the president and ending with the common laborer. And so on. For the determination of the position of an individual in the sociocultural space, it is important to know, not only with which systems he is affiliated, but also what exactly is the position he occupies within each of the affiliated systems. From this standpoint, it is convenient to consider the universe of the human agents as having two aspects: horizontal and vertical. The horizontal axis is represented by the systems with which an individual is affiliated; the vertical axis by the specific stratum which he occupies in the stratified structure of each system (intragroup stratification). These two axes permit us to determine his position accurately. When, in addition, we know the place of all the systems he is affiliated with in the whole universe of the systems (in their horizontal and vertical aspects), we know adequately the position of the individual or group.

For a discussion of the sociocultural position of human agents and the horizontal and vertical aspects of the intra- and inter-system stratification, see Sorokin, *Social Mobility,* chap. i *et passim.*

[54] For a further discussion, see pages 141 ff.

group became urgent. Hence a systematic replacement of the parochial referential points by ever larger and more adequate systems of co-ordinates has been taking place. However, up to the present time, no quite uniform and truly universal system of referential points has emerged. As for "meter," "yard," "foot," "rod," and other units of length in physical space used by different peoples, different societies at the present time employ a method of determination of the sociocultural position of an individual or group that is somewhat different concretely, though essentially the systems are of the same nature. In spite of the concrete difference in the systems used as co-ordinates by different societies, the method remains essentially the same: an enumeration of some of the sociocultural systems deemed most important in a given society to which the person or group belongs.

The most adequate variation of this method is given by the preceding analysis of the main and derivative systems of meanings and of the specific—horizontal and vertical—position which an individual occupies among the agents of each of these systems. This means that the sociocultural position of any human agent is satisfactorily determined if we know: (1) the language system to which he belongs; (2) his scientific position: whether he is of elementary, high-school, college, or university level, what his specialty is (such as chemistry or history), what his scientific position is with regard to the main problems of science, his total scientific mentality, his status as a scientist if he is such, and so on; (3) his religious position: what his religious attitude, credo, or denomination is and so forth; (4) his esthetic tastes and preferences: in what kind of art he is particularly interested (music, painting, literature, and so on), what kind of style and form he particularly favors or disfavors, who are his favorite masters, what he does himself in that field, and so forth; (5) his ethicojuridical position: his total social status, ethical codes, juridical attitude and convictions, the totality of his rights and duties, and so forth; and then the main derivative and mixed systems with which he is affiliated, namely: (6) his economic position and economic occupation; (7) his family (kinship) status; (8) his citizenship and political status; (9) his "philosophy"; (10) his membership in other associations and organizations.

If we know these "affiliations" and the specific place of a person or group in each of these systems (worker, master, president, general, and so on), we know almost all that we need to know of the sociocultural position of any person or group (among other groups and systems), provided we also know the place of each group of affiliation among all other systems and their groups. If a "census" could give us the necessary data concerning these nine or ten items, we could determine fairly satisfactorily the position of any individual or group in the universe of human agents of sociocultural systems. There of course remain such items as age, sex, race, status of health, and peculiarities of temperament and personality of the individual. But these are the biological and psychological items, and locate the individual, not so much in the sociocultural, as in the biological and psychological universes. As such, they do not directly concern his sociocultural position. Only indirectly, insofar as a certain age or sex or race is a sociocultural condition of obtaining or occupying a certain position, do these factors enter into the sociocultural position, and to that extent only are they determined —indirectly—by the above ten main co-ordinates.

Such is the adequate variation of the general method of determination of the sociocultural position of a person or group meeting the conditions of the contemporary international, cosmopolitan human universe.

It is hardly necessary to add that most of the contemporary sociocultural systems of co-ordinates used for the location of an individual or a group in the human sociocultural universe represent indeed a variation of this system. The variations are used by the official census of various countries, by the special census of various associations, by scientific investigations, by *Who's Who,* and so on.

Finally, it is to be noted that the system of the determination of the sociocultural position of human agents stands in the closest relationship with that of the system of meanings: *the sociocultural position of a person is determined through a reference to the same sociocultural system of meanings through which the place of a meaning in the universe of meanings is determined*. In this way, both components are bound together and are located through the same co-ordinates of the main and derivative systems of meanings (language plus science plus religion plus the arts plus ethics plus the main derivative systems), including the supersystem.

The only difference is that, when we define the position of the component of meanings, we put an accent on *cultural* systems and analyze in greater detail all the systems and subsubsystems of meanings with which a given meaning is associated. In defining the position of the component of human agents, we accentuate their *social* position, and introduce in greater detail all the subsubsystems to which the individual belongs and the specific position he occupies in each of them. For instance, in determining the position of an individual, it is important to know the co-ordinates of his family and kinship status, his occupational status, his economic and occupational positions, the territorial community in which he resides and is employed, and so on, plus his specific position in each of these systems.

For the location of the pure meanings, these co-ordinates are often unnecessary, while others that are superfluous for the determination of the position of an individual are necessary. However, we must remember that family, kinship, political position, economic and occupational systems, territorial community, extending to power, prestige and other subsubco-ordinates are but the derivatives of the law system, determined and fixed in all details by that system of meanings.[55]

So also by law (official and intuitive) are determined the stratified and differentiated positions within each social system. The law determines the character and hierarchy of State members, from the President down to the ordinary citizen; law determines also the hierarchy of the position from Pope to parishioner in the Church. Similarly, the family system and the economic system are determined by law. Therefore, the enumeration of these co-ordinates in defining the position of human agents or individuals is after all but a more detailed application of the same system of co-ordinates composed of five main systems of meanings, plus the main derivative systems and the supersystem. This means that the system of co-ordinates in the location of meanings, as well as of human agents, remains the same. The only difference is a more detailed indication of some slightly different subsubco-ordinates of the same system of co-ordinates.

Defining the position of an individual or group as the bearers of a certain system of meanings, we can often determine, not only the systems to which an individual belongs, but also the *metric or scalar values* of some of the "vectors" (groups) that determine his position. We can count the number of the members of a given group; the amount of property (measurable in dollars or other units) the groups

---

[55] See Sorokin, *Dynamics,* Vol. IV, chap. iii.

or its members possess; and so on. Though many of the co-ordinates of sociocultural space do not have a metric character, some of the subcordinates do have it.

The Location of the Vehicles of Meanings in Sociocultural Space. All physicochemical and biological things and phenomena that are vehicles of meanings are determined in their sociocultural position through the same system of co-ordinates: the main systems, the subsystems, and the supersystem of meanings through which the meanings and human agents are located. The church building, cross, altar, and other religious objects belong to the field of religious vehicles. Similarly, the factory building and the courthouse, with their paraphernalia, belong to the field of economics and law, respectively; and so on. The sociocultural nature of the vehicles is definitely and satisfactorily determined through the reference to the systems of meanings of which they are vehicles.

Their *physical* location in *physical* space (their "ecology") is determined by the referential system of geometric or physical space. However, such an "ecological" location of these objects in the physical space becomes possible only after they are determined as the vehicles of certain systems of meanings (religious, scientific, artistic, economic, and so forth). In other words, their sociocultural nature is located through the same system of co-ordinates through which meanings and human agents are located. Otherwise, the location of a certain physical object in physical space cannot give us any idea of its sociocultural nature or of its position. The object will be just a building, or an iron, silver, or wooden object of certain geometric form, with certain physical or chemical qualities that cannot give the slightest idea of the sociocultural nature of the object—whether it is a religious, industrial, artistic, or some other sociocultural phenomenon.

On the Nature of Sociocultural Space. The preceding analysis gives an idea of the nature of sociocultural space:

(1) Sociocultural space differs fundamentally from any variety of the physical or geometrical space. None of the latter is adequate or fitted for the location of the sociocultural phenomena in the sociocultural universe, nor is it suitable for the location of any of the three components of sociocultural phenomena. Here again we see the fundamental difference between sociocultural and physical phenomena, and

between the framework of the referential principles of the physical sciences and that of the social sciences.

(2) Sociocultural space is a manifold, composed of three main "planes," or aspects: the aspect or plane of meanings in the universe of meanings; the aspect or plane of vehicles in the universe of vehicles; the aspect or plane of human agents in the universe of human beings as agents.

(3) Within each aspect or plane, each meaning, agent, and vehicle is determined in its location or position in the respective universe through a reference to the main systems of meanings with their sub-subsubsystems (if need be) and their supersystem. In terms of physico-geometrical space, each plane has at least the same five main systems and several derivative ones with their subclasses, subsubclasses, and so on. These main systems of meanings can be called the "sociocultural systems of co-ordinates."

(4) The referential systems of meanings are the same for all three components of sociocultural phenomena.

(5) Since the referential systems of meanings locate also the vehicles and human agents of a given system of meanings, they locate the given sociocultural phenomenon, not only in the universe of pure meanings, but also—and especially—in the empirical sociocultural universe. Determining the system of meanings, the vehicles and agents of, say, the Roman Catholic religious system, we study and locate where, even in geometric or physical space, its vehicles and agents are located (buildings, property, and all the other paraphernalia of the Church; the number and location of its human agents; what areas are predominantly Roman Catholic; whether the number of Church agents increases or decreases; whether Church vehicles grow in volume or decrease; and so on).

In brief, we study not only the place of the meaning of the Roman Catholic religion in the universe of meanings, but the place of all its vehicles and agents in the empirical sociocultural world and in physical space. For this reason, the given conception of sociocultural space and its system of co-ordinates cannot be accused of being confined to the world of pure meanings. If anything, it requires a more painstaking study of the number and properties of the vehicles and agents, and their distribution in physical space, than any purely empirical study.[56]

[56] Here comes the place of "sociocultural geography" or "ecology." Properly under-

(6) The outlined conception of sociocultural space in its three planes or universes embraces the universe of meanings, which, as such,

stood, sociocultural "ecology" or "geography" is exactly a study of the distribution, succession, displacement, mobility, and change of the vehicles and human agents of the sociocultural systems as *they are reflected on the screen of geometrical space, on the territory of this planet.* The above analysis means that such a study is necessary for an adequate knowledge of the location of the sociocultural phenomena in sociocultural and physical space. Whether the phenomenon be "crime," "a certain religion," "suicide," "urban society," or what not, in locating its vehicles and agents in the sociocultural universe, we have to locate also where, on the physical territory of this planet, their vehicles and agents are located, or what they are as vehicles and agents—what is their frequency here or there, what displacements, successions, migrations, diffusions they have, from what point to what, and so on. (See Sorokin, *Dynamics,* Vol. IV, chap. v.) On the other hand, it must be clear that such an ecological or sociogeographical location of a given phenomenon is possible only when one is acquainted with its meaning-component, when one knows what constitutes "crime," "religion" "prostitution," "war," or "certain industry."

All these phenomena are either systems or congeries of meanings. Otherwise, there is no "crime," but a certain mode of physical action of one person toward another person; there is no "prostitution," but just a sex relationship, biologically very similar to that in legitimate "marriage." This means that any ecological study is possible only after the studied sociocultural phenomenon is located in its system of meanings in the universe of meanings. Furthermore, the ecological location of the vehicles or agents of a certain system of meanings can have a sense and value only when it is considered as one of the subsubco-ordinates of the system of co-ordinates that locates a vehicle or agent in the sociocultural universe. Without the above system of co-ordinates, it becomes either meaningless or even misleading. The king and his valet, the president of a business corporation and his office boy stay, especially during business hours, in the same building, at the same locus of physical space. They often even live in the same building. From this, however, it does not follow that their social position is the same. The same building, say a hall, now is used as a vehicle for a symphonic concert, now for a religious service, now for a political meeting, now as a place for refugees. From the fact that it remains in all these cases the same building, it does not follow that it is the vehicle of the same sociocultural system. From the fact that a certain portion of dwellings all have the same kind of telephone, it does not follow that, in all these houses, the telephone is used as the vehicle of the same sociocultural system. From the fact that the frequency of crime is particularly high in certain districts of the city, it does not follow that all who live in that district are criminals or that the territory of the district as such is the causative factor of crime. The fact that hundreds of families live in the same big apartment house does not mean that all these persons are the agents of the same sociocultural system and have the same position in sociocultural space. And so on.

Taken per se, irrespective of the whole system of co-ordinates locating the given sociocultural phenomenon in the sociocultural universe, a location of a certain object at a certain locus of physical space becomes meaningless and misleading. In that case, it is but a plain geography of certain physicochemical phenomena and objects, and certain biological organisms having no relationship to sociocultural phenomena.

Fortunately, the best works in "human ecology" avoid this blunder, and give us a valuable map of how the location and displacement of sociocultural phenomena in sociocultural space is reflected—through their agents and vehicles—on the screen of the geometrical space of the given territory. Finally, this reflection on the screen of physical space is always very imperfect; many sociocultural phenomena are not reflected at all on that screen. Others are reflected either very faintly, or even distorted.

For a discussion of human ecology and social geography, see R. E. Park, "Human

is spaceless so far as any physical or geometrical space is concerned; and the human agents and vehicles, which, as physicochemical and biological phenomena, are given in the physical or geometrical space. In this sense, the sociocultural universe is simultaneously *ideational and sensate,* has both aspects and represents an *integralist conception,* adequately embracing the sensory and supersensory aspects of sociocultural reality.

In the next chapter we shall see that such a space corresponds exactly to sociocultural time, which is also ideational and sensate. Only such a space (and time) can adequately locate in sociocultural universe the spatial or the time position of the sociocultural phenomena. Purely physical or geometrical space of any kind misses them entirely, because of the geometrically spaceless nature of the component of meanings.

SOCIOCULTURAL DISTANCE AND OTHER DERIVATIVE CONCEPTS OF SOCIOCULTURAL SPACE

The above conception of sociocultural space and of its system of co-ordinates defines a number of derivative conceptions related to it. One of these is the conception of sociocultural distance. *Sociologically, two or more sociocultural phenomena are near to one another if they occupy the same or an adjacent position in the sociocultural space; and they are very distant from one another if their positions in the space are in different and heterogeneous parts of its system of co-ordinates.* This equally concerns sociocultural phenomena as well as their separate components.

If the sets of meanings *A* and *B* are two Christian denominations, meaningfully, they both are located in the same system of religion, in the same subclass and even the same subsubclass. Therefore, in their meaningful nature, *A* and *B* are similar, and in this sense near to one another meaningfully, no matter how remote are their members and vehicles in geometric space. If *A* is a meaning of Baptist religion, while *B* is that of the United States Steel Corporation, they occupy very

---

Ecology," *American Journal of Sociology* (July, 1936); R. E. Park and E. Burgess, *Introduction to the Science of Sociology* (Chicago, 1924), and *The City* (Chicago, 1925). See further the articles of R. D. McKenzie, U. G. Weatherly, and E. F. Young in the *Journal of Applied Sociology,* Vols. IX and X; R. F. L. Faris and H. Dunham, *Mental Disorders in Urban Areas* (Chicago, 1939); C. R. Shaw, *Delinquency Areas* (Chicago, 1929); and M. A. Alihan, *Social Ecology* (New York, 1938). For other literature on social ecology and social geography, see in Sorokin, Zimmerman, and Galpin, *Systematic Source Book,* quoted, Vol. I, chap. v.

different places in the universe of meanings; therefore they are distant from one another, no matter how close are their buildings and agents in geometric space.

If individuals A and B are agents of the same sociocultural systems and have similar positions within each of these systems—for instance, if both are members of the Roman Catholic Church, directors of the same business firm, citizens of the same State, members of the same political party, nationality, clubs, and associations, and so on—they occupy similar positions in the sociocultural universe of agents; therefore they are near to each other socioculturally, though they may be separated from each other by thousands of miles of physical space. And vice versa, if A and B are agents of quite different sociocultural systems, or occupy quite different positions within the same system (such as a king and his valet, a master and his slave, a Trobriander and a member of the "Four Hundred" in New York), they occupy quite different positions in the sociocultural space; therefore they are separated from each other by an enormous social distance, though they may live and act in the same physical space.

Finally, if A and B are vehicles of the same system of meanings— say, both are the church buildings of the Roman Catholic Church, one in Rome and the other in Mexico City—they are near to each other as vehicles, occupy similar positions in the universe of vehicles (and show a tangible interdependence as parts of the same system), though they may be separated by thousands of miles of physical space and though, physicochemically, they may have little in common, one church being built of stone, brick, or marble, and having much resplendence, while the other is a wooden church, unostentatious and poor in its material equipment.

As analyzed before (see Chapter I), the vehicles of Harvard University are the most fantastic motley of the most heterogeneous physicochemical and biological objects, from corpses in its Medical School up to the glass flowers in its Museum; and yet, since they all are vehicles of the same system, they are near "relatives" in the sociocultural universe, and even show a tangible interdependence. On the other hand, if two objects A and B—say, a shoe and a spoon—are the vehicles of different systems, they are very distant from each other, no matter how close they are in the physical space. If A and B both are identical things physicochemically—say, poison in a bottle, a portion of which is used by a doctor to cure a patient, while another portion is used by a murderer to kill his victim—they become very different and very distant from each other, though physicochemically they are the same thing and come from the same source.

These remarks clarify the proposition and show what sociocultural distance means and which phenomena—when, and where, and why— are socioculturally distant or near. Unfolding the proposition, one can easily—and accurately—decide the problem of sociocultural distance in each particular case.[57]

WISSENSOZIOLOGIE OF SPACE CONCEPTIONS

Wissensoziologie of Geometric Space. In *Social and Cultural Dynamics,* Volume II, pages 428 ff., it has been shown that the apprehension and conception of space generally is different in ideational,

[57] It is easy for a competent reader to see that the offered sociological conception of sociocultural distance is very different from, for instance, the conception of social distance developed by E. Bogardus and others. So far as their concept of social distance means the degree of sympathy or antipathy, positive or negative feelings and attitudes between persons, their valuable studies are concerned with *psychological rather than sociocultural distance.* They define and try to measure, not what are the sociocultural positions of the individuals, meanings and vehicles, and how close or distant they are, but how sympathetic or unsympathetic are the attitudes and feelings of human beings toward one another, regardless of their positions. A king and his valet, sometimes even an executioner and his victim, may—and sometimes do—feel very sympathetically toward each other; and yet, their sociocultural positions remain very different and distant. A king often has much warmer feelings toward his mistress than for his queen; and yet the position of king and queen are much nearer to each other socioculturally than those of king and mistress.

The psychological conception of psychological distance is an example of one of the psychological conceptions of space and distance. It can also be one of the subco-ordinates of sociocultural distance, in its system of ethics. There, the feelings of sympathy and antipathy, solidarity and antagonism, love and hatred, become one of the co-ordinates of the moral nearness or remoteness of the persons or groups involved. But in that case this criterion of social distance becomes just one of the many co-ordinates defining the position of the persons in the socioethical universe, as a part of the sociocultural universe.

For a discussion of this conception of social distance, see E. Bogardus, *The New Social Research* (Los Angeles, 1926), and *The Development of Social Thought* (New York, 1940), pp. 466 ff.; J. R. Runner, "Social Distance in Adolescent Relationships," *American Journal of Sociology* (November, 1937); S. C. Dodd, "A Social Distance Test," *American Journal of Sociology* (September, 1935); and E. W. DuVall, "Child-Parent Social Distance," *Sociology and Social Research* (May-June, 1937). A slightly broader, more sociological conception of social distance is given in R. E. Park, "The Concept of Social Distance," *Journal of Applied Sociology,* Vol. VIII; A. Walther, "Soziale Distanz," *Kölner Vierteljahrshefte für Soziologie* (1931), pp. 263-270; M. M. Wood, *The Stranger* (New York, 1934); L. von Wiese, *op. cit.,* pp. 122 ff., 160 ff., *et passim;* P. A. Sorokin, *Dynamics,* Vol. III, chap. i; and *Social Mobility,* chaps. i-iii; T. Abel, *Systematic Sociology* (New York, 1929), chap. i *et passim;* and H. Alpert, "Social Distance" (unpublished thesis, Columbia University, 1935).

sensate, and idealistic cultures. Different also is their system of spatial co-ordinates. Above, in this part, it has been mentioned that space conception generally, and sociocultural space conception particularly, differs from society to society, from culture to culture.

The adequate history of the origin and variation of space apprehension is not written as yet. Nevertheless, it is possible to state that the *conception of geometric space generally and of sociocultural space particularly, with their referential systems and other derivatives, are different from group to group, person to person, and are greatly conditioned by the kind of society and culture in each given group.*

A study of the *cosmogonies and cosmographies* of different groups, beginning with the primitive tribes and ending with various historical societies, is the first evidence of this fact. Cosmographies are the conceptions of the spatial structure of the universe. Cosmographies of different nations, tribes, and societies depict the different spatial structure of the universe and that of the space itself. The spatial structure of the universe of the Vedas and Mahabharata is very different from that of ancient China or Egypt, both from that of the Zend-Avesta, or Homeric universe; and all these, in turn, differ from the spatial structure of the universe of different thinkers, such as Pythagoras or Philolaös, Plato or Saint Augustine, Newton or Sir James Jeans—to mention but a few scholars and peoples.[58] More than that: a study of the character of these representations of space shows that they have been decidedly influenced by the character of sociocultural conditions of the respective societies and thinkers. An example of such conditioning was given in Volume II of *Dynamics.* The cosmologic spatial conceptions of a predominantly ideational culture are marked by ideational characteristics; while those of a predominantly sensate culture bear upon themselves the sensate marks.[59] This is only one—though important—example of sociocultural conditioning of the spatial representations.

There are many other evidences of the same, especially if we take more detailed characteristics of the space conceptions of various groups and persons. For instance, the character of Christian beliefs in God,

---

[58] See, for instance, the spatial structure of the universe of ancient China in M. Granet, *La Pensée chinoise* (Paris, 1934); other conceptions, see Sorokin, *Dynamics,* II, 428 ff. For a history of cosmographies and spatial conceptions in Greece and medieval Europe, see P. Duhem's *Le Système du monde: histoire des doctrines cosmologiques de Platon à Copernic* (3 vols., Paris, 1913-20), *passim;* and W. Gent, *Die Philosophie des Raumes und der Zeit* (Bonn, 1926).

[59] See Sorokin, *Dynamics,* II, 428 ff.

various ranks of angels and saints, the concepts of paradise, purgatory, and inferno and the words of the Scripture all quite definitely determined a large number of the characteristics of space of Christian thinkers. The spatial structure of the universe respectively appears with the specified regions inhabited by various angels, saints, sinners, devils; with God as the center of the universe; with the region of the "supercelestial waters" and "undercelestial waters"; and so on.[60]

Similarly, the spatial representations of Mohammedan or Homeric cultures are marked by the most pronounced influence of Mohammedan and Homeric religions. Their space is but a reflection of their religious conceptions. The same is true of the space ideas of the Egyptians. One of the earliest Egyptian cosmologies represented the earth as a kind of bed, or a circle or square, with men, lions, and mountains serving as the pillars for the sky. The sky itself is depicted as either a cow or a woman or a roof. Between the earth and the sky there is emptiness. "The gates of the world through which the sun was coming and going out were represented as a kind of a door." Instead of points of the compass, there were many different regions—four or eight—on earth. For example, there was a region for the dead. Each region was depicted along the lines of the Egyptian religious beliefs. "It is clear also that in Egypt as everywhere, the boundaries of the sky and the earth more and more expanded and receded farther and farther with an expansion of the geographic knowledge."[61] With a change in Egyptian or other culture, especially with regard to religion, the spatial representations also changed.

Similar conditioning we observe among many primitive peoples. As in most ancient cosmologies, the space concept of primitive peoples is not the isotropic and uniform space of Newtonian mechanics, but always nonisotropic and qualitative, consisting of regions with different qualities that are inseparable from the regions, and these qualities are often derived from the character of their culture and society. Farther on, subdivisions of space—such as our north, south, east, west; higher and lower; and the like—are again stamped by the sociocultural conditions of the respective society.

A few examples will illustrate this: "[In some groups in Australia] space is conceived in the form of an immense circle because the camp

[60] See Duhem, op. cit., Vols. I, III, and V; and Sorokin, Dynamics, II, 431-433.
[61] H. Schäfer, "Weltgebäude der alten Ägypter," Die Antike, III (1927), 91-127.

of the tribe has a circular form; and this special circle is divided exactly like the tribal circle."[62]

This shows that here the idea of space and its forms is a direct reflection of the structure of the social organization of the tribe. Such data are fairly numerous.

Sociologists have shown that in many primitive groups space is not represented as a homogeneous milieu but it is divided in parts according to their mystic qualities ascribed to these parts: such and such a region or direction is regarded as being under the domination of such and such a spirit identified with such and such a clan of the tribe.[63]

Farther on, Durkheim rightly remarks that space without its differentiation and a system of reference to other bodies is almost unthinkable.

But whence come these divisions [of space] which are so essential? By themselves, they are neither right nor left, up nor down, north nor south, etc. All these [and many other divisions of space] distinctions evidently come from the fact that different sympathetic values have been attributed to various regions.[64]

The space of the primitives is not homogeneous, but qualitative, consisting of different regions

each charged with qualities [of this or that spirit]; each has its unique attributes and participates with the mystical powers it manifests. . . . Different directions and regions are distinguished qualitatively from one another. . . . Space is more felt than conceived; its directions are heavy with qualities.[65]

Among the African tribes, various regions are designated, instead of north, south, east, and west, as the region of "pure water," the region of the "pretender to the throne," or "the region of good seeds"; and the direction of the main river is designated by "to and from the sky."[66]

Roth indicates that distance is measured by the number of "suns" or "deeps" taken in performing the journey, the days of traveling varying in different directions, depending upon the difficulties, the number

[62] E. Durkheim, *The Elementary Forms of Religious Life* (New York, 1915), pp. 10-17 and 419-421. See there other examples.

[63] M. Halbwachs, *Les Cadres sociaux de la mémoire* (Paris, 1925), pp. 131-132.

[64] Durkheim, *op. cit.,* pp. 419 ff.

[65] L. Levy-Bruhl, *La Mentalité primitive* (Paris, 1922), pp. 91-93, 231-233, and 520-521. See there concrete facts.

[66] R. E. Dennett, *At the Back of the Black Man's Mind* (London, 1906), pp. 122-123.

of the waterholes, and other factors. This means that spatially unequal distances become equal, and vice versa.[67]

Among many primitive peoples, there is a special region in space where the dead live. This may be under the earth or over the earth, or somewhere else; or it may be somewhere and nowhere at the same time. In other cases, there are two or three or more "spirit worlds" situated somewhere. Some primitives believe that, in the world of the dead, everything is opposite to that of the living: words have opposite meanings, the sun goes from the West to the East, and so forth.[68]

Among the Melanesians,

. . . nothing is more difficult than to ascertain precisely in their language the place or the direction indicated by some of the adverbs of place. It is probably impossible to arrange them so as to show a corresponding sense.[69]

They neither know nor use the compass directions; places are named by reference to something which is socially, psychologically, or biologically important or conspicuous.

Similarly, Migeod relates that, among the tribes of West Africa, the directions of space are often called by the parts of the human body: as "head" for "top," and so on.[70]

Among other primitive peoples, roads and directions are often named for the peoples to whom they lead. A region of space does not exist in itself apart from what occupies it or happens in it, and social events are important. Thus they have a "Place of the Pretender to the Throne," "Place of Fertility," "Place of Murder," "Place of War," or "Place of the Sacred *Churingas*," "Place of the Totemic Ancestors," or other names to commemorate social events.

All this means that representations of what we would call "geometric space" are already greatly colored by sociocultural events and traits of the tribes, as well as by those of the peoples of a more advanced culture.

These representations are colored similarly even in our daily practice and representation of space. Our "downtown" and "uptown" have little relationship to the geometric down or up. Our "right" and "left" are geometrically often quite contradictory. Our places of space are

---

[67] W. E. Roth, *Ethnological Studies Among the North-West-Central Queensland Aborigines* (Brisbane, 1897), pp. 28 and 133.

[68] See various facts in Levy-Bruhl, *The Soul of the Primitive* (New York, 1928), pp. 235 and 301-304.

[69] R. H. Codrington, *The Melanesian Languages* (Oxford, 1885), pp. 164 ff.

[70] F. W. H. Migeod, *The Languages of West Africa* (London, 1913), I, 193 ff

also marked or determined by this or that sociocultural event or trait as: "Bunker Hill," "Waterloo," "Borodino," and so on; or "murder place," "the place where N. hanged himself," "the place of miracle," and so on.

Psychosocially, it is often not a geometrical latitude or longitude or altitude of this or that city or metropolis that determines its location in our daily thinking, but rather it is the city or some inhabited or historical point that determines the distances and places, longitudes and latitudes, of these spatial regions. Few, if any of us, know the longitudes or latitudes of most of the cities and regions; we all judge and orient ourselves in the spatial position of this or that point rather by the distance of the point from the city known to us (as "near London," "near Calcutta," and so on). When we come to a city unknown to us and look for a certain address, if we do not take a taxi, we ask for and orient ourselves in finding the place, not by longitude or latitude, but by the streets that lead to it, by various conspicuous buildings, squares, monuments we are told to watch for, by turning right or left, and so on. Likewise, in our daily routine, we talk of distances in terms of "time by car," "time by walk," "time by bus," and the like. Our system of addresses again is based upon the sociocultural system of the name of the street and the number of the house, rather than upon the geometric latitude-longitude of the place.

All this means that the past as well as the present representations and "operational orientation" in even geometric space are greatly conditioned and stamped by the sociocultural traits of the respective society and culture. The very units of the geometric distance—such as "foot," "yard," "meter," "sajen," "finger," "rod," and so on—bear the imprint of these conditions.

For local and daily purposes, we still use these local and parochial "sociocultural co-ordinates" of geometric space. When, however, the contact and interaction of various societies grew and expanded, the local and parochial systems of geometric space representation and orientation became increasingly unserviceable. "To the right of Jones' house, about twenty rods" serves the purpose for a village where everyone knows where Jones' house is situated. But for the whole human population, such a point of spatial reference becomes indefinable and therefore unserviceable.

The cosmopolitan and international and large society needed some universal, standardized points of spatial reference, which would permit it to locate in the space any point on this planet and sometimes outside of it. Parallel with the expansion of sociocultural interaction between greater and larger societies, the need grew and led to the progressive replacement of the local systems of spatial orientation by larger and larger, more and more universal systems of space representation and its points of reference. Hence, "bleaching of the local qualitative space of all its qualities," making the space more and more empty of qualities, more and more homogeneous and isotropic; hence the replacement of the "local" points of space reference by such points or such systems of co-ordinates as would permit any point on this planet to be located. This trend resulted finally, in the sixteenth and seventeenth centuries, in the nonqualitative, isotropic, uniform space of Newtonian mechanics, or the geometrical space, with its uniform (Greenwich or other point) system of reference.

This means that *the emergence of uniform, isotropic space of the classical mechanics itself, with its system of reference, was conditioned by the sociocultural process of growth of cosmopolitan and international society and culture.* It became a vital necessity for the existence and expansion of such a society. It could not get along at all without an international, standardized, qualityless space with its system of reference. If human societies had remained purely local in their contact, the local system of space representation and orientation would be satisfactory, and no need of an internationally standardized system of space would exist. Under such conditions, it is doubtful whether it would have emerged at all; at least, in all the primitive and historical societies at their early stages, when they were isolated from most of the other societies, we do not find any standardized system of space, with its system of referential points. In this sense, even the space of classical mechanics, which is still the only real space and system used for the earthly orientation of human beings in physical space, is itself a product of sociocultural conditions and, as such, it bears in itself all the marks of its sociocultural origin. Like bars of gold used as international currency, unmarked by any individual stamp of the local money of this or that country, the qualityless space of the classical mechanics, and especially its system of reference, is but the space of internationalized and cosmopolitan society.

The above brief sketch shows that *even geometric space concep-*

tions and systems of references have been conditioned tangibly by the sociocultural milieu of the respective populations. In this sense, even geometric or physical space, supposed to be quite objective and scientific, is but a variety of sociocultural space conditioned in its characteristics by the sociocultural milieu. It remains, however, geometric space, in the sense that it aims to determine the spatial position and positional relationships of material, physical objects and phenomena. In this respect it differs from sociocultural space, in the narrow sense of the term, as the space system aiming to determine the position of sociocultural phenomena in the sociocultural universe.

"*Wissensoziologie*" *of Sociocultural Space.* If even geometric space and the system of location of material phenomena in it are stamped by sociocultural conditions and have been changing with the change of sociocultural conditions of different societies and cultures, still more true is this of sociocultural space and its system of determination of social phenomena and their components in the sociocultural universe. More exactly, *the conception or apprehension of sociocultural space and of its system of co-ordinates has always been a reflection mirroring exactly the respective society and culture. There have been in sociocultural history as many different conceptions of these as there have been different societies and cultures.* In other words, conceptions of sociocultural space are directly determined by the structure and culture of the respective societies.

In order to prove that, let us note how persons and sociocultural phenomena are located in the sociocultural space of the primitive tribes and of many local societies:

(1) The sociocultural position of each tribe among other tribes is often determined by reference to the *totemic ancestors* of the tribe. Instead of "England" or "France," the names of many tribes are the names of their totemic ancestors, be it an animal, a plant, or some other object. They and their territory are defined as the "Lizards" or the "Kangaroos" or the "Baboons" and the like. Through such a reference, their sociocultural position is already defined to an extent sufficient for the local tribes to identify each group. The determination does not mean merely that such is the name of the tribe, but it means that the tribe is mystically connected and is a participant or reincarnation of the totem, which again means not simply a lizard or a kangaroo

or a baboon, but some transcendental creature resembling these animals or assuming their forms. The whole determination of the "spatial" position is thus made through use of a referential principle transcendental or supersensory in its nature. All who are coparticipants in it occupy a similar position in the primitive sociocultural universe.[71]

The sociocultural position of *each member among the members* is defined again through a reference of the member to the respective age, sex, rank, or other group into which the tribe is differentiated and stratified. Determination of the position in this way defines his social status and gives an idea of his rights, duties, functions—in brief, of almost all the important sociocultural properties of the person. The sociocultural position of *most of the sociocultural objects or phenomena* is again determined through the reference, either to religious and magic principles of the "sacred" and "tabooed," and their numerous derivatives, or to other sociocultural properties of the tribe. In other words, it is defined by the referential co-ordinate of their religious system (which is, at the same time, in a sense their scientific and ethical systems, not yet separated clearly from their religous system).

Through such a reference, an indefinite number of diverse objects and phenomena (regarded as "the vehicles" or "symbols" of supersensory powers) are definitely placed in their sociocultural universe. An example: all the objects that are connected with the totemic ancestors—*churingas,* certain regions, sacred mountains, springs, events— appear to be placed in "the sacred" region or class; all are believed to be interconnected mysteriously, and all are allocated to definite positions determined by their beliefs and ceremonies. A large number of other physical objects, regions, and phenomena are placed in the class of the "profane" or "evil." The position and relationships of each of such objects and phenomena—and they embrace almost their whole universe—are thus definitely determined, and determined with great detail.

An example of this is given by the "sacred places" or "totemic centers." They are the most sacred places. But they are not merely places; they are symbols that denote simultaneously the respective local patri-

[71] For a discussion of totemism, see B. Spencer and F. G. Gillen, *The Arunta: A Study of a Stone Age People* (London, 1927); E. Durkheim, *op. cit.;* R. Thurnwald, *Die menschliche Gesellschaft* (4 vols., Berlin-Leipzig, 1935), *passim;* and R. H. Lowie, *Primitive Society* (New York, 1920). See also W. I. Thomas, *Primitive Behavior* (New York, 1937), pp. 171 ff.

lineal group, the totemic animal or plant species of the group, the mystical spirits, and the place itself, with its objects and territory.[72]

In brief, sociocultural space, position, and positional relationship among the primitive groups are conceived and defined through application of the principles of their social differentiation and stratification, their religious beliefs, and other systems of their culture. All the "co-ordinates" are sociocultural co-ordinates, taken from their own society and culture. Therefore, their sociocultural space is a replica mirroring their own culture and society.

As most of these tribes are isolated from the rest of mankind, they are little individual human universes, with comparatively simple structure and culture. Being local, their system of co-ordinates of sociocultural space is also local and comparatively simple. It cannot serve as a system of co-ordinates for a cosmopolitan culture and society; it cannot locate most of the sociocultural phenomena of mankind. But for the tribes' own use, their system is serviceable and defines sufficiently well the positions of persons, tribes, and other sociocultural phenomena.

The same can be said of any other society and culture. The socio-cultural space of the Hindu caste society is stratified and little penetrable from caste to caste. The social position of a person is determined by the reference to his caste and by the position of that caste in the total caste universe. The position of sociocultural phenomena is determined through reference to the religion especially, and to other sociocultural systems that play an important role in the caste society's culture.

Sociocultural space and its system of co-ordinates in a sensate and democratic society are made up of those sociocultural systems which play an important role in it. They serve as reference points. A person's position is defined by his economic, occupational, or political group. The position of a cultural phenomenon is defined by the reference to one of the cultural systems, particularly to science, or by the utilitarian ethics and law that play especially important roles in its culture. The space is conceived as stratified but "penetrable" from stratum to stratum, according to the principle of the equality of opportunity and

---

[72] See L. Levy-Bruhl, *L'expérience mystique* (Paris, 1938), pp. 180 ff.; A. R. Radcliffe-Brown, "The Social Organization of Australian Tribes," *Oceania*, I, 60 ff.; A. P. Elkin, "Totemism in N. W. Australia," *Oceania*, Vol. III. See also C. G. Seligman, *The Melanesians of British New Guinea* (London, 1910), and works quoted in the preceding footnote.

of intensive social mobility of such a society. Generally, *the main co-ordinates in each society are those social groups (for a person) and those cultural systems (for a culture phenomenon) which play particularly important roles in such a society.* If caste is an all-important social system, then caste is used as the main co-ordinate for defining the position of a person; if an income group (rich and poor) is the most important group, then one of the main co-ordinates in such a society will be a reference to a beggar or millionaire group, to how much "the person is worth." If an educational group, or race, or "blue-blood" ancestry is one of the most important groups in a society, then these will be used as the main co-ordinates. The same is true of the cultural values. If, in a given society, the religious system is the most important—as it is in some societies—then the co-ordinates of religion are used as the main reference point. If science or art systems play particularly important parts, then these systems are used as the reference points for the location of any sociocultural phenomenon.

Not only the referential co-ordinates but even the representations of the sociocultural universe itself are stamped by the prominent traits of the social structure and the character of the culture of each respective society. Sociocultural space (often reflected in the ideas of the world "hereafter" or of "the City of God") of the caste and aristocratic societies is thought of as a pyramid of hierarchical ranks of superiority and inferiority, ranged in a certain manner corresponding to the actual stratification (castes, orders, ranks) of the respective society. If the culture of the group is predominantly ideational or sensate, the representation of the sociocultural space is also stamped by these respective traits. If the given society is mobile and has many channels for vertical movement of its members, the sociocultural space is also represented as having many doors leading from one stratum to another. If the social distance of persons in a given society is factually determined by their kinship, their similarity in religion or economic status, by their race, age, or sex, by their political position, or by their occupation, respectively, "social distance" is represented as determined by the corresponding criteria and as measured by it. In India, all members of the same caste are socially near and occupy similar positions. Social distance is measured by the position of the castes in the hierarchy of castes. Brahmin and Sudra are very distant from each other, though they may live in a close proximity. In a capitalist society, persons of similar economic standing are near to one another, while the poor and the rich are separated by an enormous sociocultural distance.

Finally, when we turn to the contemporary conceptions of sociocultural space, beginning with the above conceptions of the importers of the geometric space and ending with the conception of this work, they all are a reflection of the cosmopolitan, internationalized society and culture.

If an Australian tribe's reference to its totem defines its position in the little sociocultural universe of the Australian tribes, if its reference to the age and sex group defines the position of its members, and if its reference to the principle of the sacred and profane defines somewhat the position of the tribe's cultural values in its local or parochial universe—then such co-ordinates become quite insufficient for the location of any or all cultural values, any or all social groups, any or all human beings in the whole sociocultural universe of mankind, at the stage of international interaction of all its main groups and of cosmopolitan contact of all the cultures. Just as the local system of geometric space and its system of co-ordinates became quite inadequate in a cosmopolitan society for a determination of all the physical objects in the universe, and called forth the emergence of the "bleached" universalized geometric space of Newtonian mechanics, with its system of co-ordinates—so, with the internationalization of culture and societies, there appeared the most vital need of such a conception of sociocultural space and such a system of co-ordinates that could function in regard to any meaning, any person or group, any vehicle, or any sociocultural phenomenon. Hence the emergence and increasing attempts to create such a system of sociocultural space.

These attempts have grown with the internationalization of societies and cultures, and with an increase of contact between them. As in the case of geometric space, such attempts had already become conspicuous in the sixteenth, and especially in the seventeenth, centuries. The "social physics" of these centuries quite definitely attempted to solve this need.[73] Since that period, the attempts have been growing continuously. A part of the thinkers have attempted to solve the problem by an imitation of the space of Newtonian mechanics, or the geometry of Euclid, Lobatchevsky, Riemann, and others. They have hoped that, having "bleached" the sociocultural space of any color, of any quality,

[73] See Sorokin, *Sociological Theories,* chap. i.

of any local flavor, they would be able—as the natural scientists did with physical space—to obtain a conception of sociocultural space and its system of co-ordinates applicable to any society, any culture, and capable of locating anything and anybody in the sociocultural universe. All the above geometric, physical, mathematical, topological conceptions of sociocultural space are the result of this need and of these hopes.

We have seen that, although the need is most urgent, and although the imported geometric conceptions are indeed bleached of any local co-ordinate, nevertheless they do not achieve their objective. They are so "broad" that all the sociocultural universe slips through the meshes of their net. All the efforts of this kind have not solved the problem. Therefore, there is need for a conception of sociocultural space that can meet the need of spatial determination of all sociocultural phenomena; and that can do so, if not in the scalar way, then by being able to place each person, each meaning, each vehicle, at that "point" of the sociocultural universe to which it belongs and, through such a placement, give us a knowledge of the properties of the located phenomenon, its relationship to other phenomena, and the place of the system to which it belongs among all the systems of the sociocultural universe.

This task seems to be met fairly well by the conception of sociocultural space and its system of co-ordinates as here outlined. The conception is all the more successful in that, in some cases—especially with regard to human agents and vehicles—it permits us, not only to determine their place, but to supplement it by their metric or scalar values (like the number of the members or agents of this or that sociocultural system, or the number of its vehicles—be they cannon, dollars, tons produced, schools, churches, and so forth). For these reasons, our conception seems to meet the need better than the current "imitative conceptions."

But all of these conceptions have been the products of internationalized mankind and its culture; in this sense, they are socially and culturally conditioned. Thus the conceptions of sociocultural space with its system of co-ordinates have indeed been different in different cultures and groups; and, all in all, they have been directly conditioned by a given culture and society. Each of them, according to its need, conceived sociocultural space in its own image and resemblance. The conception of geometric space also is socioculturally conditioned, as we have seen, and also is stamped by the properties of the respective culture and society. In this sense, all such conceptions are also sociocultural. But the conditioning of the conceptions of geometric space has not been so close and decisive as that of the conceptions of sociocultural space; and geometric space is designed for the location of physical phenomena in physical space, while the function of sociocultural space is to determine the position of sociocultural phenomena (with their meaning-component) in sociocultural space. Herein lies the profound difference between them. Herein also is the reason for the failure of the imported geometric space conceptions to perform this function.

SUMMARY

(1) There are many and different spaces—physicogeometrical spaces, biophysical spaces, psychological spaces, and finally, sociocultural spaces—each with its own system of co-ordinates.

(2) All varieties of physicogeometrical space (Euclidian, Newtonian, Lobatchevskian, Riemannian, and others) aim to locate physical bodies and phenomena in the physical universe. They are the means of man's orientation in, and adaptation to, that universe. All varieties of biological (physiological) space aim to locate the vital phenomena in the universe of life and to serve as the means of orientation in, and adaptation to, that universe; more specifically, as the means of adaptation of the organs of the same organism to one another. The same is true of all the varieties of psychological space of any kind, exemplified by the space of "sympathy and antipathy" of Bogardus or by other conceptions of psychological space. Sociocultural space aims to locate the sociocultural phenomena and their components in the sociocultural universe: the component of meanings in the universe of meanings; the component of human agents in the differentiated and stratified universe of human societies; the component of the vehicles in the universe of vehicles; and finally, any sociocultural phenomenon among other sociocultural phenomena. It is a means of man's orientation in, and adaptation to, the sociocultural universe—the nearest and most important to him, even from the standpoint of a mere survival value.

(3) Sociocultural space therefore differs fundamentally in many respects from the physical, biological, and psychological spaces, including its system of co-ordinates for the location of sociocultural phenomena

in the sociocultural universe. As such, it is a space of its own kind irreducible to all other spaces. In comparison with any kind of physico-geometric space, sociocultural space differs in the following properties:

(a) Geometric space is virtually unbounded and embraces the cosmic physical universe. Sociocultural space is bounded by the human universe as bearers of meanings. Beyond this universe, it does not "extend" and has no meaning.

(b) Geometric space is isotropic (homogeneous), predominantly scalar or metric, devoid (with the exception of vectorial quantities or values)[74] of quality. Sociocultural space is mainly qualitative, as a universe of structured, qualitative systems. Only some of its co-ordinates (concerning the agents and vehicles) have a remotely scalar character, expressed in the form of either "nominal," "ordinal," or "cardinal" numbers.[75]

(c) Physical and sociocultural spaces "touch" each other in a "portion" of each of these spaces, being "out of each other" in their greater part. They overlap exactly in the portion of the location of material vehicles and human agents as physical objects in physical space. The overlapping part of physical space is limited by the inhabited territory of this planet, which is but an infinitesimally small fraction of physical space. On the other hand, physical location of the vehicles and agents locates them only in physical space, without determining their sociocultural position.

(4) The systems of co-ordinates of geometric and of sociocultural space are again fundamentally different. Any system of co-ordinates of the geometric space of any kind does not at all determine the position of sociocultural phenomena in the sociocultural universe; it defines only the position of the vehicles and human agents as physical objects in the physical universe. Such a location does not define their position, qualities, relationships, and changes in the sociocultural universe.

On the other hand, the system of co-ordinates of sociocultural space

[74] Some of the quantities (or values or units) of mechanics—for instance, the volume or mass of a body—are characterized entirely by their numerical value. They are called "scalar quantities" (grandeurs). The others—for instance, velocity and force—have simultaneously the numerical value and a certain direction. They are styled the "directional or vectorial quantities (or values)," and are represented by vector. See Lecornu, op. cit., pp. 23 ff.; and Appel and Dautheville, op. cit., pp. 1 ff.

[75] See their distinction in application to the "measurement" of sociocultural phenomena in H. M. Johnson, op. cit., pp. 342 ff.

does not define the position of sociocultural phenomena in the physical universe. At best, when complete, it gives the physical locus of some of the agents and vehicles—and never of the meanings—in their physical "ecology." The sociocultural position of the component of meaning does not have any physical locus and therefore cannot be located in any part of physical space.

(5) The system of co-ordinates of sociocultural space consists of the universe of the main systems of meanings (with their subsubsystems and supersystem). Like the systems of co-ordinates of geometric space, it may be more or less complete and all-embracing. In simple tribal societies, geometric as well as sociocultural systems of co-ordinates are comparatively simple, local, unsystematic, and "patchy," although they serve these societies satisfactorily in their orientation in the physical and sociocultural universes. For contemporary internationalized and cosmopolitan societies, such parochial systems—geometric as well as sociocultural—do not meet the need and do not permit the location of physical phenomena in the physical universe or of sociocultural phenomena in the sociocultural universe of the whole of mankind. Hence, the emergence of such systems of co-ordinates of geometric and sociocultural systems (especially beginning with the sixteenth century in Western culture) that try to meet the need of such a complex society and culture.

The Newtonian system met this need satisfactorily, insofar as physical space and its system of co-ordinates are concerned. Post-Newtonian conceptions try to improve and to generalize it still more and to make it universally applicable for any—microscopic and subatomic —physical phenomena. In the sociocultural sciences, no genuinely universal—applicable to all sociocultural phenomena—system of co-ordinates of sociocultural space has emerged as yet. The attempts to solve the need through an importation of Euclidian, Newtonian, or post-Newtonian concepts of geometric space with respective systems of co-ordinates do not and cannot solve the problem at all. Other attempts have been only partly successful. To be successful, any attempt to solve the problem must take as its starting point the universe of the main systems of meanings and use them as the main co-ordinates. In *Dynamics* and in this work, as a rough approximation to the task, the universe of the five main systems of meanings—together with the main derivative systems, plus the supersystem—are taken as the main "co-ordinates" for the determination of the position of meanings in the universe of meanings. As a rough approximation, this system permits us to locate the place of practically any meaning in the universe of these five main systems of meanings and their main derivative systems, together with the supersystem of the sensate-ideational-idealistic.

Through the same system of co-ordinates, we can locate the position of any vehicle and any human agent. Referring a vehicle or person to the subsubsystems of meanings they objectify or bear, we locate their position—of a vehicle, in the universe of vehicles; of a human agent in the universe of social groups—as bearers of the systems. In this way, the position of vehicle or person in the sociocultural universe is satisfactorily determined.

If we want further to know where the vehicles and agents are located, as physical objects in physical space, we can easily ascertain that, once their social position is located. By using consistently such a system of co-ordinates, we can, fairly satisfactorily, locate any sociocultural phenomenon in its universe. Eventually, the system of co-ordinates can be perfected and improved; but any improvement will probably be a continuation of this principle, rather than an introduction of another referential principle radically different from it.

(6) Finally, the outlined conception of sociocultural space is integralist in its character. Let us turn now to the problem of sociocultural time.

Chapter IV

SOCIOCULTURAL TIME

Plurality of Various Metaphysical, Physicomathematical, Biological, and Psychological Time

Like the conceptions of space, the conceptions of time are numerous and different from one another. There are a variety of *ontological or metaphysical conceptions of time* aiming to define its ontological or metaphysical nature: whether it is an a priori form of our mind; whether it exists objectively or subjectively; whether it is absolute or relative; whether it represents a reflection of the movement of the Soul of the World or is merely an order of succession of phenomena; whether it is continuous or discontinuous;[1] and so on. Then, too, there are several conceptions of physicomathematical, biological, and psychological time. Finally, there are several conceptions of sociocultural time, different from ontological, physicomathematical, biological, and psychological time.

In this chapter, ontological or metaphysical conceptions of time are entirely omitted, not because they are unimportant, but because their analysis lies beyond the scope of this work. We shall limit our inquiry by demonstrating: (1) that there exists indeed a plurality of different physicomathematical, biological, and psychological times, each having its own function and its own referential system; (2) that the conceptions of all these times are tangibly conditioned by the character of the sociocultural milieu in which such conceptions are originated and spread; (3) that, side by side with these "times," there is a variety of sociocultural time different from all of these, and having its own structure and functions; (4) that this time is a direct reflection of the sociocultural milieu in which it is conceived and used; and (5) that the social sciences cannot be adequately served by any of the physicomathematical, biological, and psychological times, and need an ad-

---

[1] For a discussion of these see P. A. Sorokin, *Social and Cultural Dynamics,* II, 413 ff. See also W. Gent, *Die Philosophie des Raumes und der Zeit,* quoted; L. R. Heath, *The Concept of Time* (Chicago, 1936); P. Duhem, *Le Système du monde,* quoted, I, 244 ff.; *The Problem of Time* (University of California Publications in Philosophy, 1935), Vol. XVIII; H. Hausheer, "St. Augustine's Conception of Time," *Philosophical Review* (September, 1937); and M. Souriau, *Le Temps* (Paris, 1937), chap. vii *et passim.*

equate conception of sociocultural time as one of their main referential principles.

Let us now show that there are indeed a variety of different physico-mathematical, biological, and psychological times, each having different structures, aims, and functions.

Variety of Physicomathematical Time Systems. The best-known variety of this time is the time of classical mechanics. Whether Newtonian absolute time is accepted or not,[2] the time of the classical mechanics is continuous, infinitely divisible, uniformly flowing, purely quantitative, and devoid of any qualities.[3] Mechanics' time is a measure of motion of a material point or body in terms of the motion of another material point or body, taken as a point of reference.

In dynamics, time is employed as a fundamental variable and one is here concerned only with intervals of time. Equal intervals of time are defined as those in which the earth rotates through equal angles about its axis [as a fundamental unit of time serves one second or $1/86,400$ part of a mean solar day]. The three co-ordinates which determine the position of a particle are to be regarded as continuous functions of an independent variable, the Time.[4]

Such are the essential characteristics of the time of the classical mechanics.

Different from this is the time of the microphysics of quantum and of the Minkowski-Einstein theory of relativity. Just where the difference lies for a nonspecialist, and perhaps even for a specialist, is not easy to define. The points of difference mentioned seem to be several: (1) the inapplicability of the time of macrophysics to subatomic phenomena, and therefore operational meaninglessness of the time of classical mechanics in such an application;[5] (2) the noncontinuous, "atomic," "epochal," character of the time of quanta, connected with

---

[2] See the Newtonian formula of time (absolute and relative) in Sorokin, *op. cit.*, II, 425, n. 103. Mach, Poincaré, and others rejected Newtonian absolute time as meaningless, "as an idle metaphysical conception." See E. Mach, *The Science of Mechanics,* quoted, p. 224; and H. Poincaré, *Dernière pensée,* quoted, pp. 40 ff.

[3] See the details in P. Appel et S. Dautheville, *Précis de mécanique rationelle,* quoted, pp. 38 ff.; L. Lecornu, *La Mécanique,* quoted, pp. 6, 11, and 19 ff.; Mach, *op. cit.,* pp. 222 ff.; and J. C. Maxwell, *Matter and Motion* (New York, 1878), p. 28 .

[4] H. Crew and K. Smith, *Mechanics for Students of Physics and Engineering,* quoted, pp. 97-98.

[5] See, for instance, such an interpretation in P. Bridgman, *The Intelligent Individual and Society,* quoted, p. 33; and R. A. Millikan, "Time," *Time and Its Mysteries,* quoted, pp. 16 ff.

its principle of indeterminacy;[6] (3) the greater inseparableness of time and space in the four-dimensional space-time continuum of the theory of relativity, in contrast to the separableness of time and space in the Newtonian conception; (4) in the fact that the theory of relativity "makes little of time (while thermodynamics) makes much";[7] (5) in somewhat more technical sense, a replacement of the Galilean transformation by the Lorenz transformation, and of an absolute point of reference by a relative one; or (6) several or all of these differences. Whatever the difference is exactly, the time conception, structure, and system of time measurement, together with the frame of reference, of the relativity and quantum theory is different from those of the classical mechanics.

If we pay attention to several other important traits of so-called "time systems" of physics, astronomy, geology, and biology, as, for instance, M. Souriau did, then we must agree with him that "we meet in the universe many varieties of time, a dozen, at least, with certain contradictions between them" which give but "a series of scandals of time."[8] Indeed, when we take the conceptions of the universe and of its contraction or expansion as set forth by Einstein, de Sitter, Lemaître, and Friedmann, the conception of time becomes practically meaningless.

Since, according to these theories, the radius of the universe doubles every 2,000,000,000 years, the remoter the nebulae of the universe emitting the light, the longer it takes for the rays of light to reach this planet; therefore, the remoter the galaxy, the older it is. On the other hand, before such a light from the remotest galaxy reaches us, the universe doubles in its radius. Under such conditions, the nearer the galaxy, the older it is. Which is older and which time is longer are hardly possible to decide. We are lost with our time in the mysteries of the vastest theaters of space.[9]

[6] See, for instance, F. A. Lindeman, "Symposium on the Quantum Theory," *Proceedings of Aristotelian Society*, Vol. IV, Supplement; Millikan, *op. cit.*, pp. 16-18; and, by implication, in the conceptions of A. S. Eddington and in M. Schlick, *Space and Time in Contemporary Physics* (Oxford University Press, 1930), pp. 79 ff.

[7] E. A. Milne, "Some Points in the Philosophy of Physics, Time, Evolution, and Creation," *Annual Report of the Smithsonian Institution for 1933* (Washington, 1935), pp. 219-238.

[8] Souriau, *op. cit.*, pp. 3-4 and 29 ff.

[9] *Ibid.*, pp. 7-8. From the standpoint of the relativity theory, "the time ordering of the events thus depends on the particular observer, and has nothing to do with the events themselves. . . . An individual observing two separated distant events may describe

Likewise, hardly any clear meaning of time is possible when we turn to so-called "time units" of astronomy. The unit here is the velocity of light—186,000 miles per second—the velocity in "which our earthly distances are contracted to zero, our clocks stop and cease to mark time." Such units are the "light distances" rather than time units.[10] Expressions such as "100,000 light-years as the greatest diameter of the Milky Way,"[11] or "the unit of time—megaparsec—equal to 3.26 x 10^6 light-years," are hardly conceivable in terms of time, and represent indeed the distances of light. Anyhow,[12] here we have a system of time and its frame of reference, as well as the operational mechanics for its measurement, very different from that used in the terrestrial distances and time systems.

The example of the terrestrial time system is offered by *geology*. Its time system is stratigraphic and is based upon the stratigraphic "documents of the earth"—its eras and layers superimposed upon one another. "A certain ideal order" of the position of the layers, arranged in a chronological order, separated by catastrophies from one another— such is the system of geological time. "It is fairly difficult to find *ex abrupto* any relationship between a hypothetical dance of galaxies and meteors and an obscure pile of mineral testimonies scrutinized by a geologist," and serving him as a time-reference system and "operational clock."[13] An imperfect translation into one generalized time of all these times of the classical mechanics, of quanta, of the relativity theory, of the theories of expansion and contraction of the universe, of the light-years of intergalaxy distances and times, and of geology is perhaps possible; nevertheless, it can hardly be an adequate translation, and what is more important, the time systems, the time units, the time clock, and the operational procedures remain very different in all these natural sciences.

These remarks are sufficient to show that the physicomathematical times of the natural sciences are indeed far from being identical, and represent a variety of notably different time systems.

---

one as preceding the other, while another may describe them as simultaneous. . . ." The matter becomes purely arbitrary, and "no one choice is to be preferred to any other." See Milne, *op. cit.*, p. 223.

[10] Souriau, *op. cit.*, p. 12. For a discussion of the time units and the intergalaxy distances, see H. Shapley, "On the Lifetime of a Galaxy," *Time and Its Mysteries*, quoted.

[11] *Ibid.*, pp. 44-47.   [12] Souriau, *op. cit.*, pp. 12 ff.

[13] *Ibid.*, pp. 15 ff. See there a series of other considerations.

Biological Times. Still more true is this in regard to *biological times.* Again, there are several biological times, all different from the physicomathematical times and from one another.

The time of biology is, first of all, the *time system of evolution,* represented by the "biological tree" of the origin of the species. As such, it is different from the astrophysic and geologic times.[14] Furthermore, biological time is not the empty and indifferent time of Newtonian mechanics, but is an efficient, cumulative, partly qualitative, even *epochal* (as opposed to *continuous*) time which as such incessantly creates ever new vital phenomena and "becomes a vital factor of biological reality." Here time is not a mere empty, evenly flowing, fourth co-ordinate, but turns out to be a real "becoming," filled with life and creativeness. These are "the characteristics of time not included or even not considered by the physicist."[15] For these and other reasons, a number of biologists rightly state that the time of physics is different from the time of biology.[16] A still more open revolt against physical time, in favor of an independent biological time, is voiced by Lecomte de Noüy, C. Crampton, M. F. Ashley-Montagu, J. Huxley, and others.[17]

The main argument of the revolt is that the physical time is a clock external to the vital processes; it makes equal that which biologically is unequal, and vice versa. For instance, according to this theory, all persons ten years old by physical time are supposed to be at the same stage of physiological development; and all persons—for instance, two girls, one ten and another eighteen years old according to physical

---

[14] See the reasons in *ibid.,* chap. vi.

[15] L. R. Heath, *The Concept of Time,* p. 153.

[16] See, for instance, J. S. Haldane, *The Sciences and Philosophy* (London, 1928), and *Organism and Environment* (New Haven, 1917), esp. the last chapter; J. Johnstone, *The Philosophy of Biology* (Cambridge University Press, 1914), pp. 337 ff.; F. H. Pike, *The Driving Force in Organic Evolution* (London, 1913); R. I. Lillie, "Directive Action and Life," *Philosophy of Science* (April, 1937); Milne, *op. cit.;* and H. S. Jennings, *The Universe and Life* (New Haven, Conn., 1933), p. 93.

From different standpoints, the difference is well stressed by many a philosopher, such as: J. M. E. McTaggart, "The Unreality of Time," *Mind* (1908); B. Bosanquet, *The Principle of Individuality and Value* (London, 1912); and J. Royce, *William James and Other Essays* (New York, 1911), pp. 271 ff. H. Bergson's and others' opinions are given later on.

[17] See Lecomte du Noüy, *Biological Time,* quoted; C. Crampton, "Physiological Age," *American Physical Education Review* (1908); J. Huxley, *Problems of Relative Growth* (New York, 1934); R. Goldschmitt, *Physiological Genetics* (New York, 1938); and M. F. Ashley-Montagu, "Letter on Social Time," *American Journal of Sociology* (September, 1938).

time—are assumed to be at different stages of physiological development. Meanwhile, observation shows that persons equally old according to the physical clock are physiologically at quite different stages of development. Mary, who is ten years old according to clock time, may be eighteen years old physiologically, and as ripe to give birth to a child as another girl who is eighteen years old by clock time. And conversely, the physiological age of two persons of the same age by the physical clock may be, and often is, very different.

Clearly, the more important measure from the point of view of the biologist is the physiologic rate of development, and not the total number of chronologic moments during which the organism developed. . . . A statement of the amount of the chronologic [clock] time during which any structure has existed tells us nothing of this rate.[18]

Hence, the advisability of measuring biologic time by its own clock— the clock of the organism itself—but not primarily by the clock based upon the revolution of the earth.

Lecomte du Noüy, together with A. Carrel, in their study of the rapidity of cicatrization of wounds, found that wounds of the same size and identical in other respects required different times for cicatrization with different persons. Making all the necessary allowances, they came to the conclusion that the difference in time of healing is due mainly to the *physiological age* of the persons. The older the person physiologically, the longer is the time necessary for cicatrization of the wound. A child of ten will cicatrize a wound of twenty square centimeters in twenty days; a man of twenty, in thirty-one days; a person of thirty, in forty-one days; a man of fifty, in seventy-eight days; and so on.[19]

Thus the same work (cicatrization of the same wound), to be done by the organism, requires different lengths of the physical (clock) time from the organism at different physiological ages. If, however, instead of this clock external to the organism, we take the organism itself as a clock, and the velocity of the cicatrization in it as the pointer of the clock, we come to the conclusion that "everything occurs as if sidereal time flowed four times faster for a man of fifty than for a child of ten"[20] (because the same physiological time-unit healing of one square centimeter takes about four times as much sidereal time in a man of

[18] Ashley-Montagu, *op. cit.*, pp. 282-284.
[19] du Noüy, *op. cit.*, pp. 154 ff.   [20] *Ibid.*, pp. 160 ff.

fifty as in a child of ten). Thus, when we take physiological time as a unit of comparison, physical time no longer flows uniformly. From this standpoint, one year of clock time for a child, or for persons young physiologically, is much longer physiologically and psychologically than for his parents, or for old persons.

To sum up: Physiological time is "a granular, variable, individual time, differing from the continuous, integral, universal time."[21]

The above gives an idea of the biological time and of the differences between biological and physical time. It also gives some of the reasons why physical time is not always adequate for a study of—indeed, is sometimes misleading in—the measurement of the velocity or the rate of change of biological processes.

Psychological Time. Fairly close to biological time is psychological time. We are well acquainted with the discrepancy between the *chronological (physical) and mental age of persons.* Like the chronological and physiological ages, biological time and psychological time do not often coincide. Here also "the flow of consciousness," as well as individual perception of time, is neither continuous nor proportional to the physical time. In a year, many more things happen to a child than to an old man.

H. Bergson's conception of time serves as a good introduction to an idea of psychological time, as well as to the difference between the latter and the physical time of the classical mechanics. Bergson denies emphatically that the time of mechanics is a real time, or that it is anything more than a mental diagram. Real time is neither homogeneous nor evenly flowing; nor does it have the same uniform rhythm or beat. It is qualitative and, according to the kind of consciousness, heterogeneous:

The essence of time is that it goes by; time already gone by is the past; and we call the present the instant at which it goes by. [This instant is not a mathematical instant.] The real, concrete, live present [in our perceptions] necessarily occupies a duration. The duration lived by our consciousness is a duration with its own determined rhythms, a duration very different from the time of the physicist, which can store up, in a given interval, as great a number of phenomena as we please. [For instance,] in the space of a second, red light—the light which has the longest wavelength, and of which the vibrations are the least frequent—accomplishes 400 billions of vibrations. . . . Now the smallest interval of empty time

<hr />

[21] *Ibid.,* p. 170. See there the details and several suggestive analyses.

which we can detect equals, according to Exner, 1/500 of a second. . . .
[If we could watch the succession of 400 billions of vibrations, each in-
stantaneous and each separated from the next only by the 1/500 of a second
necessary to distinguish them, it would require more than 25,000 years
before the conclusion of the operation.] Thus the sensation of red light,
experienced by us in the course of a second, corresponds in itself to a succession of phenomena which, separately distinguished in our duration, with
the greatest possible economy of time, would occupy more than 250 centuries of our history. Is this conceivable? We must distinguish here between
our own duration and Time in general. In our duration—the duration
which our consciousness perceives—a given interval can only contain a
limited number of phenomena of which we are aware. [And vice versa,
we can imagine a big mind or consciousness for which thousands of years
of human history would appear as one second. This means also that the
infinitely divisible time of mechanics is not our time or real time.][22]

[From this it follows that the homogeneous time is an imaginary idol
of our language, a mere mental diagram.]

The psychological time experienced by an individual is almost quite
opposite to the time of mechanics. In contrast to the latter, it does not
flow uniformly; it is not "empty" and homogeneous; it has no unit
similar to that of one second; it is not measured by a distance crossed
by the body; it is not infinitely divisible. In brief, it is not the time of
mechanics at all. Here are a few commentaries on these statements:

It is possible to discover within the limits of human experience great
differences in the power to apprehend time and to deal with temporal ideas.
[It varies with persons, age, groups, situations, and occasions.][23]

(1) *For our various organs of sense, there are certain limits in an
apprehension of time, and the testimony of various organs may be
different in regard to its duration:*

When separated by a certain time interval ($10\text{-}20\sigma$) touch and sound
stimuli are judged simultaneous; at a longer interval ($30\text{-}40\sigma$) they are
definitely successive; but at an intermediate interval ($20\text{-}30\sigma$) the subject
finds it extremely difficult to judge whether they are simultaneous or not,
and to decide in which order they occurred.

Integration of all these different times reported by various organs
of sense has taken place in the course of evolution and social life, but
even now it is not perfect.[24]

[22] H. Bergson, *Matter and Memory* (London, 1919), pp. 176-178 and 272-280.
[23] Mary Sturt, *The Psychology of Time* (London, 1925), p. 10.
[24] *Ibid.*, pp. 15-16.

(2) *Our judgment of duration is very inaccurate* and, in comparison with the homogeneous and quantitative time of mechanics, shows a great deviation; some durations appear to us much shorter and some much longer than the corresponding durations of the mathematical or mechanics' time. Many tests with both children and adults—including those given by Mary Sturt, E. H. Moore, J. T. Morgan, and others—show that individual organization of time is very diverse, whether it concerns the understanding of ordinary time words and symbols, the ability to form a conception of a universal time scheme extending into the past and future, or the historical data or correlation of the simultaneous and sequential events.[25]

As regards the individual apprehension of duration, it is generally very inadequate, and shows a conspicuous "subjectivity" and deviation from the "mathematical-objective" time. Under some psychological conditions, a relatively long duration of mathematical time—sometimes several minutes, even hours—are unnoticed and perceived as one moment, or time may even appear to be absent entirely. Under some other conditions, one or a few minutes of an "objective" time appear of a much longer duration. There are psychological conditions that cause time "to fly exceedingly fast, and other conditions that cause it to drag" interminably. One's emotional state, the direction and division of one's attention, the amount of fatigue, faintness, and sleep, the number of events occurring in the period to be estimated, the pleasantness or unpleasantness of the experience, and many other circumstances are responsible for such "subjectivity" in time-feeling and time-apprehension.[26]

(3) Studies of Herbart, Wundt, James, Lotze, Helmholtz, and many others have shown that psychological time is "atomic," "discontinuous," consisting of the moments of "the specious present" intercepted by those of the empty time.[27] Finally, time is connected with

[25] *Ibid.*, chap. iv. See esp. E. H. Moore, "The Accuracy of Testimony Relative to Time Intervals," *Journal of Criminal Law and Criminology* (July-August, 1935).

[26] Sturt, *op. cit.*, chap. v; R. S. Woodworth, *Psychology* (New York, 1922), pp. 439 ff.; W. James, *Principles of Psychology* (New York, 1899), I, 624 ff.; and Sturt's experiments with adults in apprehension of time (relatively short) show that, in practically all experiments, the ratio of the subjectively apprehended time differed from "the actual or mathematical time," being (in terms of per cent) 105, 96, 98, 68, 74, 91, 89, 106, 79, 85, 111, 67, 65, 45, 96, 128, etc., in various experiments with various persons. See Sturt, *op. cit.*, pp. 94 ff. For other data, see Moore, *op. cit.*, pp. 1-6.

[27] See James, *op. cit.*, I, 622-631 and 642, and his *Some Problems of Philosophy* (New York, 1911), pp. 172. See also Heath, *op. cit.*, chap. iv; and Schlick, *op. cit.*, pp. 79 ff.

memory, insofar as judgment concerning the past, present, and future or the time sequence is concerned.

Here again the time of the *isolated* individual and his time sequences would be most different from physical clock time and generally most incoherent, defective, and fragmentary in comparison with mathematical time. "A creature without memory would be unable to apprehend any duration beyond, possibly, the shortest." For such a creature, the very discrimination of the past, present, and future, as well as the feeling and apprehension of time, would be impossible. Insofar as individual memories are different, this aspect of time will be different in their individual experiences.

In the quotation from Bergson, we saw that the smallest interval of empty time which an individual can detect is about $1/500$ of a second.[28] Any shorter duration would be unapprehended, and no history and no timing of the synchronous or sequential events would be conceivable. Meanwhile, mathematical time is infinitely divisible and flows on by itself incessantly, as a series of infinitely divisible and equal units.

Without any social reference, the individual's time based on his personal experiences and "memory" would be something exceedingly bizarre and incongruous. His case would be similar to that of the famous girl found in 1731 in the forest near Châlons who did not know her name, her age, her place of birth, her past or present, nor how long she had been in the forest or elsewhere; in brief, she utterly lacked any apprehension of time duration—past, present, and future— and did not have anything but unrelated, weak, and fragmentary recollections. Or such an individual would have the incongruous concept of time we sometimes experience in our dreams, where often past, present, and future are all mixed together, and the sequence or simultaneity of events is exceedingly fantastic and utterly different from mathematical or any other time.[29]

We shall discuss this further later on. For the present, however, the above discussion should show some of the peculiarities of the time of an individual psychological experience and how sharply it differs from the time of mechanics.

[28] See James, *op. cit.,* chap. xv.
[29] See about this in M. Halbwachs, *Les Cadres sociaux de la mémoire,* quoted, pp. 1 *et passim.* See other considerations on psychological time in Souriau, *op. cit.,* chaps. vi and vii.

"Wissensoziologie" of Metaphysical, Physicomathematical,
Biological, and Psychological Conceptions of Time

Before passing to an analysis of sociocultural time, different from
and possibly most important of all the times, let us briefly point out
that all these time conceptions and time apprehensions—metaphysical,
physical, biological, and psychological—are in a sense also a variety of
sociocultural time, in that they are all greatly conditioned by the character of the sociocultural milieu in which they are conceived and
propagated. In *Dynamics* (Volume II, pages 413 ff.) it has been shown
that, in a predominantly ideational culture, the conceptions of time are
also ideational; while in a predominantly sensate culture the dominant
conception of time is also sensate. (Note there what is meant by
ideational and sensate time and the evidences.) This is one of the
evidences of the proposition offered. We can go much further in that
direction and can claim that, whatever conception of time is offered,
it is conditioned by the total character of the culture and society in
which its author lives and works. In a culture in which mathematics,
science, and philosophy are undeveloped, no elaborate conception of
metaphysical, mathematical, physical, astronomical, geological, biological, or psychological time is possible. One does not expect to find the
Newtonian conception of time in a primitive society; or the metaphysical conception of time, such as Plato's or Aristotle's, or Saint
Augustine's, or experimental measurements of physiological or psychological time perceptions among the illiterate tribes. It would be
simply impossible, because there is neither scientific, philosophical, nor
psychological ground prepared for such conceptions; nor is there even
a sociocultural need for any generalized conception of time. From a
child who does not know the *A, B, C* of arithmetic or physics or
psychology or biology, one does not expect a formulation of Newtonian, Einsteinian, Platonic, or any other generalized conception of
time.

In this sense, only in the sociocultural milieu where the status of
the sciences, philosophy, psychology, or biology is already greatly developed—and developed in a certain way—is any systematic conception
of time possible; and only there and then does it emerge and diffuse.
In this sense, all elaborate conceptions of time in any field of thought
are socioculturally conditioned and are sociocultural time in a broad
sense.

This general proposition equally concerns most of the specific characteristics of the time system accepted in this or that society and culture. We shall discuss this point further. For the present, the proposition may be illustrated by the emergence of the time of the classical mechanics in the sixteenth, seventeenth, and eighteenth centuries in Europe. In purely local, primitive societies, a synchronization of the activities of its members can be done and is being done easily, through purely local "clocks," whether they be "the time necessary to cook rice," or "afternoon," or "time of cock-crowing," "or time of sending the cattle to pasture," or "time of festival," or some other referential point from the local cosmic, biological, or social processes.

In an internationalized society in interaction with a large number of societies, such local clocks cannot work satisfactorily for the purposes of synchronization of the activities of its members. In a local society, they can serve satisfactorily to "keep the appointments" of the members with one another. Hence, with a widening of the interaction of a given society with other societies scattered over widely different areas of this planet, each having its own rhythm of social life, there has been a growing need of some clock that would permit all of them to "keep appointments," to meet, to interact, to work or consult together. With the growth of such a need, we observe a process of the replacement of the narrow and local "clocks" by those of wider and wider scope, more and more free from purely local "pointers," more and more turned toward taking for their "time-pointers" such cosmic phenomena as are independent of the local conditions, readable for all, translatable for all, and accommodating all. Hence the emergence of the purely quantitative, bleached of any local color, evenly flowing, infinitely divisible, time of the classical mechanics, with its unit, the second, based on the rotation of the earth around its axis.

Like the space of the classical mechanics, the time of the classical mechanics and its clock began to emerge with the internationalization of society and the widening of its network of contact. Hence the invention of the mechanical clock in the fourteenth and fifteenth centuries, together with the emergence of the new cosmogony, and the new physics and mechanics—all of which reached their full development in the sixteenth and seventeenth centuries. None of these conceptions of time and its clock could or did emerge in the purely local societies that had no need of such a timekeeper applicable to all societies. On the other hand, they all became an absolute necessity for all societies which became to any degree international.

This explains why the first calendar, as well as the first mechanical clock, appeared in the cities. In ancient cities, there first arose the significantly large congregation of individuals with different backgrounds. Then it was that there became manifest the necessity of creating a frame of reference that would be mutually comprehensible. Thus, among the Latins:

When city life began it was naturally found necessary to have a more exact measure of the *annus* and the religious events included in it. Agriculture was still the economic basis of the life of the people; and in keeping up the agricultural religious rites within the city it was convenient, if not absolutely necessary, to fix them to particular days. This was, beyond doubt, the origin of the earliest (?) calendar of which we know anything.[30]

Similarly, it was the necessity for regulating the religious cult that "first created the calendar in Greece."[31] And, according to Spinden, even the apparently strictly astronomical calendar of the Mayas was intended fundamentally for religious purposes.[32]

This illustrates specifically the thesis that almost all of the important characteristics of the time conception of either the natural sciences, of philosophy and metaphysics, of theology, or of psychology and biology are stamped by the needs, status, and nature of the sociocultural milieu in which such conceptions are born and diffused. With the proper variation, this is applicable to any important characteristic of time conceptions. In this broad sense, the mathematical, physical, biological, psychological, and metaphysical time conceptions all are already socially organized time systems, conditioned by the sociocultural environment in which they are conceived and diffused. In subsequent paragraphs,

---

[30] W. W. Fowler, "Calendar," *Encyclopedia of Religion and Ethics*, III, 133.

[31] M. P. Nilsson, *Primitive Time Reckoning* (Lund, 1920), p. 366. This is the best work in the field.

[32] H. J. Spinden, "Maya Inscriptions Dealing with Venus and the Moon," *Bulletin of the Buffalo Society of Natural Sciences* (1928), Vol. XIV, No. 1: "It is found that luni-solar calendars have a preëminently sacral or religious origin." In different form, some kind of similar timekeepers and time systems appeared in all the ancient societies—such as ancient Egypt, Babylonia, China, India, or Greece—when they entered the phase of a great expansion of their interactions with other societies. Hence, the development of either "water clock," "sand clock," "sun dial," and other mechanical timekeepers, together with a development of the astronomical and mathematical knowledge underlying such "timekeepers." See J. H. Breasted, "The Beginnings of Time-Measurement and the Origins of Our Calendar," *Time and Its Mysteries*, quoted, pp. 59-94; and esp. Nilsson, *op. cit.*

further corroboration of this thesis is given. For the present, let us turn
to an analysis of sociocultural time and its forms.

SOCIOCULTURAL TIME, ITS FORMS AND PROPERTIES

Preliminary Characteristics of Sociocultural Time. Since there is a
wide variety of metaphysical, physicomathematical, biological, and
psychological time, it would be strange if there were no sociocultural
time different from all these and socially most important among them.

In a preliminary characterization, sociocultural time differs from all
the other times as follows:

(1) *It conceives and measures sociocultural phenomena*—their
duration, synchronicity, sequence, and change—*in terms of other sociocultural phenomena taken for the point of reference,* but not in relation
to the ultimate reality, as does metaphysical time; nor in the relationship to the other material bodies, as does physical time; nor in the relationship to the biological or strictly psychological phenomena, as do
the biological and psychological time.

(2) *The fundamental trait of sociocultural time is that it does not
flow evenly in the same group and in different societies.* Within the
same period of mathematical time—say, one hundred mathematical
days—in the same society or sociocultural system, the amount, number,
and eventfulness of happenings can be quite different. There are one
hundred days during which the whole life of the group or of the
sociocultural system changes fundamentally; and there are other one-
hundred-day periods during which no great change happens; life flows
on without any striking events, day in and day out. The same is true
to an even greater extent of changes in different societies or sociocultural systems. One year of existence of a modern social group is
packed with more numerous and greater changes than are fifty years
of existence of some isolated primitive tribe. The rhythm of events—
through which and by which we judge the flow of time—is different,
like a symphony with a slow movement and with a fast scherzo, each
of which is felt directly and not with the help of a watch.

If we are interested in apprehending the real rhythms of each
"movement," which, as such, is a whole or "togetherness," and not
in a mere pedantic computation of how many mathematical minutes
this or that movement lasted, we shall be able to take these rhythms as
an immediate datum; and having taken them as such, we arrive at

the conclusion of the different "beats" of social time at different moments of the sociocultural system's existence. In *Social and Cultural Dynamics,*[33] it has been shown that, for instance, the tempo of the sensate phase is faster than that of the ideational phase; that there are processes with accelerating, constant, and retarding tempi.

(3) *The moments of sociocultural time are uneven; it does not flow uniformly, but has eventful and critical moments and moments or stretches of an empty duration,* a mere filling in between the eventful moments. We have them in the form of rhythms, caesurae, and othei punctuating moments of sociocultural time.[34]

(4) *Sociocultural time is not infinitely divisible.* There are long and short periods—an hour, a day, a week, one year, twenty-five or more years—which, for a given sociocultural process, are units that do not permit of further division and subdivision. One can rent a room by the day or week, but rarely by the hour or minute. One makes a contract for one year or semester, but seldom for shorter periods. Some events, like the silver-wedding jubilee or some similar anniversary, come only after a stretch of a certain number of years.[35]

(5) Sociocultural time is *qualitative through and through.*

(6) Sociocultural time is not an empty flow but an *efficient* time, which by its passage turns out to be an important creative, modifying, and transforming agency in a great many sociocultural processes. In capitalist countries, time becomes the agency of commercial interest, dividend, profit; the agency that decides often the victory or defeat of armies, the fate of persons and societies; and so on.

(7) Sociocultural time has a peculiar, three-plane structure—the plane of the *aeternitas,* that of the *aevum,* and that of the *tempus* properly—absent practically in any other conception of time.

Fundamental Functions of Sociocultural Time. Let us now develop the important characteristics of sociocultural time. The functions of sociocultural time are: (1) synchronization and co-ordination or sequential timing of one sociocultural phenomenon with the others, and especially with those that are taken for the point of reference; (2) organization of the time system for realization of sociocultural continuity and for orientation in the infinite flow of time; and (3) reflection of the pulsation of sociocultural systems and, at the same time,

[33] Vol. IV, chap. xi.
[34] *Ibid.,* Vol. IV, *passim.*   [35] *Ibid.,* Vol. IV, chaps. ix and xi.

facilitation of such pulsations or rhythms as are necessary for the life and functioning of any sociocultural system.

Since human beings are destined to live and to act collectively, one of the indispensable conditions for any possible collective action is a time synchronization or time co-ordination of the actions of the parties involved. If X agrees to meet Y, both must be at the agreed place at the agreed time. Otherwise, if X arrives five hours later than Y, neither the meeting nor collective action is possible. If workers of a factory do not "time" their coming to the place of work, collective work becomes impossible. The same is true of any collective action, be it work, a fight, a ceremony, a procession, a conclave, or what not.

The possession of means and ways to "time" the behavior of the members of any group in such a way that each member apprehends "the appointed time" in the same way as do other members has been possibly the most urgent need of social life at any time and at any place. Without this, social life itself is impossible. A mutual, co-ordinated timing of the behavior of the members of a group has been the indispensable means for an adaptation of their behavior to one another. This timing adaptation to the actions or movements of one's fellow men or enemies has been far more important than its application to natural events. It has had to be "mutual" for all persons who are in the same system of interaction. In this sense, its point of reference is social phenomena, and not something else ("when father comes, then you do so and so"; "when the cows are milked," "when the crop is harvested," and so forth). It is true that some of the natural phenomena (sunset, morning, winter, midday, night, rainy day, and so on) are often used as a means of timing. But, as we shall see, they serve only as a means of finding out when the activities or sociocultural phenomena happen; they are not used for their own sake. The timing is intended to co-ordinate the actions or the social phenomena "timed," but not the social and the natural phenomena themselves. The latter are but means of time co-ordination of the activities. When the artificial instruments of such a co-ordination were invented (watches and clocks of various types), they began to be used as such means more regularly than the natural phenomena.

The same can be *said of "time-binding" of various social and historical events,* or of the realization of sociocultural continuity and of orientation in the endless flow of time. Here the social nature of the

points of reference is even clearer. Take any chronological system—
that of the ancient Babylonians, Egyptians, Chinese, Hebrews, Greeks,
Romans, Hindu, Koreans, the Arabian, Mohammedan, medieval or
the modern European—and you find the time sequences apprehended
on the basis of some social event that is taken as the *era* or *point of
reference* before or after which the other events are placed.

The Babylonian chronology was kept according to eras. For instance, the Seleukidian era (312 B.C.) had its origin either in the Battle
of Gaza or in the murder of Alexander IV (311 B.C.). The other—
earlier and later—eras originated similarly in some social event of great
importance.[36]

The ancient Egyptians counted their years according to the years
of reign of the ruling king, each king being the starting point of a
new era.[37] The beginning of the Arabian era is the epoch of Hegira,
July 15, 622 A.D., again a social event of great importance.[38] Similarly
among the Persians, the eras were important social events. Thus, for
instance, one of their eras was the year 632 A.D., marking the last king
of the Sassanide dynasty. The other era was the year 1079 A.D., which
started with an important social event.[39]

Numerous and different (more than twenty different systems) eras
of various parts of India at various periods have again their origin in
important political, religious, or generally social events.[40] The same,
with a slight variation, is true of the Javanese Saka era (78 A.D.);[41] of
the Chinese and Japanese era (a combination of the years of the reign
of the emperor with the sixty-year cycles);[42] of the Thibetan era[43] (the
year 1026 A.D.), established by the lamas in commemoration of the
acceptance of the *Kâla-chakra* system; of the Siamese and Cambodian
eras;[44] and of the eras of the Central American ancient societies (Mexico, Peru, and others).[45] The Greek and Roman eras are well known.
We ourselves compute our era from the beginning of Christianity.[46]
The other "historical peoples" do the same.[47]

[36] See F. K. Ginzel, *Handbuch der matematischen und technischen Chronologie*
(Leipzig, 1906), I, 136.   [37] *Ibid.*, I, 222.
[38] *Ibid.*, I, 238.   [39] *Ibid.*, I, 275.
[40] *Ibid.*, I, 380.   [41] *Ibid.*, I, 414.
[42] *Ibid.*, I, 479.   [43] *Ibid.*, I, 406.
[44] *Ibid.*, I, 410.   [45] *Ibid.*, I, 433 ff.
[46] See M. Chaine, *La Chronologie des temps chrétiens de l'Egypte et de l'Ethiopie*
(Paris, 1925), and W. Mayher, *Die astronomische Zeitrechnung der Völker* (München,
1913).
[47] See Ginzel, *op. cit.*, Vols. I and II.

Finally, if we turn to primitive peoples, we see the same division of time, but in a still clearer form.

Sociocultural Time in Primitive Societies. Among the primitive peoples, the time reckoning is almost absent; instead, they have only a fragmentary and discontinuous "time indication." For this reason, they do not have either units of weeks, months, or years, in the mathematical sense. Consequently, they have no systematic chronology.

"Generally the primitive peoples reckon only where an immediate practical interest requires them to do so." Their chronology does not go far, either in the past or in the future. Asked about either an age of a man or how long ago such and such an event happened, they answer by a reference to this or that—but almost always social— event. Thus a thing happened before or after "an initiation event," "when the beard of a given person was so long," "before or after harvesting or calving," or in connection with some other social event. "Common bases for reckoning are afforded by important and striking events which have been impressed upon everyone and are present in all men's minds." Such striking events are: catching a big fish or game, war, famines, the condition of the rice fields, an epidemic of smallpox or some other disease, and so forth.[48]

Thus their system of chronology is very discontinuous, short, and vague, but with all this, the points of reference in such chronologies are almost always various important sociocultural events.

The relative independence of sociocultural time and the system of reference of physical time, the social nature of sociocultural time as a means of co-ordinating sociocultural phenomena with one another and orientating them in the stream of time, and, finally, the reflection of sociocultural life itself and of its beats in the sociocultural time structure come out clearly also in the *punctuation and subdivision of sociocultural time and in the "units" for its "measurement."* Let us glance at the facts that demonstrate these functions of sociocultural time.

The totality of the evidence concerning the methods of the primitive time reckoning shows: (1) that, *in their time apprehension, time is neither continuous, nor evenly flowing, nor infinite, nor quantitative only. And its units and subdivisions are again far from being purely*

[48] Nilsson, *op. cit.*, pp. 97-100. See in this careful study the facts and the vast literature on this subject. See also L. Levy-Bruhl, "Le Temps et l'espace du monde mythique," *Scientia* (1935), 139-149; A. I. Hallowell, "Temporal Orientation in Western Civilization and in a Preliterate Society," *American Anthropologist*, XXXIX, 647-670.

quantitative. Time is represented as discontinuous, as though formed by means of certain links, with empty stretches—not reckoned and not perceived—in between. Out of this emptiness only these moments of time (its discontinued segments) are caught which are connected with some important activities of a group. The system of time indications is a discontinuous system of *pars pro toto.*[49]

A time unit—such as an hour, a minute, or a day, or a continuous twenty-four- or twelve-hour unit, indeed, generally any unit of mathematically definite and continuous time, is scarcely known to primitive man. He uses often such a unit as "night" or even—more rarely— "day," but these do not mean "day" or "night" in our sense. "Night," to him, means just "the time between going to sleep in the evening and waking in the morning," and such a time "appears to him as an undivided unit, a point." "The complete day of twenty-four hours is unknown to him."[50] This means that his time-links are apprehended in reference to man's rhythm of waking and sleeping, but not in reference to a natural phenomenon as such. Likewise, the shorter units of time exhibit the same characteristic. They are not the mathematical and quantitatively equal time-units but again something qualitative and apprehended in reference to man's rhythm of activities during the day and night. Instead of a half hour or fifteen minutes, they would say, as long as "rice cooking" or "frying of locust," or "the man died in less than the time in which maize is not yet completely roasted" or "the time in which one can cook a handful of vegetables," and so on.[51]

Division of the day shows similar traits. Here are a few examples of the primitive division of a day into parts: "milking time," "mealtime," "rest time," "the time of the yoking of the oxen," "when the buffalo is sent to (or brought from) the pasture," "time for the cattle to drink," "time when the cattle return home (or enter the kraal)," "when man's face can be recognized," "when people go to bed," "when people awake," "going to market place," "rising from market place," and similar expressions.

Side by side with these purely social phenomena, references are made also to several natural phenomena which are closely associated with the important daily phases of man's activity and which, in this sense, are substitute references for those activities. "Sunrise," "time of

[49] Nilsson, *op. cit.*, pp. 9-10.
[50] *Ibid.*, p. 17.   [51] *Ibid.*, pp. 42-44.

lengthening of shadows," "time when the frog croaks," "cock-crowing time," "bright horizon," "time when the flies are stirring," and so on.[52] It is easy to see that most of these time divisions and time indications do not exist "objectively" outside of man's social activities and are essentially of a social nature, a frame of time location of one social phenomenon by another. A uniform and quantitatively equal mathematical hour was practically unknown to the past.

The varying hour remained almost up to the end of the Middle Ages. Our modern hour has only been in general use since about the fourteenth century, when it was first spread by a construction of the striking clock.[53]

The same social imprint is clear on the seasonal or "monthly" or "weekly" time apprehension. "The year as a numerical quantity is only the tardily attained summit of development." As such, it is unknown to the primitive peoples. What is known to them is a sequence of their seasonal activities. And season again, or other parts of our "year," are longer and shorter, from the quantitative standpoint; but for their users, they are units because the corresponding activities are units.

The Andamanese distinguish the following seasons: "Much honey" (January); "Ripening of tuber, catching turtles" (February); "Still another two kinds of wild fruit ripen" (March); "Many visits to neighboring tribes" (April); "Caterpillars-meal" (August); etc.

Hesiod's agricultural calendar gives another example. "The cry of the migrating cranes shows the time of ploughing and sowing"; "Before the appearance of the swallow, the messenger of spring, the vines should be pruned"; "When the thistle blossoms, the summer has come," and so on.[54]

Generally, the mode of life and sequence of the main occupational and sociocultural activities determine mainly what we style a "season" or longer period.

Some peoples divide our year into two; some into three, four, five, eight, and more seasons or months, according to their mode of life and its geographical surroundings ("wet and dry," "cold and warm," "windless and windy," and so forth). Especially common among the agricultural peoples has been a sequence of agricultural seasons, or the "Agricultural Year."

[52] *Ibid.*, pp. 19-39.
[53] *Ibid.*, p. 44.   [54] *Ibid.*, chap. ii.

It is most clearly defined among the rice-cultivating peoples of the Indian Archipelago, by whom the seasons are determined according to the state of the rice. It is said, for example, in speaking of an event, that it happened at the blossoming or harvesting of the rice.

Among the Bahan (Borneo), the year is divided into eight periods: the clearing of the brushwood, the felling of the trees, the burning of the wood felled, the sowing, the weeding, the harvest, the conclusion of the harvest, and the celebration of the new rice year.[55]

Or take the periods which remotely correspond to our "month." In ancient Sumer, the "year" was divided into twelve unequal and irregular "months," denoting: (1) habitation; (2) driving the irrigation machine; (3) laying the brick in the mold; (4) sowing; (5), (6), and (7) festival "months"; (8) opening the irrigation pipes; (9) ploughing; and other characteristic activities. The names themselves are clear enough to make any comments unnecessary.

In Lagash, in the pre-Sargonic period, there were twenty-five irregular "months" or parts of the year. Their names were predominantly occupational (as in the preceding case), partly sociohistorical (as "month in which the third people came from Uruk"), partly agricultural, and partly religious, festival, and cult names. Divisions and months had an irregular and fluctuating character (because these social functions were irregular and fluctuating).

In Akkad, the year was divided into thirteen parts of a character similar to the above. *Ezen* (month) meant "feast."

The ancient Israelites did not have their own names for months and took the Canaanitish names; "the counting was a shifting one, it had no reference to the solar year." There were two months called "bringing in of fruits"; two called "sowing"; two called "late sowing"; one called "pulling off flax"; and one called "barley harvest."

Among the Egyptians, "the year" was divided into three seasons, each of four months: "inundation," "seedtime," and "harvest."

Among the ancestors of the European peoples, we find a similar situation. The month names of the peasants of Macedonia include: "threshing-floor month," "vintage month," "sowing month," "Precious Cross," "Nicholas," "Saint Andrews."

Among the months of various Slavic peoples in the past, Yermolloff's investigation showed the following distribution of their names:

[55] *Ibid.*, pp. 66 ff.

(1) Eighteen names taken from the agricultural-vegetable king-dom, such as: "birch month," "leaf-fall," "oak month," "blossoming month," and "hay month."

(2) Nine names taken from the animal kingdom connected with agriculture and means of subsistence, such as: "cuckoo month" and "dove month."

(3) Seventeen names taken from natural phenomena generally, such as: "winter month," "snowing month," and "dry month."

(4) Ten names taken from the periodically recurring activities, such as: "sowing month," "plowing month," "seeding," "mowing," "the harvester," and "the sickle."

(5) Twenty-five names taken from religious and social customs and festivals, such as: "Christmas," "The Virgin," "Nicholas," "All Saints'," and "Rosalia."

(6) A few unexplained and Latin names, such as: "May," "April," and "March."

A similar picture is presented by the old German, Anglo-Saxon, Danish, and Scandinavian names of "months," and by those of many other peoples.[56]

Thus the periods of the seasons or months quite clearly show the predominantly social nature and origin of the periodization; the rhythm of social life and social events is mainly reflected in them, and serves as the main point of time reference and time apprehension. All these divisions have little in common with natural phenomena as such, are little related to them, and are little due to them in their origin and nature.

However, these months or seasons do not really divide "the year" in our sense into the above number of seasons or months. The primi-tive peoples apprehend only the sequence of the seasons, and a year, as we know it, is unknown to them. It is unimportant to them whether the total number of seasons fills the year (in our sense), whether the seasons are equal, or whether the same season in two years is of an equal length. They do not care about this quantitative equality, and consequently their seasons are unequal. The same season in two years may be of different length and placed at different points of our year,

[56] *Ibid.*, pp. 226 ff.; Ginzel, *op. cit., passim;* H. Webster, *Rest-Days* (New York, 1916); B. Landsberger, "Der kultische Kalender der Babylonier und Assyrier," *Leipziger Semit. Studien* (1915), VI (1-2); A. Yermolloff, *Der landwirtschaftliche Volkskalender der Russen* (Leipzig, 1905).

because the phases of agricultural or other occupations do not occupy an equal length of time; they shift from year to year in their place in the year time, sometimes coming a month or so earlier or later, and have different lengths. The seasons of primitive peoples are a reflection of their occupational and religious activities; and since these are unequal and shift, the seasons also shift and are unequal. Besides, primitive peoples do not know continuous time. The "between-seasons" time is neither reckoned nor measured; it is as though it was nonexistent.

This is made clear as we consider what may be regarded as an equivalent to our year.

Originally the year does not exist as a numerical quantity, the *pars pro toto* counting being resorted to, [and] the years are not reckoned as members of an era but are distinguished and fixed by concrete events. The uniting of the different seasons into a complete year only takes place gradually.[57]

Thus their year is something very different from ours:

For the Dyaks the rice-harvest is a main division of the year: in September, after the conclusion of the harvest the year is at an end. . . . [Among many other people] when they begin to cultivate the yam-fields, they begin a new year; when the yams are dug up and the dry grass is burnt away, a year has passed [though the whole time from the beginning to the end of harvesting occupies only a part of our "year"].

Generally, a year

. . . does not denote any definite number of months: the sense is rather "to plant and eat, to plant it again and harvest it." At the end of the harvest the year is also at an end.[58]

The remaining time is socially unimportant. It does not count and is not reckoned with: it is empty or almost nonexistent.

Finally, primitive time indication or time reckoning has many other "artificial" periods of time, which are still purer in their social nature. Such are "the market weeks," "rest days," feast periods," and "religious and ceremonial periods" which come either periodically after four, five, six, seven, nine, ten, sixteen, or more days ("weeks" of these lengths are found among many peoples). These break the stream of time into segments and serve as the point of reference (for location of other events in time-flows), or they come nonperiodically, in connection with

---

[57] Nilsson, *op. cit.*, pp. 86 ff.   [58] *Ibid.*, pp. 90-91.

some important social event expressed in a festival or ceremony which, in its turn, is due to some important phase in the life of the group—such as harvesting ("agrarian-festival cycle"), hunting, the end of the fishing season, and the like.[59]

For many of such festivals the members of the tribe, usually dispersed, come together. In order to be able to come together, they have to "come to an understanding" as to the time and place of the festivals. Mutual co-ordination of behavior becomes absolutely necessary. Various devices are used: a rope with a definite number of knots denoting the number of "days" or "hours" up to the moment of the festival, use of the tally, the Peruvian quipos, notched sticks, and similar primitive "watches." In the tribes where festivals have been repeated many times, the members are accustomed to the time of their celebration, and the festivals are the main marks of their time calendar.[60]

[For instance, among many tribes of Bolivia] their knowledge of the calendar is not according to days, but according to the principal festivals. In the Babylonian calendar the names of months derived from festivals spread more and more.[61]

Let us stop for a moment and grasp the meaning of all these facts. In the evenly flowing mathematical time, there are no divisions into "weeks," "weekdays," and "rest or market days"; into the periodic and nonperiodic festival days or periods; into "bad and good" or "lucky and unlucky times." Even the natural phenomena and their periodicities do not account for such "artificial periodization" and "breaking" of time. All this is due to and reflects the rhythm of the sociocultural life of the group (its economic, occupational, religious, vital, and other rhythms of activities). While we are accustomed in a degree to measure the duration of various events and processes by quantitative mathematical time units (such as hour, day, month, and year, each unit being equal to the other), among the primitive peoples, their social events and activities determine and measure the mathematical and quantitative time, making it qualitative and nonmathematical. Time there is but a mirror of the daily or seasonal or "weekly" or annual activities of the group and its members. These activities are the time units; they are the points of reference (before or after or during

[59] *Ibid.*, chap. xiii. See also F. H. Colson, *The Week: An Essay on the Origin and Development of the Seven-Day Cycle* (Cambridge, 1926).

[60] Nilsson, *op. cit.*, pp. 319 ff. See also Webster, *op. cit.*

[61] Nilsson, *op. cit.*, p. 319.

or as long as) for other social and nonsocial phenomena. Their order
determines the sequential apprehension of other phenomena. Where
we are prone to say: "The depression lasted three years, seven months,"
they would say: "What you style three years, seven months, is as long
as a depression period," where this period would be a unit by itself.
Where we would say: "The first World War started twenty years
ago," they would say: "It was as long ago as the time elapsed since
the first World War."

E. Durkheim rightly says:

Try to represent what the notion of time would be without the processes
by which we divide and measure it. . . . This is something unthinkable!
Now what is the origin of this differentiation [of time into days, weeks,
years]? It is not so much our personal experience because it is not *my time*
that is thus arranged; it is time in general. . . . That alone is enough to give
us a hint that such an arrangement ought to be collective. The divisions
into days, weeks, months, years, etc. correspond to the periodical recurrence
of rites, feasts, and public ceremonies. A calendar expresses the rhythm of
the collective activities, while at the same time its function is to assure their
regularity.[61]

H. Hubert and M. Mauss, in their study of the time representations
in magic and religion, stressed a series of the fundamental differences
between the mathematical, purely quantitative time and the religious
and magical time. Just as space in magic and religion differs from the
geometrical space by its qualitativeness (as "sacred" and "profane"
areas), similarly the religious and magical time is qualitative, not infinitely divisible, and not homogeneous. The essentials of their argu-
mentation follow:

Since rites are performed at certain periods, a timing of the co-ordinated collective actions is a necessary condition of the magical and
religious rites. These are situated in a time environment. Here lies
one of the most important sources of the origin of the calendar, of
various systems of time reckoning, or of collective organization and
externalization of time. The magical and religious calendar is one of
the earliest calendars, and continues to exist often after an introduction of the mathematical calendar. Hubert and Mauss state:

[62] E. Durkheim, *The Elementary Forms of Religious Life*, quoted, pp. 10-17 **and**
419 ff. Cf. Erich Voegelin, "Die Zeit in der Wirtschaft," *Archiv für Sozialwissenschaft
und Sozialpolitik*, 53. Bd., 1. Heft, 1924.

But for religion and magic the object of the calendar is not to measure, but to punctuate or to rhythm the time [to cut into links, sacred and profane, the time devoted to the performance of rites and the "empty" ones]. Rites are necessarily distributed in time divided by the fixed points distanced from one another; and religious representations suppose equally a rhythm of time in which durations of all kinds, and especially the divine durations, are passing [various religious periods: millenniums, calpas, periods of fastings, holidays, weeks, Easter, Christmas, etc., of the Christian and other religions].

Such a rhythm of time is very different from any mathematical division of time.

The following are the most important characteristics of religious and magical time:

(1) "The successive parts of times are not homogeneous." The parts that appear to us equal and equivalent quantitatively are neither equal nor equivalent in magic and religion. Only the "slices" of time that are considered identical in their relationship to the religious or magical value are equivalent in the religious and magical calendar (though, quantitatively, they may be quite different). This means that, for religion and magic, time is not a mere quantity, and "the cycle of the calendar periods is but one of the particular systems of the critical dates and intervals which turn around in the time process."

(2) "The critical dates interrupt the time continuity." Time in which religious and magic phenomena pass is discontinuous; it does not flow evenly, but has "cuts" in its marching. Its elements are not identical. The critical moments or links are different from those which precede and follow them. This means that a society whose existence and activities are divided into various rhythmical periods of seven or nine or another specified number of days, weeks, months, years, imposes the rhythms upon the time durations which otherwise do not have any rhythms, any "cuts," or any periodicities whatever.

(3) The critical periods (such as holidays or fasting periods) as well as the intervals between two critical dates are, each by itself, indivisible and unbreakable. They are real units. An act (of purification or sin) committed at a critical period fills the whole interval and extends its influence over the whole of such an interval (contaminates or purifies it for its whole length). Consequently, such an interval becomes impenetrable for any other influences and is a real unit of time.

Thus time here has a spasmodic character and is indivisible beyond the critical periods and the intervals between them.

(4) The durations quantitatively equal figure often as unequal, and vice versa. Only the periods whose qualities (in regard to religious and social values) are similar will be similar, regardless of their quantitative duration; and the identical quantities of time—but different in their qualities—will be dissimilar.

Thus in magical and religious representations of time, "there is something else besides the quantitative considerations of more or less." There is "a notion of the active qualities whose presence or absence makes corresponding periods similar or dissimilar." "The parts of time are not indifferent to the things which may occur in them. The parts either attract or reject them." (Hence astrological prognostications, lucky and unlucky days, or parts of time where luck and bad luck happen just by virtue of the time-moment; various taboos of performance of various actions at a certain period of time, etc.) "The dates are the signs or signatures of the things which pass by."

All this means that the idea of time and its divisions is to a great degree a *social convention*. These divisions into various periods are reflections of social rhythms of activities; these are their basis. And from this standpoint, the original and real function of the calendar was to serve as an indicator of which periods had to be celebrated by festivals and ceremonies. "The calendar was an order of the periodicity of rites," but not a measurement of time as a pure quantity. Only later on were the quality and the things associated with different periods of time detached from time, giving us the abstract, mathematical time as a pure quantity, infinitely divisible, homogeneous, continuous, and evenly passing.[63]

A somewhat similar conclusion is drawn by another disciple of Durkheim, Dr. M. Halbwachs, who considered the problem from another angle—namely, from that of memory. Memory is a most essential condition for apprehension of time, and especially for the localization of various events in the infinite time process. Since it is so, the questions arise: How is memory possible? What are its essential conditions? Is it a mere psychological quality of the individual mind,

[63] See H. Hubert and M. Mauss, "Etude sommaire de la représentation du temps dans la religion et la magie," *Mélanges d'histoire des religions* (Paris, 1909), pp. 189-229. See also Levy-Bruhl, *op. cit.*

or is it something more; and does it require some other conditions besides a normally functioning brain?

The answer to these questions is that one of the indispensable conditions of memory is a "social framework" or "social milieu."

Memory depends upon social milieu. It is in society usually that man acquires his souvenirs and in it also that they are recollected, recognized and localized. There is a collective memory and a social framework of it.[64]

Without this social framework of memory, an individual would be similar to the above-mentioned girl of nine or ten years old, found in the forest in 1731, near Châlons. In our recollection of anything, in order to remember it, and to place it in the time process correctly in regard to other things, we need several points of reference to other events and circumstances, amidst which a recollected phenomenon took place. Usually, the role of these points of reference is played mainly by various social phenomena (persons, members of the family, school, church, and so forth). In this way, the social world serves as a framework of our memory.

If, for a moment, we were to imagine that all the social points of reference have been taken away, our memory at once would be enormously impoverished, disorganized, and even destroyed to a great degree. This is especially true of the recollections experienced by us indirectly, through the testimony of other persons and groups. For instance, without "the collective memory" or "social framework," time sequences of a greater part of historical events would disappear. But even as regards our direct experiences, many of them could not be recollected, or rightly placed in the time process, without the testimony of other persons, groups, and various social objects. Our individual memory rapidly "evaporates," quickly forgets many things, and still more rapidly distorts facts that happened some time ago. In all such cases, the group and other persons who were connected with the event, and the social "documents" on which it was fixed, are the witnesses through which our memory could be "revived," enriched, and corrected. In this sense, again the social milieu is an indispensable condition of our memory and our time apprehension.

Every recollection, however personal it may be, even our recollections of our thoughts and unexpressed sentiments, is always in relation to the whole

[64] Halbwachs, *Les Cadres sociaux de la mémoire,* quoted, pp. viii-ix.

ensemble of notions possessed by many others, with persons, groups, places, dates, words, or forms of language spoken, with beliefs and ideas—in brief, with the whole material and moral life of the groups of which we are or have been members.[65]

Any reconstruction of the past, including our personal past, is almost impossible without this social framework of memory. It is impossible outside of "society," because, for any localized recollection, a verbal description of it is necessary (place, date, names, words uttered, actions done, thoughts experienced, and so forth). Meanwhile, language itself is already a social phenomenon. Insofar as it rarely can be revived and localized without this "vehicle of recollection," the social milieu is present in practically all recollections and apprehension of time. It is also shown by the fact that man's memory undergoes a disorganization when he is more or less completely detached from society.

Thus, without a "social framework," memory becomes exceedingly poor and limited quantitatively, distorted qualitatively, and in many cases generally impossible. Insofar as time apprehension itself becomes impossible without memory, we see thus that a social framework of references is an indispensable condition for apprehension or reckoning of time itself. Without a "collective memory," there would be no history; no possibility of reconstructing the past, which extends for hundreds or thousands of years back; no possibility of apprehending the sequence or simultaneity of millions of facts and events. In that case, each of us would be living in a universe exceedingly limited in time and space.

Having indicated the differences of sociocultural time from the other times, in application to the primitive peoples, let us consider now whether these differences still exist in the time apprehension of modern peoples; whether their social and mathematical times are identical; and finally, whether the mathematical time is fit for the determination of the time relationships of sociocultural phenomena.

Sociocultural Time in Modern Societies. We saw that, among the primitive peoples, time is "social" in nature. What is the situation in modern societies? Did mathematical time drive out sociocultural

---

[65] *Ibid.*, pp. 49-52. See also the experimental data on the distortion of the durations and of the sequence of events in Moore, *op. cit.*, pp. 5-6. He rightly concludes: "Timeposts [important events] and not consciousness of elapsed time intervals govern our estimates of time."

time within these societies? And does now our sociocultural time coincide with the mathematical time of mechanics?

There is no doubt that, *in the course of time, the concrete time indication has been more and more replaced by a time-reckoning system which began, more and more, to employ as a unified point of reference the rotation of the moon, the sun, and was finally replaced by the earth rotation as an exclusive point of time reference.* Parallel to that, time apprehension tended to become less and less qualitative, and more and more quantitative. Thus there seems to have been a definite trend toward "quantitative and mathematical time." As the history of the calendar shows, this process has been exceedingly slow, has moved erratically, and has resulted in various calendar systems; but its trend has, nevertheless, been toward "quantitativization" and "mathemativization" of time.[66]

Shall we conclude from this that, in the modern societies, there is no difference between the sociocultural and mathematical times; that there is only one mathematical time, fit for all purposes, making unnecessary any sociocultural time which differs from it?

Such a conclusion would be rash, *first, because the trend mentioned is not as yet completely accomplished; second, because sociocultural time still exists and is as alive as in the past, side by side with mathematical time; and third, because, as we have seen, mathematical time itself is in a conspicuous degree a variety of sociocultural time and has come into existence through a play of sociocultural circumstances enlarging the net of interaction of a society.*

We have seen that the primitive and local system of reference to the local sociocultural phenomena as a means of co-ordination and synchronization is sufficient only as long as it concerns the local group having uniform rhythms of its activities. When, however, the contact and interaction have gone beyond the one group and extended over many other groups, with different rhythms of sociocultural life, with different systems of critical dates, such a local system ceases to function satisfactorily. In one group, "the harvest festival" is (in our terms) in July; in another, it is in January. If a member of one group informs a member of another that they will meet on "the second night of the harvest festival," they evidently will never meet. In brief, when inter-

[66] For a discussion of the details, see Ginzel, *op. cit.*; Nilsson, *op. cit.*; and Webster, *op. cit.*

course extends over many groups with different rhythms of sociocultural activities and time indications, *the concrete and local systems of sociocultural time cease to perform satisfactorily the function of co-ordination and synchronization of their activities. Hence the urgent need to establish such a standardized system of time reckoning as would be equally comprehensible for all the groups involved, and would serve equally all the groups as the uniform point of time reference for the co-ordination and synchronization of their activities.*

These widely divergent groups had to turn to something that could serve as a kind of Esperanto with respect to the element of time, equally comprehensible for all of them. Such an Esperanto of time reference was found more and more in some of the natural phenomena, particularly in the motion of the moon, the sun, and of some of the stars (especially the Pleiades). These "time indicators" move independently from the different sociocultural rhythms; thus all social activities could be "timed" and synchronized with them. Hence the emergence of this "standardized" system of time reference.

The history of calendars and chronology clearly shows this development. At the beginning, when the motions of the moon, the sun, the planets, or the Pleiades were known inadequately, various peoples used them as a rough and inaccurate system of time reckoning. Hence the inadequate "lunar months" and "lunar year," or the "solar month and solar year."[67]

More and more, the sun and moon became a "common Esperanto" for the time co-ordination and synchronization of the activities of various groups. This explains why, with the "internationalization" of society, scholars began to study their motion more and more intensively; to compute and measure them more and more accurately. It also explains why astronomy and astrology began to be cultivated and developed by the priests and magicians and "scholars" of the ancient Babylonian, Egyptian, and Central American societies, as well as among the Greeks, Romans, and other peoples; this cultivation was not a mere matter of scientific curiosity, but the result of a most urgent sociocultural need. The governments, too, began to foster the research,

[67] For the history of the calendars of the Egyptians, Babylonians, Hebrews, Greeks, Romans, and other peoples with diverse durations and systems of computations, see instructive details in the works of Ginzel, *op. cit.*, and Nilsson. See also G. Friedrich, *Die Geschichtszahlen der Alten sind Kalendarzahlen* (Leipzig, 1910); W. Schultz, *Zeitrechnung und Weltordnung* (Leipzig, 1924); Mayher, *op. cit.*; and Colson, *op. cit.*

and they had to do so because an accurate knowledge of the motion of these universal time indicators became the most vital social necessity. The more intercourse was extended between the various groups and peoples, the more these uniform time indicators began to be used. When finally the system of Copernicus came into existence, the astronomical or mathematical system of time reference based upon the earth's revolution was established and accepted by all "internationalized" societies.

Such was the main trend of the evolution of the systems of time reckoning. It testifies to the fact that the evolution was due to the most urgent social need; that its main factor was the social factor in the form of an extension of the system of interaction of the societies. The emergence of this mathematical system was a reflection of the changes in the field of social interaction. From this standpoint, the standardized mathematical time is a mere variety of the same sociocultural time, as conventional as any system of time reckoning.[68]

This "socially standardized" or "mathematical" time still performs the same function of co-ordination and synchronization of human activities. One of the most important satellites of this "socially standardized time" through which it operates is its child, the *watch*. The watch is an incarnation and materialization of this standardized "quantitative" time. It came into existence parallel with the emergence of mathematical or socially standardized time. It emerged *in the urban aggregates,* where persons and groups from all parts of the universe, with different mores, rhythms, activities, and systems of time reckoning are grouped together, and where an accurate and absolutely uniform time reckoning is a vital necessity. Simmel remarks properly that it was with the city that the watch entered into existence.

The relationships and affairs of the typical urban resident are so manifold and so complicated, and, above all, urban relationships and activities are interwoven into an organism of so many parts through the agglomeration of so many persons with such differentiated interests, that the whole would break down into an inextricable chaos, without the most exact punctuality in promises and performances.[69]

[68] The very choice of the moon or the sun or other natural phenomenon for the indicator of time is a sociocultural convention. See some remarks on the conventional elements in astronomical time in Hubert and Mauss, *op. cit.,* pp. 213-219.

[69] G. Simmel, "Large Cities and Mental Life," in P. Sorokin, C. Zimmerman, and C. Galpin, *A Systematic Source Book in Rural Sociology,* quoted, I, 244.

This explains why a watch of any kind emerged in urban and "international" aggregates, and why the ancestor of the modern watch began to diffuse in Europe only after the fourteenth century—that is, only when the urbanization of Europe progressed notably. The same considerations explain why even now, in rural districts of the same country, a watch is used much less than in urban parts; and why, especially in agricultural and so-called "backward" countries, with their homogeneous population and mores, with the quiet local time reckoning and limited area of interaction, a watch is little used, is not necessary, and when possessed by any of the natives, is used as an object of luxury rather than one of necessity.

Side by side with this quantitative time, we still have a full-blooded sociocultural time, not so much quantitative as qualitative, similar to the time of primitive groups.

Factually, our living time does not flow evenly, is discontinuous, and is cut into various qualitative links of different value. The first form of this qualitative division is given by our *week*. Mathematical or cosmic time flows evenly, and no weeks are given in it. Our time is broken into weeks and week links. We live by the week; we are paid and hired by the week; we compute time by weeks; many fairs and markets take place once in a week; we walk and exercise or rest so many times a week. In brief, our life has a weekly rhythm. More than that: within a week, the days have a different physiognomy, structure, and tempo of activities.[70] Sunday especially stands alone, being quite different from the weekdays as regards activities, occupations, sleep, recreation, meals, social enjoyments, dress, reading, even radio programs and newspapers.[71] The Fourth Commandment and similar taboos of other religions separate it clearly as a "sacred day" from the

[70] See P. A. Sorokin and C. Berger, *Time-Budgets of Human Behavior* (Cambridge, Mass., 1939), where it is shown that each weekday has its own structure of activities different from that of other days of the week and similar from week to week, in the behavior of some 103 persons studied.

W. James aptly says: "An ingenious friend of mine was long puzzled to know why each day of the week had such a characteristic physiognomy for him. That of Sunday was soon noticed to be due to the cessation of the city's rumbling, and the sound of people's feet shuffling on the sidewalk; of Monday, to come from the clothes drying in the yard and casting a white reflection on the ceiling; of Tuesday, etc. . . . Probably each hour in the day has for most of us some outer or inner sign associated with it as closely as these signs with the day of the week" (*op. cit.*, I, 623).

[71] See the facts in Sorokin and Berger, *op. cit., passim*.

rest of the "profane" days of the week.[72] All this is well known to anyone by direct personal experience.

The widely current opinion that the week or other sociocultural divisions of time are determined by astronomical phenomena is far from being true.[73] A week of any kind is a purely sociocultural creation, reflecting the rhythm of sociocultural life but not the revolution of the moon, sun, or other natural phenomena. Most human societies have some kind of week, and their very difference between weeks is evidence of their independence from astronomical phenomena. There are "weeks" consisting of three, four, five, six, seven, eight, nine, sixteen, and more days. The Khasi week almost universally consists of eight days, because the markets are usually held every eighth day. A reflection of the fact that the Khasi week had a social rather than a "natural" origin is found in the names of the days of the week, which are not those of planets (a late and arbitrary development), but of places where the principal markets are held. In similar fashion, the Roman week was marked by *nundinae*, which recurred every eighth day and upon which the agriculturists came into the city to sell their produce. The Muysca in Bogotá had a three-day week; many West African tribes, a four-day week; the peoples of Central America, the East Indian Archipelago, old Assyria (and now Soviet Russia), a five-day week; the population of Togo, a six-day week; the ancient Hebrews and most contemporary civilized societies, a seven-day week; the Romans, Khasis, and many African tribes, an eight-day week; and the Incas, a ten-day week.

The constant feature of virtually all these weeks of varying lengths is that they were always found to have been originally associated with the market.[74] Colson indicates quite clearly that the earliest forms of the continuous week of which we have any knowledge had nothing to do with the moon.[75] The appearance and spread of this time unit was always in conjunction with some periodically observed social event, and did not come about through observation of the heavenly bodies. Moreover, as Hutton Webster perspicuously suggests, some phase of the social structure usually accounts for the variations in the length of the week.

---

[72] See esp. in Durkheim, *Elementary Forms of Religious Life,* quoted, *passim.*

[73] "It should not be forgotten that astronomy and the calendar are not identical. In matters of the calendar, practical utility is welcomed more than refined astronomical calculations." See Nilsson, *op. cit.,* p. 281.

[74] *Ibid.,* p. 363.   [75] Colson, *op. cit.,* pp. 3 and 112-113.

The shorter intervals of three, four, and five days reflect the simple economy of primitive life, since the market must recur with sufficient frequency to permit neighboring communities, who keep on hand no large stocks of food and other necessaries, to obtain them from one another. The longer cycles of six, eight, and ten days, much less common, apparently arise by doubling the earlier period, whenever it is desired to hold a great market for the produce of a wide area.[76]

[Our week's] septenary division has not arisen from the phases of the moon, but on the contrary the phases of the moon have been arranged in accordance with the septenary scheme.[77]

The "lunar" week differs vitally from [our] continuous week, and the earlier forms of the continuous week had nothing to do with the moon or the month.[78]

The lunar month is about twenty-nine and a half days and deviates quantitatively from the seven-day week. If the lunar month were computed in seven-day weeks, soon there would be a great discrepancy between such four-week months and the "lunar months," or the real phases of the moon.

As stated, the Graeco-Roman week originally was of eight days. At some time, around the third century of our era, it began to be replaced more and more by the seven-day cycle or week. The rhythm of social life changed, and its change led to a change in the week or the unit of sociocultural time.[79] There were probably several main sources of our week, and all of them sociocultural in character: the influence of the seven-day Jewish week transmitted through the early Christians; the influence of such ideologies as the religious cults of Mithraism and some other Oriental cults; the belief in astrology, which became quite diffused at that time and which tried to establish a seven-day period in honor of the seven planets.[80]

Like other weeks, our week is not a natural time period but a reflection of the social rhythm of our life. It functions in hundreds of forms as an indivisible unit of time, with its Sundays and weekdays. Imagine for a moment that the week suddenly disappeared. What a havoc would be created in our time organization, in our behavior, in

---

[76] Webster, op. cit., pp. 117-118.

[77] Nilsson, op. cit., p. 330, also chap. xiii on the "week." See esp. Ginzel's monumental work, op. cit.   [78] Colson, op. cit., p. 3.

[79] We have seen a similar change of the rhythm of social life in Soviet Russia when the seven-day week was replaced by the five-day week. This shows the purely social nature of "week" division of time, and also its indispensability in some form or the other.   [80] For details, see Colson, op. cit.

the co-ordination and synchronization of collective activities and social life, and especially in our time apprehension. Many of us would certainly mix our appointments, shift and change our activities, and fail many times to fulfill our engagements.[81] If there were neither the names of the days nor weeks, we would be liable to be lost in an endless series of days—as gray as fog—and confuse one day with another and one routine with another. We think in week units; we apprehend time in week units; we localize the events and activities in week units; we co-ordinate our behavior according to the "week"; we live and feel and plan and wish in "week" terms. It is one of the most important points of our "orientation" in time and social reality.

But the week is not the only form of sociocultural time unit that exists among us. The next qualitative time unit is our *month*. Month links of time are again purely artificial, sociocultural "cut-outs" of time. The duration of the month is not necessarily fixed by the phases of the moon. Mommsen states, for example, that, among the Romans, there was a calendar system "which practically was quite irrespective of the lunar course" and which led to the adoption of "months of arbitrary length."[82]

This disregard of the moon's course in the determination of month durations has continued to the present. Unequal periods of astronomical time are socially equated, as is evidenced by the practice of paying monthly salaries. The equality of months is conventional, not astronomical. Months do not exist in evenly flowing cosmic or purely quantitative time, especially such curious months as ours: one of thirty-one days, another of thirty days and one of twenty-nine and even twenty-eight days! What a curious tempo for the poor moon to follow if our months were a prescription for her how to wax and wane, or copies of her real movement. As a matter of fact, our months run in one way and the moon moves in quite a different way; but they have little in common and consequently do not embarrass each other. "Our

[81] F. H. Colson summarizes the functional importance of social definitions of time intervals: "How do we ourselves remember the days of the week? The obvious answer is that something happens on one or more of them. If by some means or other we lose count in the course of the week, Sunday is unmistakable, even if personally we have no religious feeling for the day. So, too, school half-holidays or early-closing days force themselves on the notice of those who are not directly affected by them. But if nothing happens it is very doubtful whether a week-sequence could maintain, much less establish, itself." See *ibid.*, p. 63.

[82] T. Mommsen, *History of Rome* (New York, 1885), I, 279. In connection with this subject, see all of chap. xv.

twelve months have no relation to the planets from which they receive their names,"[83] and many varieties of months among other peoples are again "artificial"—that is, social creations, which in the past reflected faithfully the sequence of main activities of a group.

Like the week, a month is an indivisible unit of sociocultural time. We live by months and have hundreds of monthly rhythms in our social processes. We use them as the point of reference in our time orientation and time apprehension. If we eliminate months from the year, a great deal of confusion results in our time orientation and co-ordination of social activities. Like the week, our months are again colored by qualities. There are "good and bad," "lucky and unlucky," "easy and hard" months. Months of vacation and labor, social life and cessation of social life; months of city life and of country life; and other qualitative monthly pulsations of social life of a given society.

The same is true of the *year*. We saw that many people do not have any year, while many others have quite different years, showing nothing in common with either the lunar or the solar year. Some employ the *lunar,* others the *solar* year. This variety of the year already shows its social nature.[84] If one of these years is based on the sun's revolution, this is just a convenient way of acquiring a "common-time denominator" for different societies. In this sense, it is also a social convention. But if this convention coincides with "nature" to some extent, in other respects our year is again a purely social or artificial creation. Take, for instance, the *beginning* of the year. Where and when in nature, or in the sun's revolution, is it prescribed to begin January 1 at midnight and to end December 31 at midnight? Nowhere and never. It is a "social" convention, different among different peoples. Does it play some part in our time orientation, behavior, and social life? Certainly, and a great one, similar to the week and the month.

The rhythm of social life is cut in yearly links. There are annual sociocultural rhythms.[85] The point is, not that the mathematical length of these rhythms is equal to so many mathematical seconds or hours,

---

[83] Colson, *op. cit.,* pp. 1-2.

[84] Even now, there are several "years": "the tropical year" (365.24219879 days), the sidereal year (longer roughly by twenty minutes than the tropical year), the anomalistic year (365 days, 6 hours, 13 minutes, 53 seconds and a fraction), and finally the civil years of the Gregorian and Julian calendars, which are again different from the others and from each other. This shows a conventionality of even our years.

[85] See Sorokin, *Dynamics,* Vol. IV, chaps. ix and xi.

but that the rhythms of annual duration are one unbreakable unity corresponding to the annual rhythm of social life.[86]

Take further a series of years. How do we orient ourselves in their infinite sequence? The years stretch endlessly back into the past and on into the future. How do we find our place on this infinite time-bridge? Through natural signs? Not at all. We orient ourselves through reference to this or that important or conspicuous social event: "before the first World War," "after the Russian Revolution," "the time of the Reformation," of "the French Revolution," "the Middle Ages" ("Middle" is used in a very relative and purely sociocultural sense), "before and after Christ," and so on. In thousands of forms, we make such "references."

In a more uniform way, we refer to our *era* as "A.D. 1942." Other societies do the same, with their own socially important points of reference. It is curious to note that, *in this field, there does not exist any "natural" or "mathematical" universal point of reference.* This means that our long "cut-outs" of time are purely social and have only social buoys for our orientation.[87] Possibly for this reason, the eras of different peoples are still different. Without the eras, we find ourselves lost on the endless "bridge of time." With their help, we apprehend a part of this endless bridge, from the era to a given moment and some short distance beyond the era (a few centuries, or from two to four thousand years), the other part of the bridge remaining in a state of empty darkness for us.

The same is to be said of the *seasons,* which mean the *social* rather than the *natural* seasons.

Our *day,*[88] *hour, minute,* and *second* are also artificial durations, standardized, it is true, with the help of the watch, but still "artificial" because, in astronomical time, there are no such divisions. A series of

[86] For instance, when in England January 1 was introduced as the beginning of a new year, there was a riot, and the noble lord (Chesterfield) was nearly cut to pieces to the cry of: "Give us back our three months." See C. Nordman, *The Tyranny of Time* (London, 1925), p. 33.
This shows how arbitrarily we shift, lengthen, and shorten our time.

[87] "In the eternal wave which rocks us, carries us along and soon swallows us up, there is no rock to which we can fasten our frail barque; the very buoys we put out to measure our course are only floating mirages; and on the mysterious foundation of things our anchors slide along and fail to bite." See *ibid.,* p. 217.

[88] There are several days even now: from sunrise to sunset, the mean solar day, the sidereal day, and our "watch-time day," which very often depends on the accuracy of the watch.

our special days, *holidays*—"Memorial Day," "Christmas," "Washington's Birthday," "Fourth of July," and so forth—have again nothing to do with the purely quantitative time, and represent only certain qualitative marks of time purely social in their nature and quite real in their distinctness and in their functions as the points of time reference.

Take a further division of the day into twelve or twenty-four hours.[89] Such a division and the hour units are again "artificial," or a social convention. Still more obvious social conventions are *Central, Eastern,* and *Pacific standard time.* A still greater social convention is *daylight-saving time,* which shows how we "contract" and "expand" time, adding or subtracting one or more hours and shifting the time from one point to another.[90]

Any *calendar* system is full of such "conventional" marks, and the time process is constantly being intercepted by them. These marks—but not the number of mathematical units of time—serve as the points of our time reference. Any calendar is determined by and reflects the social pulsations of the life of a given group.

Within the same territorial aggregate, *composed out of different religious, occupational, economic, national, and cultural groups, there are different rhythms and pulsations, and therefore different calendars and different conventions for the sociocultural time of each of these groups.* Every year Harvard University issues its calendar. Compare it from year to year, and you will see how time is shifted there, by the mere decision of the administration. Compare further a Harvard calendar with one operating, say, among factory workers. They are very different in regard to holidays, the beginning and end of the "school" and of the factory year, vacation periods, and in other respects. The calendar of the Roman Catholics in Boston—in part, at least—is differ-

[89] "Nothing in the nature of things as presented to us obliges us to divide the day into 24 hours. The hour is a perfectly arbitrary unit of time, just as the metre is an artificial unit of length which nothing suggests to the exclusion of any other." See Nordman, *op. cit.,* p. 101.

[90] Again in our establishing the watch time we are quite conventional. In Paris, the difference between the official noon and true noon on November 3 is 16½ minutes, plus 9 minutes and 21 seconds—a total of nearly 26 minutes. This difference attains 47 minutes at Strasbourg. If the clocks marked the "true hours by the sun" at every place, they could not show the same hour simultaneously in different towns, or even in different parts of the city. "These differences are more serious than one would think. In the neighborhood of London, they amount to 6 seconds for each mile of travel either towards the east or towards the west. In Paris, local mean noon occurs 37 seconds earlier at the bridge of Charenton than it does at the Point du Jour." See *ibid.,* p. 111.

This shows why even our clock time is conventional to a considerable degree.

ent from that of the Protestant Bostonians, and both are different from those of the Jewish or Russian Orthodox Bostonians. Similarly, the calendars of the Boston Chinese or Hindu are different from each other and from the calendar of the Europeans.

The above shows, indeed, that in our modern society, side by side with quantitative time (which itself is in a degree a social convention), there exists a full-blooded sociocultural time as a convention, with all its "earmarks": it is qualitative; it is not infinitely divisible; its units are different from purely quantitative units; it does not flow on evenly, as a mere quantity; it is determined by social conditions, and reflects the rhythms and pulsations of the social life of a given group. The quantitative aspect of this time can be "translated" into the units of mathematical time; but such a "translation" remains just that, and often adds little either to its reality or to its service as an agency of time orientation, time co-ordination, and synchronization of the collective activities of the members of the group and outsiders. This social time and its dates have always existed independently of quantitative time.

WHY PURELY QUANTITATIVE TIME CANNOT REPLACE SOCIOCULTURAL TIME AND IS INADEQUATE FOR A STUDY OF SOCIOCULTURAL PHENOMENA

After the preceding analysis, it is easy to understand why purely quantitative time cannot entirely replace qualitative sociocultural time, either in the performance of its sociocultural functions or in the study of sociocultural phenomena. If we try to replace sociocultural time by a purely quantitative time, time becomes devitalized. *It loses its reality, and we find ourselves in an exceedingly difficult position in our efforts to orient ourselves in the time process, to find out "where we are" and where are the other social phenomena on "the bridge of time." Likewise, any co-ordination and synchronization of the collective activities becomes exceedingly difficult.*

Imagine for a moment that all the above social conventions in regard to time are taken away; the beginning of the year, the week, the month, Christmas, special dates and holidays, the era, and so on. Imagine further that we cease to orient ourselves in time by reference to any social event or phenomenon. What would be the outcome? We would be lost in time. We would have an unlimited number of the units of mathematical time at our disposal: billions, trillions, quintillions of seconds. With mathematical precision, we can use our fund of seconds to measure the various durations. But from what point shall we start measuring and to what end? Since mathematical time is continuous and flows evenly, its flow is intercepted by no "marks," no "critical dates," no "points of reference," no "eras," no "beginning of the year," no "holidays," no "events," no caesura from which we can start our measurement and through which we can localize the events on the time bridge.

More than that: if a point of reference were given, the purely quantitative measurement of time and time localization of events would be an exceedingly difficult operation. To say that, from this moment up to such and such a moment, there remain or have elapsed 10,563,744 mathematically equal minutes or days, while for another event the time distance is 3,649 mathematical hours, for a third 476 days, and for a fourth 375 mathematical years, would be difficult to remember; and it would be still more difficult to keep such an infinite number of figures in our memory for use in our activities and orientation. Since the units are identical and colorless, the difficulty would be still greater. Each man would have to become a counting machine, using a great part of his time just for these computations of various dates and time distances between various phenomena.

This picture shows why translation of our colorful sociocultural time into units of purely quantitative time would disorganize our time orientation, our collective activities, and social life generally. Instead of giving us advantages, it would put us into a very disadvantageous situation. As long as a society exists and has its own rhythms, important and unimportant events, tensions and relaxations, critical and noncritical periods, "sacred and profane" moments, ordinary and holy dates—just so long will sociocultural time, with all its characteristics, be a living reality, ineradicable and irreplaceable by the abstract, purely quantitative mathematical time, little fitted either for our orientation in the time flow or for the performance of the most important social functions of social time.

This suggests also some of the inadequacies of purely mathematical time for even a scientific description of sociocultural phenomena.

(1) The first inadequacy of purely quantitative time, as shown in the above imaginary situation, with its dates and conventions, and its absence of sociocultural time, is that it makes an interpretation and

description of many social phenomena practically impossible or meaningless. To say that, "between phenomena X and Y, 604,800 seconds have elapsed" means much less and is more difficult to remember than if we say "a week has passed." It would be simpler and more meaningful if we said "one month" or "one year," rather than giving an enormous number of seconds, hours, or days for such periods. In millions of forms, various concrete sociocultural references—such as: "He came after N.," "See you at Christmas," "At the end of the lecture," "We will talk it over at lunch"—are more easy and convenient for either co-ordination of the activities or for orientation in the time flow.

(2) The second disadvantage is that many a time relationship cannot be described precisely in terms of purely quantitative time. If we say: "Event X occurred 1,942 years after event Y," the statement describes the time distance between the X and Y events. But it does not tell us whether Y happened 1,000 or 500,000 B.C.; consequently, we do not know when X happened. The statement does not give the point of reference for determination of Y-time on the infinite time bridge; consequently, it does not define X either. Without such a point of reference in the form of this or that "era," the whole statement—like millions of similar statements—becomes indeterminate. Neither the sun nor the moon nor other natural phenomenon can give such an era (because we do not know any definite episode in nature which by itself can function as an era). Hence the necessity for some sort of sociocultural date for such a starting point. Without it, the time relationship of most of the phenomena becomes indefinite.

The same is true of many other time relationships. For instance, I do not see how it is possible to describe without some point of reference such time relationships as we describe in the statements: "second part of the week," "at the end of 1931," "hunting season," "This happened during my vacation," "It took place at Christmas," "I shall lecture on Friday," "at 10 P.M. Eastern standard time," "after Commencement," and so forth. It is evident that these statements are meaningful and define rather well the time situation or sequence or simultaneity of two or more phenomena. We understand them perfectly. Their "translation" into such and such a number of seconds or hours would add nothing but the burden of memorizing these figures.

On the other hand, these time relationships cannot be described in terms of purely quantitative time, stripped of all sociocultural conventions, because such a time does not have either "the beginning of the year" or "the week" or "Christmas" or a "hunting season" or "Friday" or "Commencement" or even "Eastern standard time" (the boundary line where Eastern time ends and Central time begins is also a mere convention). All these dates are social conventions and are nonexistent for pure quantitative time. The time relationships discussed are therefore indescribable in terms of this time.

(3) The third disadvantage of purely quantitative time is that it robs time of all its qualities and makes it "deadly gray" and homogeneous. Through this "bleaching," it leads to many unnecessary difficulties and faults. First, since purely quantitative time is equally gray and homogeneous everywhere, there is no possibility of marking it by means of some critical date or conspicuous sign as the point of reference. This leads to the impossibility, just discussed, of description and location of many sequences, simultaneities, and time relationships. Furthermore, where the description is possible ("X happened 3,567,894 hours after Y"), it overtaxes our memory and becomes an unbearable burden. But the main shortcoming is that such a disqualification of time greatly disfigures reality.

In addition to its quantitative aspect, our time has certain qualitative aspects. In our individual and collective experience, various portions of "the time bridge" are not identical in their quality; there are the portions that are "sinful" and "holy," "happy" and "unhappy," "Sabbath" and "weekday," "Christmas" and "Lent," "time of harvest" and "time of sowing," "time of labor" and "time of rest," "waking hours" and "sleeping time," and so on. All these qualities are, in our experience, inseparable from time. Just because they are inseparable, many portions of time have their own qualitative individuality. They are permeated with the pulsating rhythms—different for different periods—of life and reality itself. The knowledge of the main kinds of sociocultural rhythms—no matter whether periodical or not—is by itself a very important knowledge concerning the sociocultural phenomena.[91] Stripped of their specific qualities, all rhythms and punctuations would disappear, and the whole sociocultural life would turn into a kind of a gray flowing fog in which nothing would appear distinct.[92] From the standpoint of science, there is a decided disadvan-

[91] See Sorokin, *Dynamics*, Vol. IV, chaps. viii, ix, xi, and subsequent ones.
[92] Here, from quite a different standpoint, my conclusions about living time—

tage in replacing a living reality by its dead and imperfect diagram.

(4) The fourth disadvantage of purely quantitative time is that it disfigures and impoverishes sociocultural reality in an additional way: *through dividing the indivisible durations of processes and through dissolving the living unities of sociocultural time in the ocean of mechanically identical units of mathematical time.* We have seen that the units of sociocultural time are many and different: day, week, month, year, Christmas, vacation, and so forth. Many periods of sociocultural time, sometimes of a long mathematical duration and easily divisible mathematically, are socially indivisible. They are living unities. When a quantitativist breaks such units into a certain number of seconds, hours, or other equal units, he breaks the living unity of this time portion, distorts the reality, and loses the nature, "wholeness," "meaning," and *"Gestalt"* of such periods. Like a blind partisan of "mathematical anatomy," he cuts all the organisms into equal pieces and, through computation of the number of the pieces, tries to understand the nature and the differences between organisms.

Let us clarify this statement a little. There are many sociocultural time units that are breakable and divisible mathematically but indivisible socioculturally. We rent a room by the day or week or month or year. Perhaps we do not stay a whole day, but only thirteen hours and twenty-five minutes; yet we pay for a day. The same is true in regard to a week, month, and other sociocultural durations agreed upon and unbreakable for the sociocultural purposes involved. We are hired by the hour, by the day, by the week, semester, and so on. If the worker works only fifty-six minutes or sixty-three minutes, he is paid for the one hour agreed upon. The same is true for other sociocultural units; they function as unbreakable, no matter whether the actual duration of the services is a little longer or shorter. Interests or dividends are paid by the quarter year; the residence requirement of a college is one year.

Imprisonment for certain crimes is again definite, be it three months or five years, and is unbreakable under ordinary conditions. In business, promotions are given after a certain fixed unit of time—no

---

qualitative time, so full of its own rhythms—considerably approach Bergson's concept of real time, which is also qualitative and inseparable from the pulsations, tensions, and relaxations. "Real movements . . . are quality itself, vibrating, so to speak, internally, and beating time to its own existence through an often incalculable number of moments." See Bergson, *op. cit.,* pp. 268-271 ff.

earlier and no later. The right to vote and to exercise one's rights as a citizen, the right to marry, and the right to become Senator or President, are likewise fixed at a certain age limit, which cannot be shortened. These twenty-one or thirty years that an individual has to reach are a rigid requirement for the purpose in mind. All these time units are divisible mathematically but not socioculturally; one cannot obtain a three-seventh portion of the right to marry on reaching the three-seventh portion of the twenty-one-year unit fixed by law. Any attempt to divide such units into units of purely quantitative time will destroy them, and with them will vanish the essential aspect of sociocultural reality.

Another way of making a similar mistake is as follows: In a non-mathematical way, we often divide man's life into "childhood," "youth," "maturity," and "old age." From a quantitative standpoint, such a division is certainly imperfect; but is it meaningful? Does it give us a good knowledge of the principal stages of man's full life? Does it describe these stages accurately? Does it "pack" each stage— youth, childhood, maturity, old age—with a series of the most important qualities, making each distinctly separate from one another and meaningful for us? Yes, it does that. Each stage in this description is a unity. If we broke it into many parts, then "childhood," "adolescence," etc., would be dissolved in these units, and what would remain would be perhaps a division of man's life into one hundred or one thousand or one million parts; but these parts would be just meaningless numbers and nothing more. If all the qualities of each stage were eliminated, the result would run something like this:

Expressed in units of the mean solar seconds or minutes or hours or days, the mean duration of man's life is so many seconds (hours, days, years); the median duration of man's life is so many seconds (hours, days, years); the modal duration of man's life is so many seconds (hours, days, years).

One can pile up other quantitative indexes of man's life and use all kinds of formulas for their computation. What do we get by this quantitativization of our description? Some indexes showing what is the mean, the median, and the modal duration of man's life, as compared with the number of mean time intervals between two successive passages of the sun across the meridian (solar day). And that is about all.

We have broken man's life into mathematically equal units of time and computed its duration in these units, and as a result, man's life has slipped between our fingers. It simply disappeared; all that is left is a row of numbers, like millions of other rows indicating the mean, the median, the modal duration of a frog's life, rainfall, symphonic concert, a given tree, lecture, automobile, and what not. The meaningfulness, the essential stages through which it passes, all the characteristics of ·these stages—in brief, almost the whole content of *man's life*—disappeared in our numbers, through our breaking the natural durations (and stages) in man's life into the purely quantitative units of seconds, minutes, days, and years. Our numerical precision we bought at an exceedingly dear price: the loss of all the main phases of man's life. From whatever standpoint, this knowledge of these phases and of their sequence is as valuable, at least, as the numbers of hours of man's life duration.

If the above quantitative data were supplementary information concerning the quantitative duration of each of the phases, they would have been a valuable addition. But such a supplementation already means a shift from a purely quantitative to the qualitative-quantitative time; therefore it is inconsistent with the purely quantitative time. In addition, it would find almost unsurmountable difficulties in measuring exactly what is the mean or median duration of childhood, adolescence, maturity, and old age. If, in some way, these difficulties can be overcome, another error will be committed—to be discussed further— namely, that of equalizing what is unequal and making unequal what is equal.

What has been said of the phases of man's full life can likewise be said of all the nonperiodical rhythms in sociocultural processes discussed in *Social and Cultural Dynamics*.[93] Each of the double, triple, quadruple, and more complex sociocultural rhythms is also a unity. An adequate knowledge of the character and structure of the rhythms in any sociocultural process is one of the most important bits of cognition of the process, no matter whether the rhythms are periodical or not, whether they have some average duration or not, whether we know the mathematical duration of it and of its phases or not. The very knowledge of the kind of rhythms in a given process is of paramount value as such. If we would close our eyes to the quality of the rhythm,

[93] Vol. IV, chaps. viii ff.

to the qualities of its phases, and to its other qualitative aspects—indivisible from one another—we would miss the rhythm entirely, and would have in our hands only rows of dead figures without any definite meaning and significance. Still less would we be able to grasp such phenomena as "the change in togetherness," as the time sequence of the qualitatively different phases, as even time uniformities and time tempi, not to mention that we would miss completely the super-rhythms studied. When to these qualitative synchronicities or sequences we can add purely quantitative information about their duration in the units of the quantitative time, such additional information is valuable. But that is only one kind of information, and far from being the most important one. Besides, as we have seen, such information is often unavailable.

The same can be said of hundreds of other durations of various social phenomena. Their living durations, with all their richness of qualities and indivisibility of movement, as in a great symphony, disappear when they are dissolved into the mere number of mathematical time units.

Try to describe in terms of these mechanical units such units of sociocultural duration as "courting," "kiss," "marriage," "death," "ceremony," "revolution," "reaction," "decay," "conflict," "depression," "revival," "festivity," and thousands of other phenomena. Many of them would be difficult to "measure" quantitatively. When they can be measured, the "measurement" (provided one honestly eliminates all the qualities) would at best give only one of many properties of the process (its quantitative aspect), and that at the cost of other no less important properties, if one is consistently quantitative. Such a description results only in a row of numbers—among millions of other numbers—which do not touch either the essence or the "body and soul" of the phenomenon.

Another illustration of the same indivisibility of some units of sociocultural time in economic processes is given by A. Marshall's analysis of the phenomena of economic equilibrium, as dependent upon "long" and "short" periods over which the market is taken to extend:

The nature of the equilibrium itself, and that of the causes by which it is determined, depend on the length of the period over which the market is taken to extend. We shall find that if the period is short, the supply is limited to the stores which happen to be at hand; if the period is longer, the supply will be influenced, more or less, by the cost of producing the commodity in question; and if the period is very long, this cost will in its turn be influenced, more or less, by the cost of producing the labor and the material things required for producing the commodity. These three classes, of course, merge into one another by imperceptible degrees.[94]

Furthermore, he develops in detail the role of these long and short periods in regard to prices, and shows a series of important differences in the equilibrium of normal demand and supply with reference to long and short periods.[95]

Granted that this analysis is correct, we can ask what kind of time Marshall had in view in this discrimination of the "long" and "short" periods: purely quantitative, or a variety of social time? Though Marshall himself does not stress the social nature of his periods (partly because he did not have a sharp idea of the difference between social and quantitative time), nevertheless, there is not a slightest doubt that the nature of his periods is mainly social and not only quantitative. In other words, for Marshall, a quantitatively long period of time can be a short period, and vice versa. Why? The following quotation from R. Opie's comments explains:

As early as 1881 Marshall was conscious of difficulties in economics because events are not continuous in time. He would write of normal results in order to meet the problem, but "admitted that there are several difficulties in the way of a precise definition of the period of time to which normal results apply." . . . The confusion worried him, because he was continually turning his mind towards the conflict between theoretical construction and the applicability of theory to "practical life." When he distinguished long and short periods he was not using clock-time as his criterion, but "operational" time in terms of economic forces at work. Supply forces were given the major attention, and a time was long or short according as it involved modifiability or fixity in some chosen forces on the supply side. The greater the modifiability of the supply forces the longer the period of time under discussion, *irrespective of the length in clock-time.*[96]

From this, we see that these "short" and "long" periods have little to do with the quantitative time, and that they cannot be expressed in a definite number of its units or be broken into smaller units, because then each long or short period would cease to be such and would lose

[94] A. Marshall, *Principles of Economics* (London, 1925), p. 330.

[95] See *ibid.*, Bk. V, *passim*, and particularly chap. v.

[96] Redvers Opie, "Marshall's Time Analysis," *Economic Journal*, XLI (June, 1931), 198-199.

its bearings upon the prices and equilibrium. Each period is to be taken as a whole, as an unbreakable unit of social or economic time.[97]

(5) The fifth disadvantage of purely quantitative time is that it devitalizes time as a potent creative factor and in this way misinterprets time and, with it, certain aspects of sociocultural processes. This is the same disadvantage the biologists have already noted, when they say that mathematical or purely quantitative time is an "empty affair," while in biological evolution, time is the potent factor that changes organisms and leads to a cumulation of these changes:

The more we reflect on [the idea of duration and the empty time of a physicist], the more we see that mathematical time is only a way of seeing things apart from each other. Things become extended in time as they become extended in space. Whether occurrences capable of analysis by the method of physics are what we call past or future occurrences, they are all given, in that each of them is only a phase of the others. Duration belongs to the organism. The past is known because all that occurred to the organism still persists in its organization. The future is unknown because it has still to be made. Duration is therefore a vector—something having duration and the organism progresses out of the past into the future.[98]

Still more conspicuous is the potent role of sociocultural time in the field of sociocultural change. Extension of its duration leads, not only to a cumulation of change and modification of the processes and systems, but duration as such modifies the quantity and quality of many a sociocultural phenomenon. An example of this is given in economics: "Time in economic process is not an empty stretch in which the process is merely reflected but time is the dimension which determines the economic process in each of its variation points."[99]

The concrete illustration of that principle is given, for instance, by the phenomenon of profit on capital. Among the most important theories of the source of profit are: the theory of abstention from an immediate consumption of goods (Senior and others), and the theory of a difference in value of the commodities produced at the present and in the future (E. von Böhm-Bawerk and others).[100] Both theories introduce the time factor as a real source of the interest or profit. The

---

[97] As R. Opie says, in Marshall's mind there was a confusion of this "operational" time with the clock time, and thence resulted his worries. In spite of this, he rightly proceeded in his classification and analysis of long and short "operational time."

[98] Johnstone, *op. cit.*, p. 337.   [99] See Voegelin, *op. cit.*

[100] See the theories in E. Böhm-Bawerk, *Kapital und Kapitalzins* (3d ed., Innsbruck, 1914); also R. Streller, *Statik und Dynamik in der theoretischen Nationalökonomie* (Leipzig, 1926), pp. 102 ff.

reasons for it, according to Böhm-Bawerk, are generally that the present goods are more valuable than the future ones. More specifically, the difference in value of the present and of the future goods is due: (1) to the difference in the relationship of demand and supply at the different moments of time; (2) to the fact that "we generally undervalue our future needs and the means which lead to their satisfaction"; and (3) to the fact that, "as a rule, the present goods are, on the technical ground, more preferable means for satisfaction of our needs and therefore have a greater marginal utility than the future goods."[101] Thus the time factor, as such, increases (or decreases) the value of the commodities produced and creates profit or interest. Time becomes one of the most important elements of the economic phenomena.

This active role of time in economic processes comes out in many other forms, for example:

In the social struggles of our days time plays a very important rôle. For a worker his labor hours are very poor in life enjoyment [erlebnisarm]. Only in his free time has he a possibility to enjoy life and fill his free time with the experiences and memories which appear to him valuable. Only this time appears to him as a real life, when he can get something out of life. [Struggle for a shortening of his labor hours is not so much a struggle for reduction of his labor energy as much as for time.]

An artizan, an artist, a scholar does not experience this lust for free time. For these professions the work is an enjoyment [die Arbeit das Erlebnis]. The hours of work are creative, meaningful, valuable. For many of the members of these professions the labor-hours are the most creative. "Free time" for them is a "lost time."[102]

This shows that the ever-flowing mathematical time is falling into quite different qualitative portions for us, with different tone, value, and subjective apprehension of time. We long for "the enjoyable hours" and dread the "unenjoyable periods" of time.

The same is true of business cycles and many other phenomena. Whatever may be the factors of business cycles, one of them is a discrepancy between demand and supply, and this discrepancy is again due to the time factor. At the beginning of the production of a certain commodity, production's amount is calculated on the basis of the existing market demand; but owing to a lapse of time between the begin-

[101] Böhm-Bawerk, op. cit., pp. 440-445 and 454. See there other theories of W. S. Jevons, Otto Efferz, K. Wicksell, and others.
[102] Streller, op. cit., p. 126.

ning and the last stage of the production, there comes a change in the demand or supply, which results in the discrepancy.

More than that, some economists try even to define the very essence of the capitalist economic system in terms of time:

> The faster the demand changes, the more numerous are the needs, the greater becomes the risk to bring to the market the goods produced at a wrong time, the more capitalistic becomes the economic system (*Wirtschaft*). . . .

In the Middle Ages, goods were produced directly for the consumer, and there was no risk of a great change in demand. Now they are produced for an anonymous market liable to considerable fluctuations in demand in the course of time. Hence the importance of time for capitalist economy:

> Without any contention for the exactness of the expression, it is possible to see in "Economies with Time" (*"in dem Wirtschaften mit Zeit"*) the criterion of Capitalist economy. Not a production of the means of production distinguishes the modern economy from that of 200 years ago, but the fact that now they manage business with time (*dass man heutzutage mit der Zeit wirtschaftet*) and consequently time is given a value.[103]

The same may be said of almost all sociocultural processes, especially in sensate cultural and social systems. It has been shown elsewhere[104] that the tempo of change in sensate culture is particularly fast, and time (as *tempus,* see further, pp. 215 ff.) becomes the most potent agency of change in such cultures and societies. Literally, "time becomes money" and something even much more important than money. This active and creative role of sociocultural time is left out of account by purely quantitative time. Therefore, if this role of time is not properly considered, many a change and many a sociocultural process becomes incomprehensible and unaccountable.

(6) The sixth disadvantage is that *quantitative time, applied alone to sociocultural processes, makes equal what is unequal, and vice versa.* From the standpoint of such a time, the lives of two men, each living sixty years, are equal in their duration; two moments of the same quantitative duration in the life of a society are also equal. Meanwhile, we well know that, measured by the amount and quality of experience,

---

[103] *Ibid.,* pp. 124-127. See also R. Streller, *Die Dynamik der theoretischen Nationalökonomie* (Tübingen, 1928), *passim;* and J. Schumpeter, *Business Cycles* (2 vols., New York, 1939), *passim.*

[104] See Sorokin, *Dynamics,* Vol. IV, chaps. ix and xi.

ideas generated, emotions lived through, changes, tragedies, comedies, and dramas experienced, deeds done, adventures experienced, two lives of the same quantitative duration may be, and often are, of very different duration. One life-career may be filled mainly by an empty "killing of time"; the other may be packed with human experience in all its multitudinous forms. In the same sixty years, one life is packed with an amount of experience and change which, in the empty life, would need three, ten, one hundred times as long a quantitative time as these sixty years. Insofar as the quantitative time considers only the quantitative duration of the lives, it equalizes two exceedingly unequal values.

The same can be said of any two equal quantitative durations, whether in the life of different persons or even of the same individual. There are minutes or hours packed with eventfulness; and there are minutes or hours empty of any incident. The same problem is solved, or thought through, or accomplished, by one person in a few hours; by another, in a much longer stretch of quantitative time, or sometimes not at all. A man of genius performs in a short period a task which, for an ordinary man, requires a much longer time; sometimes the ordinary man cannot do it at all, no matter how much time he is given. In different form, the same inequality of quantitatively equal periods of time comes out in the following manner: *Human life is literally an incessant competition for time by various activities with their motives and objectives.*

The human organism is an apparatus capable of performing exceedingly numerous and diverse activities, from eating and copulation up to the actions of religious prayer, creation of scientific, artistic, and other values. Potentially, the number and diversity of the activities it can perform are enormous. So, too, are the concrete motives or reasons for its activities.

Each of these activities, with its motive, requires some time for its performance. Since the total quantitative time allotted to human life is limited, no individual can perform at any moment of his existence all the potentially possible activities with their motives. These crowd one another, and compete for the time necessary to carry them on. At any moment of our existence, we are forced—consciously or not—to choose from a multitude of possible activities and motives one or two, and to leave all the others unrealized. At any moment of our existence, an incessant and relentless struggle goes on among numerous and different activities and motives for time, and through that, for the opportunity "to be or not to be" carried on. Each one tends to monopolize for itself our organism and the time necessary for it to be born from potentiality into actuality. At any second or minute of a man's life, one or a few activities emerge victorious, while all the others are ignored and left unborn (for that moment). Thus, if in a given hour or half-hour, we choose (consciously or not) to read, hundreds of other possible activities are left unborn during that period.

Viewed in this light, human life is a process of incessant struggle for existence of various motives and activities. The outcome of such a struggle for any and all moments of our existence determines the character of our "life-scenario" for a particular moment and for the totality of moments within our life-span. If for most of these moments our organism is seized, say, by stomach-filling activities and their motives, the life-scenario will be the dull story of a life spent in the manner not essentially different from animal life. If most of the time the conquering activity is, say, creative work in science, art, religion, or philosophy, the story of such a life will be the story of life spent mainly in attempts (successful or not) at creation of the respective scientific, religious, or artistic values. The two "stories" will be as different as can be.

Observation shows that, *within the same segment of quantitative time, it is possible to carry on, not one, but two or more different activities, satisfying different needs and resulting from different motives.* Thus man can walk and at the same time think about different problems, talk with a companion, improve his health, and satisfy his esthetic taste by enjoying the scenery. A man like Mozart or Beethoven composes his concerto or symphony and, through that, simultaneously earns money for satisfaction of his necessities, satisfies his creative urge, creates a great masterpiece, achieves fame, and often prays to God in this form, as was the case with Mozart's *Requiem* or Beethoven's *Missa Solemnis* and *Quartet in A Minor*. A person can eat his meal and at the same time read his paper or book and, through reading, study this or that problem and satisfy simultaneouly a number of other motives and quests and needs. An individual can listen to the radio and at the same time knit, eat, or drink, or carry on several other overt activities to the satisfaction of several and diverse motives and "drives." Especially easy is such a simultaneous carrying on of two or more activities when one is of a half-mechanical nature, as most manual unskilled work is. The hands may be busy with their task while the mind may pore over several problems unrelated to it or other organs, and the rest of the organism may be engaged in still more different activities.

The ability to carry on two or more activities simultaneously varies with different individuals and groups. Some, like Caesar, can carry on seven different activities simultaneously; others cannot perform simultaneously even two simple tasks. It is evident that *two equal segments of quantitative time during which "X" pursues only one activity, "A," while "Y" performs "A," and "B," and "C," are unequal. Meanwhile, if we disregard this fact, they are certainly equal quantitatively.* Such a "cumulation" of several activities and experiences within the same unit of quantitative time means practically an extension of the quantitative time in the possession of a person. If the "cumulated" activities were performed one after another, so much more quantitative time would be necessary in comparison with the time used in "cumulated activities."

The majority of persons whose life is meaningful, eventful, and creative, carry on two or more well-chosen activities simultaneously, no matter what their social station—whether they are rich or poor, slaves or masters, or what. Still more can this be said of the majority of the men of genius and creators of cultural and social values. Here, perhaps, is one of the secrets why some of them have been able to achieve and create so much in spite of their limited and sometimes very short span of life, as in the case of Mozart, Pushkin, Purcell, Mendelssohn, and others. *Such a cumulation of activities means practically a considerable extension of the ordinary span of life of each of them,* sometimes doubling, trebling, quadrupling the one-activity duration of their creative period. With the proper modification, the same can be said of ordinary persons. If any normal individual can carry on simultaneously, side by side with, say, his physical work some intellectual work—even in the form of a mere thinking out of some problem, or listening to a lecture or talk or music—he not only enriches his experience and performs more but, so to speak, doubles the time, in the sense of performing in one period two activities that would require more time if they are performed one after another.[105]

[105] Here is a point of considerable practical importance for all those who complain of a lack of time generally, or who seek time for educational and other purposes. If a person is capable of carrying on such double or triple activities simultaneously, through this "cumulation," he can increase his time for all such purposes many times more than

In all such cases, we have a phenomenon similar to that which we encountered in the analysis of biological time. L. du Noüy and others have indicated that persons of the same age chronologically often have quite a different physiological age, and vice versa. Likewise, the psychologists have pointed out that persons of the same chronological age often belong to quite different mental ages. Still more conspicuous is this discrepancy between the purely quantitative and sociocultural durations in sociocultural processes.

What has been said of individuals can likewise be said of the sociocultural systems. In the life of societies, there also are pregnant periods packed with eventfulness and with the simultaneous performance of several cumulated activities. The periods of revolution and of the "turning points" in history are examples of this. Sometimes in the short period of a few years or months, the given sociocultural system experiences more changes and lives more intensely than in the decades of the stagnant periods of its history. In the nineteenth century alone, the number of scientific discoveries and inventions was much larger than throughout all the centuries from the fifth century B.C. to the sixteenth century A.D. One century is packed with discoveries and inventions, the others leisurely go by, their "empty" (in this respect) stretches being punctuated only once in a while by a few inventions and discoveries.

The above shows how purely quantitative time makes equal what is unequal, and unequal what sometimes is equal. In so doing, it disfigures the reality, misleads us by such equalizations and inequalities; and perhaps misses the most important characteristics of this or that process.[106] At any rate, a mere comparison of the quantitative duration of two or more sociocultural processes measured in the terms of the units of quantitative time is, by itself, of little value, and of even

---

through shortening by one or two hours the official time of his work. One measure does not exclude the other.

[106] The above makes evident the inadequacy of all statements and procedures based on purely quantitative time, such as regarding a society as old if it existed chronologically for a long period of quantitative time, and as young if it existed chronologically only a short stretch of quantitative time. Socioculturally, the first society may be younger than the second in some cases. Similarly, the assumption that any society or culture has to take a long time for its passing from one stage into another, because another society passed it only after decades and centuries, is also sometimes fallacious. From the fact that several centuries were necessary for society *A* to pass from a given phase to another, it does not follow that another society, *B*, cannot make the passage in a much shorter period of chronological time, and vice versa.

negative value, if we do not consider adequately what we compare and measure.

(7) The seventh inadequacy of quantitative time, like physical space, is that *it does not permit us to locate many a sociocultural phenomenon in time.* This is the most important shortcoming, which brings out the most specific characteristic of sociocultural phenomena and of sociocultural time. We have seen that physical space cannot locate meanings at all. Likewise, *any variety of quantitative time cannot at all locate in time the meaning of the meanings, the meaning of the sociocultural phenomena, and especially certain forms of meanings and phenomena.* If we ask when and where in time such phenomena as "validities" and meanings of meanings are located, what their duration is, and when they emerge and disappear, we receive no answer, except, perhaps, that they are "timeless," "eternal," "everlasting," or just "out of the time category."

Among numerous classes of sociocultural phenomena, we meet this class of meanings, as pure meanings, and as components of any empirical sociocultural phenomenon. As an example, we can take "validities." Any adequate scientific statement is supposed to be valid or true anywhere and at any time. "Two and two make four" is supposedly valid now, was valid in the past, and will be valid in the future, no matter whether a given society or person knows it or not. To know or not to know a certain validity is one thing; the validity of the proposition is another.[107]

The discovery of a validity is a temporal matter, which can be located in time. For instance, the validity of the law of gravitation was discovered by Newton in such and such a year A.D. But the validity of the law is assumed to have existed before the discovery and continues to exist after it. Where, then, on the time-bridge is this validity located? Any adequate truth, any genuine scientific proposition, is assumed to be forever valid. The meaning of any meaning is assumed to remain identical to itself. Even a fallacy as such is assumed to remain fallacious for all time. If the concrete sociocultural phenomena that come and go, appear and disappear, can easily be placed in any system of time, these "eternal" or "semi-eternal" validities, values, meanings, and fallacies cannot be located at all in any quantitative

[107] For a discussion of this point, see esp. E. Husserl, *Logische Untersuchungen* (3 vols., Halle, 1922).

system of time; or, if they can, they require some quite different kind of time. What, then, is the nature of these mysterious "timeless" validities and meanings and values whose "timelessness" is claimed even by a host of empirical scientists, in regard, at least, to the scientific truths and scientific propositions? If they are "timeless," then exactly what does this "timelessness" mean, and how can timeless phenomena be an element or component of the empirical sociocultural world which, as empirical, is assumed to be not "timeless"?

In brief, with regard to all meanings as meanings and values as values, validities, truths, and falsities, quantitative time of any kind is helpless. It cannot either locate them in time or measure their duration; nor can it compare their time durations. It simply does not catch them in its time net. Not catching them, it cannot indicate how and in what way they differ from those phenomena that are temporal and therefore can be measured (rightly or wrongly) in terms of quantitative time and located on "its bridge." Hence, the dilemma of a sociologist:

> He is forced either to construct such an all-embracing and manifold system of time which would permit in some way to "locate" in its referential system the purely empirical ("temporal"), as well as the "eternal" and "semi-eternal," classes of sociocultural phenomena or to append to his system of empirical time some "pseudo-time" construction in which the validities, meanings, and other timeless values can be placed and sociologically accounted for. In either case the result is a sociocultural time system which is fundamentally different from the purely empirical time system of a natural scientist.[108]

(8) Finally, the eighth shortcoming of the quantitative time system is that, *in many cases, it gives a purely accidental information of accidental synchronicity or time sequence of two or more sociocultural phenomena, without any knowledge as to whether the phenomena are connected with one another meaningfully and causally or are mere congeries to one another, accidentally happening "simultaneously" or in a certain time order.*[109] The value of such an accidental time adjacency of two or more phenomena is very limited, theoretically and practically. Sometimes it is negative, when from a time adjacency of two phenomena we conclude they are connected with each other; or from a

---

[108] P. A. Sorokin, "Rejoinder," *American Journal of Sociology* (May, 1938), 970.
[109] See Sorokin, *Dynamics,* Vol. IV, chaps. ii, iii, iv, *passim.*

time separation of these phenomena we conclude they are not connected with each other meaningfully or causally.

Such are the inadequacies of quantitative time when it is applied to sociocultural phenomena, whether for practical purposes of sociocultural life or for a scientific study of sociocultural phenomena. Hence the urgent need of the construction of a system of sociocultural time.

CONSTRUCTIVE HYPOTHESIS OF SOCIOCULTURAL TIME IN ITS RELATIONSHIP TO QUANTITATIVE TIME

The solution of the problem of sociocultural time appears to me to be achieved along the following lines.

Aeternitas, Aevum, Tempus. The integralist or adequate system of sociocultural time consists, like the system of sociocultural space, of three different planes: *aeternitas, aevum,* and *tempus*.[110]

(1) *Aeternitas,* or ideational time, is the plane of time on which all the eternal validities, verities, pure meanings, and pure values—even pure falsities—are "located." It is the world of everlasting, unchangeable, timeless *Being* of the pure meanings as meanings. They are not in *tempus,* but in *aeternitas.* They remain forever identical to themselves and do not have any simultaneity, any "before" or "after," any flow, any sequence, anything temporal in the sense of *tempus.*

(2) The *aevum* plane is co-participant in the ideational world of pure meanings and in the changing world of sensory perception. The *aevum* plane of time is idealistic time. This is the plane of time on which most of the empirical sociocultural validities, verities, and values are located in the time system. When we take the most valid scientific or ethical propositions actually discovered and held in the possession of men, we think of them as a rough but valid approximation to the absolute truth or value. In their secondary characteristics, they are expected to change, but in their essentiality, they are regarded as being eternal and everlasting validities that endure an indefinitely long period of time, and will remain such wherever and whenever they are discovered. Such empirical validities, verities, and values are "semi-eternal"; they have in them something from the unchanging Being of the *aeternitas* and something from the ever-changing Becoming of the *tempus.* The most valid propositions of science, the basic laws and categories of human thought, the "immortal" art values, the co-eternal

---

[110] For the medieval division of time into these "species," see *ibid.,* II, 413 ff.

values of ethics or religion—all these have this property of the *aevum* and are located on the *aevum* plane of time. To that extent, the *aevum* is an unavoidable plane of the adequate system of sociocultural time.

(3) Finally, in regard to the location of the purely sensory phenomena, the *tempus* is the proper plane of the system of sociocultural time. These sensory phenomena belong to the world of Becoming, Flux, Change. They are passing butterflies. They proceed and are located in *tempus*. In the physicochemical *tempus* flow the physicochemical phenomena; in the biological *tempus* are the biological phenomena; and in the sociocultural *tempus* move the sociocultural phenomena in their empiricosensory aspect. This sociocultural *tempus* is thought of in accordance with the respective sociocultural conditions, and is different for different societies and cultures; it bears upon itself their stamp, and it changes as these conditions and their rhythm change. In a cosmopolitan, international sociocultural milieu, it is watch time par excellence; in an agricultural or primitive isolated community, it is the time of their agricultural and primitive calendar of activities. Now it is "daylight-saving time," now "Eastern standard time"; and there are many other "times," all relative, changing, fleeing enumerators of the fleeing empirical conventions and agreements of the interacting social groups. This sociocultural *tempus* may have dozens of concrete forms. In most cases, these forms can be translated into the most standardized quantitative form of time—our clock time—as the product of the internationalized cosmopolitan society and its latest and most serviceable convention.

Such is the integralist system, the only adequate system of sociocultural time that permits us to locate all classes of sociocultural phenomena, including the pure meanings, on their proper plane in a time system. Without this three-floor system of time, we either cannot locate in the time system the pure meanings and semi-eternal verities, validities, and values of the sociocultural world, or we have to declare them "timeless" and exclude them entirely from the time category. By such an exclusion, one neither avoids the difficulty nor solves the problem, one neither locates the sociocultural phenomena in time nor indicates the nature of the phenomena and their relationship to one another and to the time plane to which they belong. It merely throws them "into a heap" whose nature and composition is unknown. By systematically introducing the above three-plane time system, we avoid many of the difficulties and add no liability. Indeed, we gain, not only a more general, adequate, and all-embracing time system, but through allocation of the above three classes of sociocultural phenomena, we establish a certain relationship between these, with the help of the time planes, and thereby obtain a certain cognition of important properties of these phenomena. Since the pure validities and semi-eternal approximations of them are given anyhow in the sociocultural world, the mere *tempus* is quite inadequate for their time location, and it is better to have a time system that accounts for their position than to throw them into the unrelated and unknown heap of the timeless mysteries.

In offering this "three-plane system of time" I do not offer anything new, but simply reintroduce the dominant system of time held by most of the medieval thinkers: their *aeternitas, aevum,* and *tempus.* For a comprehensible reason, in the dominantly sensate culture of the last few centuries—the culture that is mainly an incessant Becoming—the *aeternitas* with its eternal Being, and the *aevum* with its synthesis of Being and Becoming were almost entirely dropped, and the whole time system was reduced to the mere *tempus,* as the sensate conception of time.[111]

For the time being, the thinkers of these sensate centuries have decided that the *tempus* is adequate and that there is no need to restore "the metaphysical absurdities" of the "Dark Ages." Now we see that such a belief is inadequate, and we are forced to extend the system of sociocultural time beyond the *tempus,* adding to it the planes of the *aeternitas* and of the *aevum.* There are several reasons for such an extension:

(1) The extension is explained first of all on purely empirical grounds. We cannot "locate in time" a large part of sociocultural phenomena and one of their main components, the pure meanings.

(2) As purely empirical investigators, we see that in the sociocultural reality there have existed and continue to exist the ideational, the idealistic, and the sensate conceptions of time—the first two being, not exceptions, not something rare and infrequent, but as widely "diffused" in various cultures and societies as the sensate conception of time.

(3) We see also and are forced to acknowledge the inseparable coexistence in any reality, especially in sociocultural reality, of the eternal categories of Being and Becoming, of continuity and discontinuity, of

[111] See *ibid.,* II, 413 ff., and chap. v.

permanency and change, of eternalism and temporalism. Either one is inescapable and unavoidable. Merely throwing into "the timeless heap" everything that cannot be put into the Procrustean *tempus* does not help; it does not avoid the difficulty. Hence the necessity of the offered "three-plane system of sociocultural time." It is needless to add that the system is by nature integralist, like the sociocultural space or causality previously analyzed.

Sociocultural Tempus. Leaving now the planes of the *aeternitas* and of the *aevum,* and concentrating on the *tempus* plane of sociocultural time, we find that this *tempus,* in contradistinction to the *tempus* of physicoquantitative sciences, is qualitative, always involving some meaning, that it is not evenly flowing; and that it is punctuated by critical dates and caesurae, and represents always a comparison of sociocultural duration or tempo of a given process "measured" by some other sociocultural process taken as a point of reference.

Whether we study the duration or velocity of a given sociocultural process or of a given sociocultural system in process, the duration and tempo of the process studied are "measured" always in sociocultural time by the duration and tempo of some other sociocultural process taken as a point of reference. If we say that the tempo and duration of the embraced processes is faster than those of the embracing processes, that the sociocultural duration of the superrhythms is longer than that of the subordinated and subsubordinated rhythms, and that the tempi of change of most of the sociocultural processes in the sensate phase are faster than the tempi of change of the same processes in the ideational phase—then all these comparisons and relative "measurements" of the faster and slower, of the longer and shorter durations, are made, not on the basis of the computation of the number of seconds or years of the quantitative time, but on the basis of the comparison of these rhythms and durations with one another (when the processes are comparable and commensurable).[112]

In a supplementary way, these processes, in their durations or tempi, can be translated into the Esperanto of the purely quantitative time, but this is possible only after the processes are compared with one another, after one of these is made a point of reference, and after the essentials of their time interrelations are established in terms of sociocultural time. Now and then they can be translated into the language

[112] See *ibid.,* Vol. IV, chaps. viii and xi.

of purely quantitative time (when possible), and in this way supplementary information can be obtained. The same principle holds in sociocultural time, when we establish the time-nearness or remoteness of two or more sociocultural events from one another. These are established again through some sociocultural event taken as a point of reference.

As such, the *tempus* of sociocultural time performs all the important practical and theoretical functions it is expected to perform. Consequently, it cannot be driven out and entirely replaced by purely quantitative time.

Quantitative and Qualitative Tempus. The relationship between the sociocultural *tempus* and purely quantitative time of the physical sciences can be summed up in the form of the following proposition: *Whenever and wherever it is possible, we shall use both, the sociocultural tempus and the purely quantitative time, as mutually supplementary; when the application of the quantitative time is impossible, we shall use the sociocultural tempus.*

That the sociocultural *tempus* is practically unavoidable in its application to sociocultural phenomena has been shown above. Without it, neither the orientation in time nor an establishment of the time—adjacency or remoteness—neither comparative durations nor co-ordination of the activities is possible. On the other hand, when we can translate adequately the data of sociocultural *tempus* into the Esperanto of quantitative time, we gain an additional knowledge of the respective processes. We can compare them with one another in the units of the quantitative time, and can compare sociocultural processes with biological and physicochemical ones. All this represents a valuable additional cognition of the processes studied. However, we have seen that quantitative time is not always applicable.[113] In such cases, we are forced to satisfy ourselves with the purely sociocultural *tempus* aspect of the phenomena studied.

Pluralistic Reference Systems of Tempus. We have seen already that the points of reference of sociocultural *tempus* are numerous and diverse. Theoretically, any other comparable sociocultural phenomenon can be taken for a point of reference. This means that *sociocultural tempus has no universally standardized point of reference, as, for instance, a second in a quantitative time.* Such a plurality of the potential

[113] See *ibid.*, Vol. IV, chap. xi; also pages 200 ff. of this book.

points of reference should not be interpreted as cognitively valueless or as not serving the main function of time.

The main functions of any point of time reference, whether in quantitative standardized time or in sociocultural time, with its lack of universally standardized points of reference, is to help find out which of the phenomena studied happened before, simultaneously, or after the others; the extent of their duration; and their relation in time with regard to nearness or remoteness.

For any given society, this objective is sufficiently well served by its own points of reference and for all of us by the total pluralistic reference systems when they are translatable into one another. Here are the simplest examples of that satisfactory service of sociocultural pluralistic reference systems: "Professor X was late for his class." "After the Battle of Waterloo, Napoleon was sent to the Island of St. Helena." "Before he was graduated, he had been offered a good position." "Oscillations in the birth rate go on much more slowly than in the field of business." "Blossoming of the Greek culture came after that of Egypt and Babylon; that of Roman culture came after the Greek; and the growth of our culture came after all these." "Plato and Aristotle, on the one hand, and Lao-tse and Confucius, on the other, were partly contemporaries." "The Italian Renaissance preceded the Reformation." "Pseudoclassicism in French literature reached its climax in the time of Louis XIV." "Zeno, the founder of Stoicism, and Epicurus, the founder of Epicureanism, were born about the same time." "The life-process of every group consists of the periods of labor intercepted by the period of rest."

In all these statements, not a single figure is used. And yet, they have a meaning and even time orientation of a sufficiently definite character. This shows that it is possible to describe and to locate an enormous number of sociocultural phenomena in sociocultural time, in spite of this time having no standard unit. Plurality of its units permits us to locate them sometimes much more easily and definitely than through mathematical time, with its standardized unit. Plurality of the units is like a totality of many signs of different kinds which always permit one to find the way out of the wilderness of events. If one sign is unsuitable, then there always are many other signs to which the phenomenon may be referred and through which its time position may be determined. In all these statements, as well as in all description of the time sequences, simultaneities, and time relations of sociocultural phenomena through the pluralistic system of sociocultural time, we are not forced to drop or to erase the qualitative traits of the phenomena referred to or described. That they remain, with all the wealth of their qualities, is hardly possible in purely quantitative time descriptions.

After the above analysis, we understand why *most of the descriptions, analyses, and interpretations of social and historical events given by the science of history are presented in terms of sociocultural but not mathematical time,* and why such a method of time location of the events has been satisfactory. The exact numerical dates are a small part of history, and even these dates (the year when an event happened) are, as we know, a mixture of sociocultural and quantitative time (for example, "the first World War, 1914-1918 A.D."). Most of the sociocultural events of history are located in terms of sociocultural time. Examples: "When Hannibal approached Rome." "After Moscow, the fate of Napoleon was sealed." "The terror of the Jacobins was ended by the Thermidore coup." "The first Triumvirate was followed by the second." "Christianity was legalized by Constantine the Great." One would be extraordinarily stupid to declare such historical descriptions devoid of cognitive or scientific value. They show the scientific and practical serviceability of the pluralistic points of time reference used in sociocultural *tempus.*

Epochal Events as Reference Points. Though theoretically any sociocultural event or process can be taken for a point of time reference, practically, for various reasons, not all sociocultural phenomena serve this purpose equally well in large societies and cultures. Theoretically, I can take for an era "the death of my Uncle John." For my own purposes, this event can serve for a point of time reference in regard to many other events and processes. But for all the people outside of myself and my family, such a date is meaningless and unknown, unlocatable in the time process, and therefore incapable of defining the time relationship of almost all the sociocultural events in the history of my nation and especially in that of many different societies. Even for my own use, an enormous number of events that happened a long time before or after this "death event" are hardly locatable in time.

In order that a sociocultural phenomenon may serve successfully the role of the time-reference point, it must be an event known to a large number of people in a given society. In order that the event may serve this role for several or all societies, it must be known to all these *societies.* Only when an event is known can it be a convenient, definite, and serviceable point of reference, either for a given society or for several societies. This is the reason why all the known "era events"— such as the birth of Christ among Christian societies, the death of Alexander or the Battle of Gaza among the Babylonians, the Olympiades among the Greeks, the founding of Rome among the Romans, the Hegira among the Mohammedans—these and other "era points of time reference" are all events known to a large number of members of a given society or to several societies.

Events that are known to many people or societies are, as a rule, *those that have a lasting and enormous meaningful-causal consequence* *for the sociocultural life of the given society.* Just for this "era-making" consequence, such events become well known and indelible in the flow of sociocultural life. For this very reason, they become the era-making or the epoch-making caesura in the historical process. Only events of such enormous and lasting consequences can be—and in fact are—the most serviceable points of time reference.

A System of Sociocultural Time Co-ordinates. Let us take now the next and final step in this analysis. What kind of events have meaningful-causal consequence for the sociocultural life of society? *Only* *the events that change enormously or that serve as landmarks of such* *an enormous change in one of the vastest of the sociocultural systems,* *or especially in the supersystem existing within the given population(s).* Even the most critical event in the life of the individual—say, the establishment or bankruptcy of a little business firm, or the birth or death of a member of a plain citizen's family—cannot be and is not such an event. Its consequences are limited to the little circle of acquaintances of the firm or family in question. On the other hand, a critical event in the life-history of a vast sociocultural system—be it religion or science, be it the empire or nation, be it the total system of arts or law or of economic organization—has a series of lasting and enormous consequences in the lives and activities of millions of its agents or bearers or members. It becomes a landmark of the profoundest change in the life-career of such a system and in that of its bearers. For this reason it is noticed, and becomes known to a vast multitude of persons and societies. Being known, it becomes a definite, serviceable point of time reference for all of them.

This applies exactly to all the points of time reference of "eras," "epochs," "periods," or of even such divisions of history as the "ancient," the "medieval," and the "modern." All these points of time reference are exactly the most important events marking a fundamental change in history—as in a great religious system (the Christian, Buddhist, or Mohammedan eras), in a great empire system (the death of Alexander, the Battle of Gaza, and the Egyptian or Japanese or Roman eras), in the life-history of scientific and artistic systems (the Renaissance), or in a cultural supersystem. (With regard to the latter, the division into "ancient, medieval, and modern" periods of history is indeed based upon the passage of the Graeco-Roman and the Western cultural supersystem from sensate to ideational, through idealistic, to sensate phases. As such, the passage is not abrupt; the boundaries between these periods are also somewhat smudged and do not have a signpost reading: "Here, in this year exactly, ends the medieval period and begins the modern.")

Thus, quite unexpectedly, we begin to understand why the existing points of time reference, like eras and epochs, have been such as they were. The answer is that these events are the landmarks of the most profound change in the life-career of one of the vast sociocultural systems or even of the supersystem. Guided by trial and error, the "horse sense" of the societies and nations unerringly chose for their points of time reference the events which logically had to be chosen as the most adequate and most serviceable for that purpose.

Quite unexpectedly also we arrive at the *system of sociocultural time co-ordinates very similar to that of sociocultural space co-ordinates. In both cases, the referential system is made up of one or of several of the vastest sociocultural systems and of the supersystem.*[114] The spatial position of a given sociocultural phenomenon is determined by its relationship to one or several of the vast sociocultural systems. The time position of the given sociocultural event is "located" through the reference to an important event in the life of one or several vast sociocultural systems, or of the supersystem. Such a result is most significant for the validity of our analysis, as well as for an understanding of why the space- and time-reference systems in sociocultural life have been such as they were.

[114] For the system of sociocultural space co-ordinates, see Chapter III of this book.

A number of other considerations make such referential points still more comprehensible:

(1) The critical events in the life of the vast systems or of the supersystem are lasting as a landmark. Therefore they can serve as a continuous reference point, in contradistinction to events or processes that come and go, and that are quickly forgotten and obliterated in their most infinitesimal consequences.

(2) By definition, the critical events in the life of the vast socio-cultural systems or of the supersystem are the focal points of the work of enormous processes meaningfully-causally connected with one another; and, as such focal points, they continue to be connected with these processes after their occurrence. In other words, these critical events are not only continuous reference points but also the continuous focal points of cross-connection of an enormous number of sociocultural forces and processes from which they are inseparable and which in turn are inseparable from the era-making events. Almost none of the sociocultural processes of the Christian or of the Mohammedan world can be separated from the event of the birth of Christianity or that of Mohammedanism. The whole sociocultural life of the respective socie-ties has been marked by Christian or Mohammedan religion. The same is true of the era-events of other populations and societies. Hence the exceptionally good serviceability of such points of reference.

Since each of these historical points is well known, we can easily establish the time relationship between them—as between the Greek, the Roman, the Babylonian, the Christian, and the Mohammedan era-points—translating all these eras into the terms of our era. For ex-ample, in our era system, the Hegira occurred July 15, 622 A.D., the Olympiade era in 776 B.C., the Roman era in 753 B.C., the Buddhist era in 543 B.C., and so on. In this way, we can easily have a continuous system of the time-reference points, in spite of the diversity and local character of the existing eras.

Universal Time System. As mentioned, with a progress of the internationalization of society and the extension of the process of interaction over practically all mankind, the local systems of time reference have been replaced more and more by systems less and less local and more and more international. In other words, the small local sociocultural systems have been more and more replaced by vaster and vaster sociocultural systems and their critical events as the points of time reference. At the present time, sociocultural interaction, for most of the vast societies, has become practically world wide. Such a situation calls more and more for a sociocultural system of time reference which is also international and world wide, applicable to all societies and sociocultural systems, past, present, and even future.

The establishment and diffusion of the purely quantitative system of time reference was one step toward the alleviation of this need. With qualitative sociocultural time as its foundation, it permits us in many cases to translate the local and "temporary" time references into this universal Esperanto. However, it does not solve the qualitative aspect of the problem of the international system of time reference. Which event, for instance, should be taken as the "era point" for all societies? Which event as the "epoch" points? Which system or super-system is to be taken as the other point of reference, either for periodization of history or for the boundary line between two different phases or stages in the history of mankind; and so on?

For the present, we can go on with several existing "eras" and "divisions of history," translating them into this or that reference system like our own. But such a translation is cumbersome and somewhat wasteful. Hence, the need of establishing a truly international system of sociocultural time-reference. Such a need will be solved, however, only when the process of internationalization has progressed a great deal further, or at least to an extent where all local jealousies, patriotisms, and the prejudices have greatly subsided and are obliterated. Under such conditions, some critical event that affects the whole of mankind may be taken as the "universal" era, and on its basis, with the help of the quantitative time, a systematic universal chronology may be elaborated and accepted. Until then, we shall continue to go on with the pluralistic systems of sociocultural time references, translating them into one another when there is a need for such a translation. Since sociocultural time is the direct reflection of the real beats and pulsations of sociocultural life itself, it is inevitable that, as long as there are different local societies and cultures, there will be the different local systems of sociocultural time. Only if and when the sociocultural life of the whole of mankind becomes truly one will the sociocultural time system become truly universal for all people. Such are the essentials of the integralist system of sociocultural time.

Chapter V

REFERENTIAL PRINCIPLES OF INTEGRALIST SOCIOLOGY

A Brief Summary

THE FOREGOING analysis of the principles of sociocultural causality, space, and time reveals the fundamental difference between these principles and the corresponding concepts of the natural sciences. It clarifies also what we mean by the homology of referential principles in the two fields. What is said of these principles applies equally to all the other basic methodological concepts of the sociocultural and natural sciences, such as that of *equilibrium*. This principle, as it is used in the natural sciences, is either entirely inapplicable to the study of sociocultural phenomena or else has to be drastically transformed into something that bears only a remote resemblance to the concept of equilibrium in the natural sciences.[1] The same is true of practically any corresponding referential principles in the two fields. They run parallel and are homological, but are nevertheless profoundly different. This means that adequate cognition of sociocultural phenomena requires its own set of basic principles, especially adapted to the peculiar nature of sociocultural phenomena, and therefore distinct from the referential notions of the natural sciences. The substitution of such a set for the present framework of one-sided, pseudoempirical sociology and social science means a profound revolution in the field of these disciplines.[2]

A tentative sketch of the principles of such a set follows. For the sake of brevity, let us denote such a school of sociology and social science by the term *integralist,* in contradistinction to the one-sided, pseudoempirical school. The exposition should begin with the system of truth, as the basic referential principle of any scientific discipline.

The Integralist System of Truth, Cognition, and Sociocultural

---

[1] Cf. Sorokin, *Social and Cultural Dynamics*, IV, 670-693.

[2] Like any political revolution, it is opposed by the powers of the old regime in sociology and social science. When they cannot cope with it through creative measures, they attempt to suppress it by censorship and other mechanical means. So it was in the past, and so it still is.

Reality. Instead of being built primarily upon the empirical system of truth and sensory sociocultural reality, the integralist sociology rests upon the integralist conception of sociocultural reality and the integralist system of truth as developed in *Dynamics.*[3] The integralist school claims that sociocultural reality, including man as its creator, bearer, and agent, is a *complex manifold.* It has its *empirical* aspect, to be cognized and studied through *sensory perception* and the *methods of the truth of the senses:* sensory-empirical observation in all its forms— experimental, statistical, clinical, and otherwise. The *logicorational aspect of sociocultural phenomena,* represented by all consistent systems of thought—scientific, philosophical, religious, ethical, artistic, and so forth—is to be apprehended through the *discursive logic of human reason,* including mathematical, deductive, and inductive logic and analysis in all their valid forms.[4] The integralists go even further. Logical thought, they say, is indispensable for cognition of even the empirical aspects, since without human logic and dialectic, no empirical cognition, no collection and analysis of relevant facts, no adequate observation, no valid experiment is possible. Without mathematical and so-called "symbolic" logic, deductive and inductive logic, no sound empirical judgment, theory, concept, or generalization is conceivable. Hence the indispensability of the truth of reason in social science and sociology. Even the most empirical, most behavioristic, most mechanistic theories in this field have always employed rational truth (though generally in an imperfect or perverted form). The incoherent jibbering of idiots may perhaps dispense with this type of cognition, but such a phenomenon has no relation to real knowledge.

Finally, sociocultural reality has its supersensory, superrational, and metalogical aspect. It is represented by the great religions, absolutistic ethics, and the truly great fine arts. We must not forget again that these have composed one of the vastest and most important segments of sociocultural reality. We must also keep in mind that these great religions, ethical norms, and fine arts are irreducible either to the mere

[3] Sorokin, *op. cit.,* Vol. IV, chap. xvi.

[4] The sociologist must not forget that science, philosophy, and other systems of thought are also sociocultural phenomena. So far as they embody a logical, consistent, rational idea, they constitute logical, consistent, rational compartments of sociocultural reality. Comprehension of this aspect is possible chiefly through logical thought, because only thus can one understand the meaning of a scientific or other theory. It takes mind and thought to understand mind and thought. Sensory perception, for instance, may give us the image of a book, but not the systems of meanings objectified in this vehicle.

complex of sensations or to a set of purely rational and logical propositions. In this sense they are superrational and supersensory. This
*supersensory, superrational, metalogical phase of sociocultural reality,
including man himself, must be apprehended through the truth of
faith—that is, through a supersensory, superrational, metalogical act of
"intuition" or "mystic experience," representing a type of cognition
"sui generis," profoundly different from sensory perception and the
logical activity of reason.*[5]

The sociocultural world, including man, certainly exhibits such a
supersensory, superrational, and superlogical aspects, of which we get
a glimpse partly through our own intuition and particularly through
the intuition of a small, select group endowed with charismatic grace
and represented by the "geniuses," "seers," "mystics," and certain
"visionaries," the founders and creators of religious and moral codes;
by the truly great thinkers; and also by eminent poets, composers,
artists, and the like. Normal intuition respecting the comparatively
familiar phases of sociocultural reality is vouchsafed to almost all
human beings; exceptional intuition concerning the complex verities
of sociocultural and cosmic reality is possessed only by the élite, such
as Buddha or Lao-tse, Plato or Saint Augustine, Saint Paul or Master
Eckhart, Phidias, Bach or Beethoven, Dante or Shakespeare, or Sir
Isaac Newton. In Chapter XVI of Volume IV of *Dynamics,* it is
shown that intuitions, often untranslatable into words or concepts
(like a profound mystic experience, a great symphony, a Parthenon,
and other creative processes of human genius also inexpressible in
words), are the foundation of the ultimate postulates and axioms of
science, religion, ethics, and the arts. It is likewise demonstrated that
they are the creative sparks which stimulate our sense organs and our
logical faculties to erect an empiricological superstructure of valid
propositions upon this intuitional basis. Attention is also drawn to the
fact that the creators of science, philosophy, religion, and moral codes,
as well as the foremost artists and poets, are at the same time dis-
coverers of an aspect of reality hitherto unknown.[6]

Through the creative discoveries of these select few, we obtain some
cognizance of this, the most mysterious and profound, aspect of sociocultural and cosmic reality. To many a downright empiricist, such an

---

[5] For a discussion of this, see *ibid.,* Vol. IV, chap. xvi; and Vol. II, chaps. i-iii.
[6] See *ibid.,* chap. xvi.

admission of the truth of faith *(horribile dictu!)* may appear equivalent to the injection of ignorance, superstition, and the like into the social sciences. Yet if they are *real empirical* observers of themselves, of their fellow men, of the structure and development of science, philosophy, religion, ethics, and the fine arts, they cannot deny either this source of cognition or the existence of the aspect of reality discovered through it. It is as much an empirical datum or fact as any other datum or fact, and equally unquestionable.

We know also that many an eminent sociocultural explorer discovered many an essential truth about sociocultural reality primarily through intuition—not through any mechanical tabulating machinery, empirical experiment, juggling with statistical data, or application of the "technique of the case study in field work." Neither Chinese nor Hindu sages, neither Plato nor Aristotle, grasped the fundamental verities concerning man, society, and culture by means of these "scientific techniques." They grasped them principally through intuition and the logic of human reason, assisted by observation.

To dispense with one of these sources of cognition of sociocultural phenomena means deliberately to forfeit one of the channels through which we obtain our knowledge and thus to blind ourselves to the most important aspect of sociocultural reality. Those who desire such mutilation and distortion of their knowledge are naturally free to follow this path. The integralist social scientist welcomes any contribution to his understanding of the sociocultural manifold through all three possible sources of knowledge. Science is enriched by any creativeness—employing empiricism, logic, or intuition—because any act of creation, as has been said, is a discovery of the unknown, of what is merely latent or potential until a great genius displays to us the hidden verity, now as the mystic Godhead, now as Plato's *Republic,* now as the Parthenon, now as Bach's *Mass in B Minor,* now as Newton's *Principia.* These aspects of sociocultural reality—often inexpressible in words—were its hidden potentialities; otherwise they could not have been actualized or discovered by a genius. Once they are actualized and embodied in empirical systems, they enrich our knowledge of sociocultural reality fully as much as all the "mechanical research of mediocre clerical manipulators" put together.

These three systems of truth and reality, with their three sources of cognition, though distinguishable from one another, are essentially one and inseparable. The distinction is but a division of labor of the cognizing mind. Specializing in the field of its own competence, each of the systems is dependent upon the others, not only for a fuller knowledge of reality, but also for the sake of verifying the validity of its results by comparison with those of the others.[7] In this sense, the three systems of truth represent a single integralist system of cognition and truth, and the three aspects of the sociocultural world are but aspects of one integral sociocultural reality.

In stressing this cardinal point, we obviously diverge from the beaten path of one-sided empirical truth, returning to the integralist system propounded by Plato and Aristotle, and by Erigena, Saint Thomas Aquinas, and Nicholas of Cusa—a system congenial in several respects to many contemporary currents of philosophical, scientific, and religious thought whose representatives are mentioned in Chapter XVI of *Dynamics*.

Such a conception does not call for any rupture with empiricism and sensory truth. On the contrary, it rigorously insists that the sensory aspects of sociocultural reality should be studied chiefly by means of empirical methods and techniques. Merely to speculate about this and that empirical phenomenon, and the relationship between them, is a fruitless and precarious activity. The same is true of a purely "intuitive" perception. In these respects, the integralist school is no less empirical than the most rigorously empirical school. But in contradistinction to one-sided empiricism, it denies that empiricism is the only system, giving us the whole truth and nothing but the truth. Besides it there are other, no less important, systems of truth which reveal aspects of the sociocultural manifold that are inaccessible to empirical knowledge. Thus, instead of dispensing with anything valuable, in the cognitive sense, in any of the systems of truth, the integralist method contains them all and is hence fuller and more adequate than any of them taken separately.[8]

[7] As mentioned in *ibid.*, chap. xvi, taken separately each of these three sources of cognition is often misleading. Therefore the best procedure is to use all of them and, whenever possible, to check the results of one source by the testimony of the others. Hence the necessity of their co-operation and "mutual aid," and the advisability of not accepting the findings of one source of knowledge until they are corroborated by other sources.

[8] These considerations refute those critics who characterize my theory of the systems of truth as a variety of skepticism. They derive such a conclusion from the fact that, according to my theory, there is not one but three systems of truth, which alternately rise and decline. Contrary to the tenets of skepticism or agnosticism, each of the systems

The Integralist Conception of the Properties of Sociocultural Reality. From this basic postulate of the integralist theory, its other principles follow. First of all, there is the integralist conception of sociocultural reality, which manifests itself in several forms.

(1) It conceives sociocultural reality as a complex of so-called "material" and "immaterial" aspects. In contrast to one-sided empirical social science or philosophical pure meaning, it does not regard or define sociocultural reality as simply a sensory or material or perceptional complex of singularistic individuals and material objects, as empiricists do (or should do if they are consistent); nor does it reduce an empirically given sociocultural phenomenon to a mere immaterial complex of ideas, values, and meanings, as pure "meaningologists" do. As we have seen, it defines sociocultural phenomena as a synthesis of "immaterial," "nonsensory," "timeless and spaceless meanings," objectified in "material," "sensory," "perceptional" vehicles and agents.[9] The fact that none of the so-called "strict" empiricists in the field of social science has been able to avoid the meaning aspect, and that no idealist has been able to avoid the material aspect, is a particularly instructive demonstration of the fallacy of the purely empirical or purely intuitive or exclusive rational approach.

(2) The integralist conception of reality, moreover, recognizes the *"givenness" (the datum) in this reality of three different aspects:* the empirical or sensory, the rational or logical, and the supersensory, metalogical, or transcendental aspects. Such an integral conception is reached through the avenue of meanings. In our definition of sociocultural reality, meanings together with their vehicles are one of the most important components, without which no sociocultural phenomenon is possible. In analyzing the meanings, we find that some of them concern the purely empirical, perceptional aspect—be it a business firm, a person, or an event (such as a murder, a play, or a wedding). Other

---

of truth, within its legitimate field of competency, gives us genuine cognition of the respective aspect of reality. Taken all together, they furnish still fuller and more adequate knowledge than each taken separately. This cognition is not a fictitious preoccupation with artificial constructs of pseudoreality, manufactured by the mind itself, as predicated by skepticism, agnosticism, and a priori Kantian philosophy of the *als ob,* or "as if," but is a cognition of genuine reality, in its authentic aspects, a true *adequatio rei et intellectus.* We are never out of touch with true reality, though we never grasp it in all its infinite manifoldness, in its "infinitude of infinitudes." Such a system of truth, cognition, and reality is the very antithesis of skepticism!

[9] Cf. Chapter I of this book; and Sorokin, *Dynamics,* Vol. IV, chaps. i-ii.

meanings represent exclusively logical and rational phases, such as the phenomena of logic, mathematics, scientific or philosophic theory, and so on. All these rational phenomena are a "sector," or aspect, of this reality. Finally, a large portion of the meanings concern supersensory, metalogical, or transcendental subjects: "God," "the soul," "the ultimate reality," "sin," "salvation," and the like. They constitute a substantial portion of sociocultural reality in the form of revealed religions, mystic values, magical beliefs, transcendental philosophical systems, and the like.

One may like or dislike any of these aspects; but no sane person and no sound empirical observer can fail to perceive that all these aspects are given as *data* in sociocultural reality. A one-sided empiricist may dismiss the transcendental aspect as prejudice, superstition, or illusion. But if he is a good observer, he must admit that such transcendental meanings and values as those relating to saints, devils, the soul, salvation, and sin have occupied a very large place in the empirically given sociocultural reality—in the form of religious, mystic, magical, ethical, philosophical, esthetic, and even scientific beliefs, systems, and congeries, objectified in millions of vehicles and agents.

(3) Through its distinction between sociocultural systems and congeries, the integralist conception *unifies the valid parts of the concepts of the empirical "sociocultural atomists" and "rational and totalitarian integralists"; of the partisans of totalitarian or rational unity, order, and uniformity of sociocultural phenomena; and of the proponents of their complete casualness, contingency, and nonuniformity.* Since sociocultural systems are, by definition and in fact, consistent unities— logical, rational, and orderly—and since they are given in the total culture of any area, sociocultural reality possesses rational, orderly, consistent aspects, or sectors. Insofar as this is true, the rationalists and uniformists are right. Since the total culture of any area reveals also congeries, which, by definition and in fact, are casual, devoid of any unity, order, and uniformity, sociocultural reality has also an aspect, or sector, where contingency, nonuniformity, and accident reign supreme. Insofar as this is true, the "atomists" and "casualists" are right. When, however, either of these factions extends its claims beyond the legitimate limit, and views the sum total of sociocultural reality as either entirely rational, uniform, and orderly, or entirely contingent, incoherent, and accidental, it is emphatically mistaken.[10]

[10] Cf. Sorokin, *Dynamics*, Vol. IV, chaps. iii-v *et passim*.

Thus in one consistent conception, the *integralist school of sociology embraces the valid parts of the purely empirical, singularistic, atomistic, and sense-perceptional conceptions; of the purely rational, logical conceptions emphasizing rationality, logic, orderliness, and uniformity; and, finally, of the purely intuitive, mystic, metalogical conceptions of reality as the transcendental "City of God," as stressed by the "sociologies" of the truth of faith. The integral sociocultural reality is obviously richer than any one of these partial concepts.*[11] It is a co-

---

[11] The integralist sociology not only embraces the valid parts of each of these conceptions, but explains how each of these one-sided theories has come about. The integralist *Wissensoziologie* offers the following fundamental explanatory principle: *The essential character of the sociological system of each prominent thinker is largely a function of two variables: of the system of truth and reality assumed by the thinker; and of the totality of his existential, especially sociocultural, conditions.* If the system of truth of the thinkers of thē most diverse cultures and periods is similar (say, the system of sensory truth), their theories will exhibit many essential similarities, in spite of the profound difference of their existential conditions. If the existential conditions are similar, the theories will display a series of similarities, at least in secondary points, in spite of the dissimilarity of their major premise—the system of truth assumed. Finally, if both the system of truth and the existential conditions of the thinkers are similar, their theories will be similar in all important characteristics.

The reasons for the proposition are as follows: (1) since the sociological system of the thinker is, for the most part, notably consistent, the system of truth and reality he assumes is the major premise that "defines the rest of the system." Otherwise, it would not be a consistent system but a congeries. (2) Insofar as any thought is a reaction of the mind to the phenomena it is confronted with, the totality of the existential conditions under which the thinker is born, lives, and thinks cannot fail to stamp his thought generally. The proposition demands a drastic modification of such *Wissensoziologie* as that represented by K. Mannheim, who, as I understand him, attempts to account for any "ideology" and "utopia" in terms of certain existential conditions such as class position and mobility, hardly mentioning the major premise—the system of truth—assumed by the thinker. See K. Mannheim, *Ideology and Utopia* (New York, 1936).

Inductive verification of the proposition bears it out very well. The conditions of existence of the thinkers of Brahmanic-Buddhist India and Taoist China, of Hesiod and Homer, of the Mohammedan Suffist mystics (such as al Hosayn Mansour al-Hallaj), of the Christian Church Fathers (Hippolytus, Origen, Tertullian, Saint Augustine, and others), were certainly as different as they could be. Their system of truth, however, was similar, as the system of truth of faith. Hence the essential similarities of their respective "sociologies." They all pay scant attention to the empirical "City of Man" and to empirical man as such; they all concentrate on the supersensory and superrational, transcendental aspect of sociocultural phenomena, on the supersensory "City of God"; they all view empirical sociocultural objects and phenomena as illusions, as pseudovalues: they all solve the problem of causation by ascribing the cause to a superempirical "Brahma," "Destiny," "God" or "gods," "Providence," and so on.

The same is true of the empirical thinkers who assume the truth of the senses. However different were the conditions of life of the ancient Hindu "positivists" and empiricists, such as Kautaliya [cf. B. K. Sarkar, *The Positive Backgrounds of Hindu Sociology*, Allahabad, 1937]; of the ancient Chinese empiricists, such as Mo-Tze and his school, called the "Chinese Sophists" [cf. esp. A. Forke, "The Chinese Sophists," *Journal of Royal Asiatic Society*, XXXIX, 1 ff.; and M. Granet, *La Pensée chinoise*, quoted, pp. 432 ff.]; of the Sophists and positivists of ancient Greece and Rome; of Thrasymachus, Protagoras, Gorgias, Lucretius, and the Epicureans; of the empiricists of

existence of rational, nonrational, and superrational elements; of the sensory and the supersensory; of uniformity and nonuniformity; of order and chaos; of the "immanently necessary" and of the casual and contingent.

(4) Similarly, the integralist sociology *organically reconciles sociological nominalism with realism,* stating that sociocultural systems are realities *sui generis,* whereas congeries are singularistic and nominalistic, and possess no structural or functional reality as a whole. *It reconciles sociological determinism and indeterminism,* giving *suum cuique.* Immanent self-regulation and self-determination of the systems is indeterministic, because it is *their own self-determination;* whereas their external determination, and especially the external determination of the congeries, is imposed from outside and is therefore deterministic.

The same is done by integralist sociology with regard to *idealism and materialism;* for an empirical sociocultural phenomenon is made up partly of the component of meanings, which are immaterial, timeless, and spaceless, and devoid of any properties of material phenomena, and partly of the components of vehicles and agents (viewed as material bodies and biological organisms), which are material and possess all the important properties of matter (both inorganic and organic).

---

the West, from Machiavelli to Karl Marx, and of most of the contemporary empirical social scientists—their theories, nevertheless, exhibit a series of basic similarities. They all reduce sociocultural reality to its purely empirical aspect; perceive it as a singularistic and "atomistic" complex; deal with concrete material topics; and give an empirical tabloid interpretation of the origin and development of social life, culture, and man, viewing them in the light of an economic, materialistic, and mechanistic interpretation of history.

Finally, the same is true of the idealistic integralists, such as Plato, Aristotle, Erigena, Saint Thomas Aquinas, Ibn-Khaldun, G. B. Vico, and the more modern representatives of this school of thought.

In brief, the assumed system of truth of the thinkers defines the situation for the superstructure of the theory they build upon it. It makes comprehensible also why their superstructure is what it is—why, for instance, the sociologies of the partisans of the truth of faith are mainly those of the transcendental "City of God," whereas those of the empiricists are of the empirical "City of Man," with all the paraphernalia of the type to which each belongs. In my course on the history of social thought, this proposition is systematically verified for the principal sociological systems of India, China, Greece, Rome, Europe, and America. It explains virtually all the important characteristics of the theories of each prominent social thinker. [For a corroboration of the proposition in a different setting, cf. H. Leisegang, *Denkformen* (Berlin, 1928); also Sorokin, *Dynamics,* Vols. I and II, where the same proposition is demonstrated in respect to forms of the fine arts, concepts of time and space, and other "first principles," and the systems of ethics and law.] Their character is equally conditioned by the system of truth of the respective culture.

Likewise, the integralist theory reconciles *sociological singularism (individualism) and universalism, temporalism and eternalism*. Ontologically, the individuals exist either as isolated Robinson Crusoes (though an absolutely isolated individual is not a sociocultural phenomenon) or as parts of a sociocultural system; likewise, a sociocultural system exists, but as a system, as a whole. The sociocultural world of pure validities and values is eternal, timeless, and spaceless—an eternalistic being; their vehicles and agents are temporal, and belong to the world of becoming.

Finally, the integralist school embraces and assigns to its proper place sociological *absolutism and relativism*. True reality is the "infinitude of infinitudes"; as such, it is absolute, metalogical, and metasensory, and as Reginald the Dominican said, is defined by itself *(absoluta specificantur a se, relativa ab alio)*. It is the source of absolute values as the measure, principle, and criterion of empirically given values of whatever kind—empirical knowledge, religion, ethics, law, art, and so forth. They all are measured by the absolute; they all are mere "approximations" of it, relative in time and space, ever changing, valid today and outmoded tomorrow. Even the famous dictum: "Everything is relative in this empirical world" is likewise relative, since the dictum itself is included in the "everything" and is a part of the empirical world.

This relativity, however, presents gradations in all the principal meaning values accessible to us; a more adequate knowledge or value is nearer to the absolute than a less perfect knowledge or value. The nearer it is to the absolute, the more it is an "end"; the farther it is from it, the more it is a "means."[12]

(5) A *similar reconciliation is effected by the integralist theory in regard to other important principles, such as the ideational (metalogical and metasensory), sensate (sensory), and idealistic (rational and integralist) conceptions of time, space, causality, number, vitalism, mechanism, and so on*.[13] Each of these different conceptions of the several categories is valid when applied to its own proper sphere. The integralist concept of time, space, causality, and other categories organically embraces all three supersystems and thus reconciles them,

---

[12] For these principles and their fluctuations, cf. Sorokin, *Dynamics*, Vol. II, chaps. iv-ix *et passim;* and Vol. IV, chaps. ii, iii, xii, xiii, xviii, and xix.

[13] Cf. Chapters I-IV of this book; also Sorokin, *Dynamics*, Vol. II, chaps. xi-xii.

assigning to each its appropriate sphere and precluding the invasion by any one of them of fields to which it is unsuited.

(6) Finally, *the integralist sociology organically reconciles the linear, the cyclical, and other conceptions of the direction of sociocultural processes, giving "suum cuique" in its interpretation of creatively recurrent sociocultural processes:* they are unique at any given moment if all their characteristics are considered; they are age-old if only the dominant patterns are taken into account. Some links of the creatively recurrent processes are linear, others are cyclical; but on the whole, they are ever new variations of age-old themes.[14]

CONCLUSION

The preceding chapters, supplemented by the four volumes of *Dynamics,* give a sufficiently clear idea of what the integralist theory is and what it should be. Though the referential framework of sociology runs somewhat parallel to that of the natural sciences, and consists of the same categories of truth, connection, system and congeries, causality and chance, change, time, space, and the like, these principles are substantially different, as regards content and meaning, in the social sciences from those of the natural sciences. Mere mechanical borrowing and importation of principles from the natural sciences cannot serve the purpose of the scientific study of sociocultural phenomena; for when literally transposed from the one field to the other, they prove to be inadequate. The invariable result is the distortion of these principles as they are given in the natural sciences; the creation of an amateurish and superfluous pseudophysics, pseudomechanics, pseudomathematics, and pseudobiology, running parallel with the real natural sciences; and, finally, a virtual failure to grasp the essence of sociocultural phenomena in their static and dynamic aspects.

This means no disrespect, however, to the natural sciences. On the contrary, it preserves the real spirit of science in general and of the natural sciences in particular. After all, the most highly developed natural sciences have become what they are, not through blind imitation of a physicist by a chemist, or of a chemist by a biologist, or of a biologist by an astrophysicist, but through the discovery and application of the theory and technique adequate to the nature of the phenomena

[14] Cf. Sorokin, *Dynamics,* Vol. I, chap. iv; Vol. II, chap. x; and Vol. IV, chaps. xiv-xv.

studied. In the last analysis, the specific principles and methods of the several natural sciences are far from being identical; indeed, they are notably different from one another. The same is true of the social sciences.

Together with the factual study pursued, in the light of the referential principles of social science in general and of sociology in particular, throughout my *Dynamics,* this outline should afford a sufficiently clear idea of what is the precise nature of sociocultural phenomena, why a strictly imitative application of natural-science principles is inadequate for their investigation, and what are the specific principles and methods of a scientific examination of these phenomena. In order to be truly scientific, such a study must conform to the canons of the integralist school.

NAME INDEX

SUBJECT INDEX

Unless stated otherwise, such terms as congeries, system, and so on mean sociocultural congeries, system.

[243]